Items should be returned on or before the last date shown below. Items not already requested by other borrowers may be renewed in person, in writing or by telephone. To renew, please quote the number on the barcode label. To renew online a PIN is required. This can be requested at your local library.
Renew online @ **www.dublincitypubliclibraries.ie**
Fines charged for overdue items will include postage incurred in recovery. Damage to or loss of items will be charged to the borrower.

Leabharlanna Poiblí Chathair Bhaile Átha Cliath
Dublin City Public Libraries

Dublin City
Baile Átha Cliath

Date Due	Date Due	Date Due
25 APR 09	21 FEB 2015	
20 MAY 09		
16 FEB 2011		
5 OCT 2011		
30 APR 2012		
24 AUG 2012		
23 OCT 2012		
04 JAN 2016		

VISIONS AND REVISIONS

Irish Writers in their Time

Series Editor: Stan Smith

This innovative new series meets the need for comprehensive, up-to-date accounts of Irish writing which combine readability with critical authority and information with insight. Each volume addresses the whole range of a writer's work in its various genres, setting its vision of the world in biographical context and situating it within the cultural, social and political currents of the age, in Ireland and the wider world. The series is not confined to any one critical approach or interpretative model but represents the diversity of recent thinking about Irish literature across the centuries, as revisited and revised by modern scholarship.

Combining monograph and edited collections, the series draws on the expertise of both established and younger critics, presented in terms accessible to the general reader. It will prove indispensable for students and specialists alike.

1. Patrick Kavanagh
(Editor: STAN SMITH)

2. Elizabeth Bowen
(Editor: EIBHEAR WAISHE)

3. John Banville
(JOHN KENNY)

FORTHCOMING

4. Sean O'Casey
(JAMES MORAN)

5. James Joyce
(Editor: SEAN LATHAM)

6. Jonathan Swift
(BREAN HAMMMOND)

Patrick Kavanagh

Edited by
STAN SMITH
Nottingham Trent University

IRISH ACADEMIC PRESS
DUBLIN • PORTLAND, OR

First published in 2009 by Irish Academic Press

44 Northumberland Road,
Ballsbridge,
Dublin 4, Ireland

920 NE 58th Avenue, Suite 300
Portland, Oregon,
97213-3786, USA

www.iap.ie

British Library Cataloguing in Publication Data
An entry can be found on request

978 0 7165 2892 0 (cloth)
978 0 7165 2893 7 (paper)

Library of Congress Cataloging-in-Publication Data
An entry can be found on request

Printed by Biddles Ltd, King's Lynn, Norfolk

Contents

List of Contributors   vii

Acknowledgements   x

1. Introduction: 'Important Places, Times'
   Stan Smith   1

2. Life and Work: The Poetics of Sincerity
   Elmer Kennedy-Andrews   21

3. Kavanagh's Poetics and Prose: Against Formulae
   Alex Davis   39

4. The Moment of *Kavanagh's Weekly*
   Gerry Smyth   55

5. Kavanagh and the Irish Pastoral Tradition
   Oona Frawley   72

6. *The Great Hunger* and Mother Ireland
   Edward Larrissy   93

7. An 'Unmeasured Womb': *A Soul for Sale* and the 1937
   Irish Constitution
   Michael Murphy   107

8. The Later Poetry and its Critical Reception
   John Goodby   121

9. 'In Blinking Blankness': The Last Poems
   John Goodby   145

10. 'The Door and What Came Through It': Aspects of Influence
    Bruce Stewart   163

    Select Bibliography   189

    The Patrick Kavanagh Centre   199

    Index   201

List of Contributors

Alex Davis is Associate Professor in Modern English at University College Cork. He is the author of *A Broken Line: Denis Devlin and Irish Poetic Modernism* (2000)and co-editor of three collctions of essays on modernist poetry, most recently (with Lee M. Jenkins) *The Cambridge Companion to Modernist Poetry*(2007).

Oona Frawley, a graduate of the University of Colorado at Boulder, took her doctorate at the City University of New York. She is currently a post-doctoral Research Fellow at Trinity College, Dublin, with interests in Irish Literature in English, Edmund Spenser, cultural memory and cognitive science. She is the author of *Irish Pastoral: Nostalgia in Twentieth-Century Irish Literature* (2005), and has edited *Selected Essays of Nuala Ní Dhomhnaill* (2005), *A New and Complex Sensation: Essays on Joyce's Dubliners* (2004) and *New Dubliners* (2005).

John Goodby lectures in English at Swansea University. He is the author of *Irish Poetry since 1950: From Stillness into History* (2000), and editor of a special Irish poetry edition of *Angel Exhaust* (1999), *Dylan Thomas: A New Casebook* (2001) and *Irish Studies: The Essential Glossary* (2004). He has published two books of poetry and translations of Heine, the Algerian poet Adel Guemar, and *No Soy Tu Musa/I'm Not Your Muse* (2008), an anthology of the work of eight Irish women poets translated into Spanish with the Cuban-American-Irish poet Carlota Caulfield. His monograph *Work of Words: Re-reading Dylan Thomas* will be published in 2009.

Elmer Kennedy-Andrews is Professor of English at the University of Ulster, Coleraine. His books include *The Poetry of Seamus Heaney: All the Realms of Whisper* (1988), *The Art of Brian Friel* (1995), *The Poetry of Seamus Heaney: A*

Reader's Guide to Essential Criticism (2000), and Fiction and the Northern Ireland Troubles: (De-)constructing the North (2003). He has edited and contributed to critical collections on Seamus Heaney (1992), Contemporary Irish Poetry (1992), The Poetry of Derek Mahon (2002), Irish Fiction since the 1960s (2006), Paul Muldoon: Poetry, Prose, Drama (2006) and a forthcoming collection on Ciaran Carson (2008). His most recent book, Writing Home: Poetry and Place in Northern Ireland, will be published later this year.

Edward Larrissy is Professor of Poetry at Queen's University, Belfast, and Research Director of the Seamus Heaney Centre. He is the author of Yeats the Poet: The Measures of Difference (1994). His latest book is The Blind and Blindness in Literature of the Romantic Period (2007). He is editing a forthcoming volume of essays on Yeats for the Visions and Revisions series.

Michael Murphy has published three collections of poetry: After Attila (1998), Elsewhere (2003) and Allotments (2008). His poems are included in The New Irish Poets (ed. Selina Guinness, 2004). He is the author of a number of critical studies, including Poetry in Exile (2004) and most recently Proust and America (2007). He is editor of the Collected George Garrett (1999), the Collected Poems of Kenneth Allott (2008), and with Deryn Rees-Jones he co-edited Writing Liverpool: Essays and Interviews (2007). He teaches at Nottingham Trent University and lives in Liverpool.

Stan Smith holds the Research Chair in Literary Studies at Nottingham Trent University. He has published studies of Edward Thomas, of Yeats and of Modernist poetry, two books on W.H. Auden (1985; 1997) and has edited The Cambridge Companion to Auden (2004). His recent work includes an edition of Storm Jameson's novel In the Second Year (2004), Irish Poetry and the Construction of Modern Identity (2005), Globalisation and its Discontents (ed.) (2006) and Poetry and Displacement (2007). Right/Left/Right: Revolving Commitment: France and Britain 1929–1950 (ed. with Jennifer Birkett) appeared in 2008, as did a collection of poems, Family Fortunes (Shoestring Press).

Gerry Smyth is Reader in Cultural History in the Department of English at Liverpool John Moore's University. He has published and lectured widely on different aspects of the Irish experience, although most of his recent research has been on the subject of music. His publications include *The Novel and the Nation* (1997), *Space and the Irish Cultural Imagination* (2001) and *Noisy Island: A Short History of Irish Popular Music* (2005). He is currently working on a collection of essays about Irish music for Irish Academic Press. His chapter in the present collection is a revised version of the essay which first appeared in his *Decolonisation and Criticism* (1998).

Bruce Stewart lectures at the University of Ulster. He is assistant editor of *The Oxford Companion to Irish Literature* (1996) and has published articles and essays on writers and themes of all periods. He served as Secretary of the International Association for the Study of Irish Literature (IASIL) (1994–2000), and as Literary Director of the Princess Grace Irish Library in Monaco (1997–2005), where he directed many conferences and edited the transactions in the Library's series together with *The Irish Book Lover: An Irish Studies Reader* (2004). He has published *James Joyce* (2007) and is presently working on a monograph on Joyce and a study of Irish poets. Born in Dublin, he has lived and worked in Britain, America and the Middle East. He created and maintains the Ricorso website at www.ricorso.net and is interested in the development of digital tools for Irish literary studies.

Acknowledgements

The quotations from the writings of Patrick Kavanagh are reprinted by kind permission of the Trustees of the Estate of the late Katherine B. Kavanagh, through the Jonathan Williams Literary Agency.

The publishers would like to acknowledge Pluto Press, who gave permission for reproduction of Gerry Smyth's chapter, originally published in *Decolonisation and Criticism: The Construction of Irish Literature* in 1999.

CHAPTER ONE

Introduction:
'Important Places, Times'

STAN SMITH

IMPORTANCE

'Yeats has crushed every Irish poet except Paddy Kavanagh', wrote Mary Kenny in the *Guardian* in August 1965: 'they have all listened to his pernicious advice about learning their trade, and worse, about being the indomitable Irishry'.[1] Patrick Kavanagh has for long represented an alternative version of Irish poetry to the high melodrama and attitudinizing of W.B. Yeats. Low key and ostensibly equable in tone, half concealing a sly acerbic wit, addressing the unromantic and commonplace Ireland of everyday, Kavanagh's lyric poetry has represented a domestic, if undomesticated, alternative to the high-falutin' rhetoric of the Yeatsian mode. Kavanagh's verse appeared to embody a poetics pitched to the quotidian world of de Valera's 'Catholic Republic', famously extolling the virtues of the 'parochial' in contrast to the siren call of the metropolitan and cosmopolitan which so attracted the 'provincial' mind-set, and, like Joyce, finding inspiration in the streets and alleys of lower-class Dublin and the stony acres, literal and metaphoric, of a sparse rural economy, like Flann O'Brien, preferring the bicycle as a mode of poetic transport to the high horse of the 'last Romantics'.

Seamus Heaney was singled out by Kenny ('a Belfast schoolteacher who is 26') as a prime victim of the Yeatsian enchantment, with a quotation from an early poem of his which, 'though it thrills my lyrical heart ... is not tough enough; there is too much Yeatsian image and cadence'. By contrast, Kavanagh represented the kind of tough realism that Kenny privileged. Heaney has come a long way since then, of

1

course. In an important lecture (and subsequent essay) delivered in the Ulster Museum in 1977, 'The Sense of Place', he conferred his by then considerable authority on the increasing consensus that Kavanagh was a benignly enabling influence for contemporary Irish writers – though not necessarily the greater poet, of greater importance to them than Yeats. Heaney commended Kavanagh's sonnet 'Epic' as an exemplary 'affirmation of the profound importance of the parochial':

> Kavanagh's work probably touches the majority of Irish people more immediately and more intimately than most things in Yeats ... Kavanagh's fidelity to the unpromising, unspectacular country-side of Monaghan and his rendering of the authentic speech of those parts gave the majority of Irish people, for whom the experience of life on the land was perhaps the most formative, an image of themselves that nourished their sense of themselves.[2]

In their introduction to the *Penguin Book of Contemporary Irish Poetry*, the poets Peter Fallon and Derek Mahon extended the contrasts, concluding that 'More than MacNeice, more than Yeats, Kavanagh may be seen as the true origin of much Irish poetry today'. In particular, following Heaney, they selected 'Epic', which they quoted in full, as a poem which 'gave sin-gle-handed permission for Irish poets to trust and cultivate their native ground and experience'. In locating its 'historical milestones' in the 'chronicle of a particular parish', they argued, the sonnet represented 'a liberation to younger poets like John Montague and Seamus Heaney'.[3] Their introduction usefully quotes Kavanagh's distinction between the parochial (good) and the provincial (bad), which has now become an almost obligatory mantra of commentators on his work, as well as of the poets who claim to have learned from him:

> Parochialism and provincialism are opposites. The provincial has no mind of his own; he does not trust what his eyes see until he has heard what the metropolis – towards which his eyes are turned – has to say on the subject ...
>
> The parochial mentality on the other hand is never in any doubt about the social and artistic validity of his parish. All great civiliza-tions are based on parochialism – Greek, Israelite, English. Parochialism is universal; it deals with the fundamentals.[4]

Among those 'younger poets' who have learned from Kavanagh, Dublin-born Paul Durcan has asserted that 'I don't like the poems of Patrick Kavanagh. I believe in them.' Writing of Kavanagh's death, his poem 'November 1967' recalls overhearing in a bar 'an old Northsider tell his missus / "He was pure straight; God rest him; not like us."'[5] Elsewhere, Durcan has enthused about the singer Van Morrison's rendition of Kavanagh's poem 'On Raglan Road' as bringing together 'the two finest poets in Ireland in my lifetime', adding that 'No other Irish poets – writing either in verse or in music – have come within a Honda's roar of Kavanagh and Morrison'. Durcan's justification for this assertion is, in his characteristic style, rumbustiously eclectic:

> Both Northerners – solid ground boys. Both primarily jazzmen, bluesmen, *sean nós*. Both concerned with the mystic – how to live with it, by it, in it; how to transform it; how to reveal it. Both troubadours. Both very ordinary blokes. Both drumlin men – rolling hills men. Both loners. Both comedians. Both love poets. Both Kerouac freaks. Both storytellers. Both obsessed with the hegira – from Monaghan to the Grand Canal, from East Belfast to Caledonia. Both originals, not imitators. Both first-time cats, not copycats. Both crazy. Both sane as sane can be. Both fascinated by at once their own Englishness and their own Irishness. Both obsessed with the audience and with the primacy of audience in any act or occasion of song or art. Both fascinated by the USA. Both Zen Buddhists. Both in love with names – placenames as well as personal names: Cypress Avenue, Inniskeen Road; San Anselmo, Islington; Boffyflow and Spike, Shancoduff; The Eternal Kansas City, The Rowley Mile; Madame George, Kitty Stobling; Jackie Wilson, Father Mat; *O Solo Mio* by McGimpsey, John Betjeman on Drumcondra Road.[6]

(That reference to a shared 'Englishness' might merit a book in its own right.) Kavanagh, Durcan suggests, in a shrewd stylistic aside, 'is a maestro of the improvised line. In fact, the only new development in recent Irish poetry was Kavanagh's introduction of the jazz line … Kavanagh was a great tenor sax who was content to blow his horn in the sunlit angles of Dublin street-corners in the 1950s. He was the King of Anonymity.' In the present collection, John Goodby's first chapter discusses the debt Kavanagh's metrical innovativeness owes to folk song and the kind of 'urban epic, peasant ballad' alluded to in the poem 'Auditors In', while Michael Murphy considers in passing what Kavanagh himself spoke of as his 'judicious use of slang and of outrageous rhyming' as a means of evading literary respectability.

In a soberer vein than Durcan's, that poet of the Dublin suburbs, Eavan Boland, has testified to the importance of Kavanagh's work for her own emerging poetics, confiding in an interview that 'Kavanagh was a crucial poet as far as I was concerned. He still is. He was the living witness of the achieved poet for me.'[7] More combatively, the short-lived, energetic and influential little magazine of 1970s Dublin, The Lace Curtain, which brought the work of such Irish modernists as Brian Coffey, Thomas MacGreevy and Denis Devlin to a wider readership for the first time, was alert from the start to Kavanagh's significance for its own contestation with the prevailing Yeatsian rhetoric. Driven by a mission to recover or reinvent a modern urban demotic flexible enough to address the Ireland of mid-century in all its complex aspects, The Lace Curtain carried in its opening issue a fierce attack by the Dublin-born and then Dublin-based, US-oriented poet James Liddy on the 'charismatic figure' of W.B. Yeats. Liddy wrote disparagingly of 'The embroidery of heroics', 'carried like an Ikon in the corridors of the Academy', of a poetry where 'All is theatrical, charade', in which 'There is no slow forming self committing itself to a definitive human attitude'. By contrast, this 'Open Letter to the Young about Patrick Kavanagh' found an alternative poetics in the work of Liddy's former drinking companion, 'a poetry in which real ideas from living come at us':

> This kind can be direct statement with a reference behind to the story of what happened to the poet. It relies on the mind staying alive, on the man making the statement keeping his emotional intelligence alive.
>
> My particular dogma concerning the kind of poetry that could be called the poetry of passionate memory is that it is more delicate and sensual than the poetry of description and analysis. Much is gained if the ideas in their language and imagery are clear and evocative yet mysterious, taking away as they give. You must think of the difference between an apparent simplicity and a simple-mindedness. You cannot imagine how hard it is for us, who suffer and occasionally

write, to bear the simple creatures who want a predetermined scheme, ambiguity and irony, in a poem. These writers of exercise poems make us angry or indifferent, according to mood.[8]

In antithesis to the Yeatsian orthodoxy, Liddy wrote, Kavanagh's 'personal vision did overcome, after "A Soul for Sale", the modishness of the Literary Revival, going back to the imagination of "The Ploughman" at a richer innerness'. Liddy's summary offers a succinct résumé of what was distinctive in Kavanagh's visionary quotidian for the writers emerging in the 1960s and 1970s: 'The landscape of his poetry is familiar enough. The corner of a field, light peeping under a canal bridge, swallows in the garage, coffee shop girls, blackberries appearing, Yeats's great dream house infested by swinishness. A world alive and green and true to despair.' In the same spirit, *The Lace Curtain*'s editors, Michael Smith and Trevor Joyce, commended in the second issue of the magazine the 'almost miraculous moral tenacity and integrity' of Kavanagh's life and work, seeing in his survival the 'individual achievement' of a writer 'wise enough and great enough not to care for the plaudits and "respect" of uncivilized and hypocritical Dublin "educated" society'. *The Lace Curtain*, they concluded, 'salutes the living spirit of [this] great writer'.[9]

Despite its preoccupation with the mundanity of an Ireland which for the whole of his life had opted for the backwaters of cultural isolationism and credal conformity, Kavanagh's poetry offers a powerful sense, as he put it in the frequently quoted words of the poem 'Epic', of having 'lived in important places, times / When great events were decided'. These lines are much cited in the present collection also, for good reason, because they epitomize the figure, both actual and literary, that Kavanagh sought to cut for himself, a figure incisively examined and in part deconstructed in John Goodby's forensic investigations of the later poetry.

The survival to which Smith and Joyce allude was not without its price. In his wide-ranging essay on the condition of the modern Irish writer, 'How's the Poetry Going?', reflecting on how contemporary Dublin had treated Behan, O'Brien and Kavanagh, the Belfast-born poet Gerald Dawe observed: '"Mighty characters": how often have we heard that phrase used patronisingly of Irish writers?' Things, Dawe continues, may have changed since Kavanagh's death in 1967, but as Kavanagh knew, 'changes can often be mere window-dressing', and he quotes *Self-Portrait* to illustrate Kavanagh's own knowledge of what was involved in this cultural myth-making:

> I realise it would not have been easy for a man of sensibility to survive in the society of my birth, but it could have been done had I been trained in the technique of reserve and restraint. A poet is never one of the people. He is detached, remote, and the life of small-time dances and talk about football would not be for him. He might take part but could not belong.

'This is Kavanagh speaking', Dawe observes: 'the poet many see as being quintessentially of the People; applauded and held up as an example of the true "bardic" Irish tradition', but

> For Kavanagh 'the real problem' is 'the scarcity of a right audience which draws out of a poet what is best in him. The Irish audience that I came into contact with tried to draw out of me everything that was loud, journalistic and untrue.' In perhaps the most damning comment of all, Kavanagh declares: 'What the alleged poetry-lover loved was the Irishness of a thing. Irishness is a form of anti-art. A way of posing as a poet without actually being one.'

'What comes through much of Kavanagh's poetry is his realisation that there was not going to be a "natural community" for him as a poet. He had instead to *create* one', Dawe continues. 'But the point is that this challenge is unavoidable for any poet. It is in effect the condition for writing poetry in this day and age.'[10]

Together with his brother Peter, Kavanagh sought to address this dearth, and to effect some kind of remedy, in the thirteen issues of his paper *Kavanagh's Weekly*, which came to an end in July 1952. Gerry Smyth's chapter in the present collection, a revised version of an essay originally published in the volume *Decolonisation and Criticism* in 1998,[11] traces the history of this short-lived journalistic project, which it sets in the wider social and cultural contexts of post-war Dublin and Ireland. The post-colonial perspectives of Smyth's essay, reflecting the general ethos of writing about Ireland by younger scholars in the 1990s, opened up new and still relevant ways of looking at these crucial years in the formation of the modern Irish state and nation.

The final issue of *Kavanagh's Weekly* carried the wry banner-headlined editorial, 'The Story of an Editor Who Was Corrupted by Love'. This post-mortem on the newspaper's quixotic mission concluded dryly that 'Our main problem was two-headed. First, there was the absence of writers and secondly, the absence of an audience', adding that, in Ireland, 'It is the need of the audience which produces the [poet's] voice ... although there is no ultimate audience there is just enough coquetry to draw out writers who are then left with a hunger which cannot be satisfied within that society'.[12] That Kavanagh had, by the end of the last century, largely suc-ceeded, at least posthumously, in creating such an audience is confirmed not only by his permanent presence on the Irish schools' curriculum, but also by the high tribute paid to him by Mary Robinson, the President of the Republic, when dedicating the Kavanagh Centre in Inniskeen in 1994: 'Let us remember him as he deserves to he remembered: not as an ornament to our literature – although he certainly is that – but as a poet who is still living among us, through his powerful and challenging poems and the force of his artistic conscience'.[13]

PLACES

Donagh MacDonagh, the son of an executed Nationalist rebel celebrated by Yeats in 'Easter 1916', introducing his anthology Poems from Ireland in 1944, welcomed 'The publication of [Kavanagh's] important poem, The Great Hunger by the Cuala Press', which 'placed him in the first rank of Irish poets'. Kavanagh's provenance was significant for MacDonagh: 'A Monaghan man, he speaks with the ruggedness of the country and the strength of the poet who can afford to break the rules.'[14] The Dublin-born Paul Durcan, as we have seen, picked out a shared Northernness as char-acteristic of both Kavanagh and Van Morrison, in a salutary reminder that geography is not totally subject to transitory and capricious political demarcations. Kavanagh's status as a 'Northerner' has been a matter of debate and even contention for many commentators, as various contrib-utors to the present collection indicate. Kavanagh was born and raised in Inniskeen, in County Monaghan, the southernmost of the historical nine counties of Ulster, artificially divorced from the 'wee six' counties of the diminished 'British' statelet established by the Anglo-Irish Treaty of 1922. According to Edna Longley, Seamus Heaney, growing up in rural south Derry, within the British Pale, 'chiefly derives his own Ulster regional root from Patrick Kavanagh's Monaghan parish'.[15] Heaney's three major essays on Kavanagh, 'From Monaghan to the Grand Canal' and 'The Sense of Place' in *Preoccupations*, and 'The Placeless Heaven: Another Look at Kavanagh' in *The Government of the Tongue*, certainly all speak, directly or indirectly, of how the young Heaney found in Kavanagh's poetry a liberating mode of writing about one's home ground which 'gives the place credit for existing, assists at its real topographical presence, dwells upon it and accepts it as the definitive locus of the given world'.[16] 'I have no need to write a poem to Patrick Kavanagh; I wrote *Death of a Naturalist*', Michael Allen reports Heaney as saying.[17] In the present collection, Bruce Stewart examines in some depth Heaney's writings on, and perception of, Kavanagh, and takes issue with some of the inferences Heaney has drawn from his work.[18]

John Montague, a Northern poet whose Catholic, Nationalist origins lie in County Tyrone, has also testified to the precedent afforded by 'the ahistorical genius of Kavanagh just across the border'.[19] Gerald Dawe, from an urban Protestant background, concluded, in an article originally published in *The Crane Bag* in 1983, that, 'given the testimony of contemporary poets such as John Montague and Seamus Heaney, Kavanagh stands as the most important figure in Irish poetry of the last three decades'. Kavanagh's presence is 'continuously reaffirmed in the work of some of the finest younger poets writing in English, such as Paul Durcan and Paul Muldoon', he wrote, compelled, he added, 'to state the obvious', that the poets he has mentioned are 'predominantly northern'.[20]

Of the ten poets represented in Paul Muldoon's *Faber Book of Contemporary Irish Poetry* (1984), only Durcan, Thomas Kinsella and Kavanagh emanate from south of that arbitrary border. Muldoon, himself of Catholic stock from County Armagh, within the 'British' zone, showcases Kavanagh, whose work has by far the largest representation in his volume, as a tutelary presence for those poets who emerged north and south in the 1960s. Edna Longley too has insisted on the importance of Kavanagh's South Ulster, 'border country' origins, responding to Neil Corcoran's description of him as 'a kind of honorary Ulsterman' with the assertion that there is 'nothing honorific about the title'. Though Kavanagh comes from a homogeneously Catholic area, she argues, where some Unionists moved north after partition, 'the county retains a Northern grasp of sectarian differences'. Lying within the historic arc of influence of Presbyterian Scots colonization, on the edge of the drumlin belt and the Gaelic lordships, both culturally and topographically 'Inniskeen, in fact, sits within a more authentic "borderlands" than the actual Northern Irish border'.[21] In the present collection, John Goodby addresses Longley's argument, while Bruce Stewart's chapter examines the issue in some depth in relation to the nature of Kavanagh's influence on, and significance for, both Northern and Southern writers, representatively figured in his discussion by Heaney and the Kerry-born Brendan Kennelly.

The play between Kavanagh's South Ulster rural origins and his urban Dublin relocation lies at the heart of his work, and is a central theme of critical discussion. This is revealed particularly in the debate about the interactions in his work of urban and rural pastoral, and of pastoral and anti-pastoral modes, a topic considered in some historical depth in Oona Frawley's chapter in the present volume.

Jonathan Allison has proposed the intimate relation between pastoral and anti-pastoral modes in Kavanagh's writing. As Allison observes,

> Traditionally, pastoral is a matter of rural life and shepherds, idyllic landscapes in which people corrupted by court and city life are changed and renewed. It suggests a healing antithesis to the corrupting influence of urban experience, but has been characterised simply as poetry of the countryside (however defined), and does not always envision an idealised and falsified, conflict-free zone, transcending the tensions of history, though it can do that, too. 'Antipastoral', on the other hand, suggests a poetics of undermining, in which pastoral conventions are deployed or alluded to, in order to suggest or declare the limitations of those conventions, or their downright falsity. If pastoral suggests that rural life offers freedom, antipastoral may proclaim it is a prison-house, and the farmers slaves.[22]

Epitomised by such eighteenth-century exemplars as Oliver Goldsmith's The Deserted Village, George Crabbe's The Village and some of John Clare's verses, the anti-pastoral mode, Allison suggests, is well illustrated by lines from Stephen Duck's The Thresher's Labour (1736), which tell us that 'No fountains murmur here, no Lambkins play, / No Linnets warble, and no Fields look gay'. 'A defining feature of such poetry', he says, 'has been its realistic treatment of labour, protest against idealising poetic traditions, and in some cases outcry against political conditions related to land enclosure'. The American critic and poet Edward Hirsch interprets the Irish Literary Revival's conception of the peasant as a politico-cultural artefact, an imaginary figure invented largely in reaction to British stereotyping. His abstract summarizes the article's argument as follows:

> In the late nineteenth and early twentieth centuries the Irish peasant was a figure encoded with literary, social, and political meaning, and to speak or write about that central image of Irish identity in the context of the time was to participate in a special kind of cultural discourse, far removed from the changing realities of rural life. The portraits of the peasant generated by different Irish poets, drama-tists, fiction writers, and antiquarians were often radically opposed to one another; in fact, each writer undertook to rewrite or to reconceptualise the peasant characters imagined by predecessors and contemporaries. Thus W.B. Yeats and Douglas Hyde created portraits that not only rivalled each other but aimed primarily at overturning the prevailing English colonial stereotype reflected in the stage Irishman. These portraits were in turn rewritten by John Synge, even as Yeats's, Hyde's and Synge's were reworked in diver-gent ways by James Joyce, Flann O'Brien, and Patrick Kavanagh.[23]

In this interpretation, it was not an actual Irish peasantry but an imagi-nary figure, 'fundamentally "created" and characterized for posterity' by the Revivalists, in 'a complex cultural discourse motivated by crucial economic, social, and political needs, as well as by pressing cultural con-cerns', which was subjected to deconstruction by writers in the wake of Joyce and Flann O'Brien:

> One thinks of Patrick Kavanagh's assertion that his 'childhood experience was the usual barbaric life of the Irish country poor'... Sean O'Faolain's vehement contention that the 'Noble peasant is as dead as the Noble Savage'...Seamus Heaney's 'archaeological' poems and Michael Longley's three 'Mayo Monologues' that implicitly criticize idealisations of Ireland's past and its people, or of the relentlessly bleak vision of Irish rural life and society in John McGahern's first three novels.

In consequence, argues Hirsch, 'One legacy of the Revivalist's glorification of the country people has been a nearly endless intertextual regress in Irish literature.'[24]

In his history of twentieth-century Irish literature, A. Norman Jeffares summarized The Great Hunger as 'a sombre, powerful anti-pastoral poem about his life on the land'. What the protagonist, Paddy Maguire, 'sexually frustrated, married to fields and animals', embodied was certainly 'not a unique personal tragedy in the Ireland of Kavanagh's youth', Jeffares observed. Nevertheless, in 'focusing on the barren routines of its lonely bachelors with an ironic sympathy', the poem presented 'an over-dark, hopeless picture, and Kavanagh 'later thought that, though it had "queer and terrible things" in it, it lacked "the nobility and repose of poetry".'[25] This interplay of 'fictive' and 'realistic' modes in the depiction of rural life is explored in Oona Frawley's chapter, which sees pastoral and anti-pastoral poetry as inseparable elements in a literary tradition stretching back to the earliest Irish literature and still apparent in contemporary folk tale and song. In situating this double aspect of Kavanagh's poetry within an ancient Irish tradition, she offers a rereading of the usually marginalized early verse that locates it centrally in relation to The Great Hunger, the poem which first established Kavanagh's presence as an authentic, original voice. In a vigorous contrast with English pastoral, Frawley sees the Irish version as expressing not the 'trope of nostalgia – literally, "homesickness" – for an idealised, vanished world that was imagined', but 'a quite literal homesickness' for those homes and landscapes of which the native Irish were dispossessed, by conquest, ethnic cleansing and plantation. A colonized people and, subsequently, a post-colonial nation, she proposes, must look at pastoral nostalgia in a crucially different way, 'not ... merely as a literary device, but as a political tool, a way of commenting on social circumstance'. In dismissing 'the Irishness of the thing' which his first book, Ploughman and Other Poems, had cultivated, Kavanagh posited such performative Irishness as 'a form of anti-art. A way of posing as a poet without actually being one.'[26] Nevertheless, a poem like The Great Hunger is not, for Frawley, a complete repudiation of Revival literature, nor simply the embodiment of an anti-pastoral poetic. It constitutes, rather, a complex updating of a long tradition of Irish pastoral which 'grants space to both the aesthetic admiration of nature and the recognition of the idealizing process that such admiration entails, set alongside a more realistic, direct confrontation with the actualities of the natural world'. There is a fruitful tension in the present volume between this line of argument and Edward Larrissy's exploration of the ramifications of the poem and such related works as 'Lough Derg', which Larrissy sees as set in stubborn contradiction to the fantasy realms of the Literary Revival, besotted with Yeats's 'dream of the noble and the beggar-man'.[27]

Michael Murphy's chapter explores the critique of the 1937 Constitution implicit in Kavanagh's collection *A Soul for Sale*. Murphy detects what he calls a 'rent', a fissure or tear in the fabric of being, in Kavanagh's poetry, represented by the expectation of an epiphany that remains forever withheld. In his Christmas poems, he says, 'it is always Advent or Christmas Eve, never Christmas morning. This to many is how Ireland must still have seemed after the Passion of the Rising and the Civil War.' Such 'rents' in the fabric of the world can be read, Murphy argues, as Kavanagh's means for realizing what Seamus Deane has called 'an internal schism that bears within itself an interpretation of Irish literary history', a schism 'between fantasy and realism' which 'duplicates the Free State's battle with the Irish Renaissance'.[28] John Goodby's second contribution extends this politico-cultural contextualization to the important last poetry, which Kavanagh referred to as his 'noo pomes', the Canal Bank and *Kitty Stobling* poems. Alex Davis finds a similar dialectic of realism and fantasy in Kavanagh's prose. In his *Self-Portrait*, Davis points out, Kavanagh described his novel *Tarry Flynn* as 'not only the best but the only authentic account of life as it was lived in Ireland this century', its 'realism' contrasted with the 'stage-Irish lie' of his earlier, semi-autobiographical work, *The Green Fool*. While finding the latter self-assessment unduly harsh, Davis in addressing Kavanagh's prose examines both 'realistic' and 'fictive' elements in such works, and relates them to the preoccupations of his critical and journalistic writings, to outline the contours of a poetic which spans both poetry and prose.

TIMES

In 1986 Seamus Deane was in little doubt that Kavanagh was 'at odds with the spiritual heroics of the foundation period of the State and ... perfectly in accord with the general desire to climb down from the [Revivalists'] dizzy height of mythology, the glories of battle, elaborate

readings of tradition and labyrinthine pursuits of Irishness and to concentrate instead on the stony grey soil of his native Monaghan and the
actualities of living the here and now', permitting a new generation of
writers, as John Montague put it, to be 'liberated into ignorance'.[29]

Declan Kiberd has described Dublin in the 1930s and 1940s as a
place 'In the familiar manner of other post-colonial capitals ... overrun
by unplanned migrations of rural folk, who had no sooner settled than
they were consumed by a fake nostalgia for a pastoral Ireland they had
"lost".' Assuming a largely hostile posture, Kiberd wrote of Kavanagh as
'the test-case here':

> [A]t first, when he was still close to his Monaghan roots, he
> denounced the false consciousness of the peasant periphery, but
> after a decade or more in Dublin, he fell back into line with it,
> going to extraordinary lengths to recreate Baggot Street as an urban
> pastoral, as 'my Pembrokeshire'. And that invented Ireland proved far
> more attractive to poetry-readers among the new Dubliners than
> had Kavanagh's bitter indictment of rural torpor in The Great Hunger.[30]

Richard Kearney takes a different line in his Postnationalist Ireland. Anthony
Cronin's memoir Dead as Doornails, Kearney wrote, 'graphically captures the
oppressive sense of malaise which dominated this period – a time when
censorship was rife, clericalism rampant and the world war no more than
a "ghastly unreality"', towards which 'the demythologizing Dublin set
of Cronin, Kavanagh and O'Brien developed an adversarial stance' that 'cultivated wit, iconoclasm and a deliberate estrangement from accredited
wisdoms'. 'They wiped the domestic slate clean', he argues, 'a middle
generation cutting through the lush vegetation of tradition to clear
spaces where new voices might be heard'. Self-Portrait, for example,
announced in 1962 Kavanagh's 'total repudiation of what he termed
"this Ireland thing", casting the Literary Revival as 'a trap sprung by the
"Celtic Twilighters"' and declaring 'The Ireland "patented by Yeats, Lady
Gregory and Synge" ... a "thorough-going English-bred lie"':

> He rejected the revivalist shibboleths of genuine peasant and aris-
> tocrat. 'Irishness', he quipped, was no more than 'a way of anti-art',
> a means of playing at being a poet without actually being one. To
> the mythologizing spirit of the Revival, Kavanagh opposed what he

called 'the comic spirit': an attitude which scorned the self-impor-
tance of Grand Narrative, preferring the carelessness and ordinar-
iness of the immediate. This deflation of posturing he described as
the 'difficult art of not caring'. Only a fidelity to the parochial and
local, to experience in the lower case, could hope to arrive at that
highest because simplest of all conditions – 'complete casualness'.

But it was not only the Revivalist mythos which he rejected: in 'Dark
Ireland' for example, Kearney says, 'he regrets the insular mentality of
the new bourgeois state':

> The provincialism of middle-class Catholic Dublin – as Kavanagh
> discovered when he tried to launch his journal *Kavanagh's Weekly*
> there in the 1950s – was quite as inimical to art as the aesthetic elit-
> ism of the fashionable Ascendancy. The mean-minded materialism
> of the former class was simply the obverse of the effete spiritualism
> of the latter. Whenever Kavanagh himself chose mythic figures –
> which was rare enough – he generally drew from Greek rather
> than Celtic mythology, and always with a view to showing how the
> Grand Narratives of myth are inextricably bound up with the vicis-
> situdes of everyday life.[31]

Antoinette Quinn's critical study of Kavanagh as a 'born-again
romantic' was informed by the unequalled knowledge of Kavanagh's life
and work revealed in the exhaustive biography she published in 2001.
Both books consider Kavanagh's encounters with the issues discussed
above in rich and complex detail.[32] Elmer Kennedy-Andrews's biographical essay in the present volume provides a succinct survey of Kavanagh's
life and times, identifying the salient social and cultural as well as personal contexts of his work, in its shifts from rural to urban locations.
Kennedy-Andrews offers shrewd explanations for the changes in
Kavanagh's own assessments of his work, in particular his disavowal of
The Great Hunger, and provides a convincing account of the illumination,
crucial for the later poetry, which Kavanagh experienced in 1955 on the
banks of the Grand Canal, at the time of his treatment for lung cancer.
He provides, too, a lucid narrative of Kavanagh's various contretemps
with the Dublin literati and with the sometimes sordid realities of both
Irish and British metropoles.

Marjorie Howes has given a forceful description of the tight little puritanical Ireland of Kavanagh's maturity, from March 1932 under the rigid regimen of Eamon de Valera, in which economic austerity, religious and political orthodoxy and sexual repression went hand in hand. In 1929, the Censorship of Publications Act had extended government censorship from film to printed matter, banning the advocacy and advertising of contraception and the publication of works of an allegedly licentious nature. *Tarry Flynn* was briefly banned as 'indecent and obscene' by the Irish Censorship Board; while Kavanagh recorded in his 'Author's Note' to the first *Collected Poems* (1964) that in 1942, just after the publication of *The Great Hunger*, he was visited by 'a couple of hefty lads' from the local constabulary enquiring about its authorship. The Criminal Law Amendment Act (1935) made the importation or sale of contraceptives illegal; the Conditions of Employment Bill (1935) set a limit on the number of women workers in industry and banned married women from most jobs; while the provisions of the 1937 Constitution forbade the enactment of any law to permit divorce.[33] The 1937 Constitution, Howes records, 'combined a republican political agenda with a Catholic moral tone', and sought to establish the 'special position of the Holy Catholic Apostolic and Roman Church as the guardian of the faith professed by the great majority of the Citizens'.[34]

Terence Brown, as Edward Larrissy points out, has said that 'if there is a case for viewing a major work of art as an antenna that sensitively detects the shifts of consciousness that determines a people's future, *The Great Hunger* is that work'.[35] Larrissy's account of *The Great Hunger* and related poems examines in depth the cultural and psychological famine enshrined in what has been long regarded as his magnum opus, despite the poet's own disavowals of it as 'underdeveloped Comedy, not fully born'. 'Those who come to Patrick Kavanagh's work for the first time', Larrissy observes, 'often assume that the title of *The Great Hunger* (1942) refers to the great Irish famine of the 1840s', a century earlier. He agrees instead with Kavanagh's biographer, Antoinette Quinn, that this is a retrospective, if inevitable and appropriate, identification, and that the poem's protagonist, Paddy Maguire, suffers first and foremost from a 'spiritual hunger' for which the famine itself becomes the larger symbol.

The 'hunger' was also a sexual one, induced by social and economic conditions which for centuries had imposed unwelcome celibacy on large sections of the Irish rural population, until the boom years which followed accession to the European Union in 1973. Marjorie Howes's account of these circumstances is vivid and succinct:

> Another aspect of Ireland's sexual conservatism that sets it apart from contemporary developments in other nations was its relationship to several unusual and much-discussed Irish demographic and social patterns. Comments on these trends persistently outline other anxiety-producing relationships between Irish sexual behaviour and national character. The anthropologists Conrad Arensberg and Solon Kimball used the term 'familism' to describe the ways in which the economic imperatives of post-famine rural life structured cultural norms about such phenomena as aging, parent–child relationships, group social events, and, most important, gender boundaries, matchmaking and marriage.

Under 'familism', she explains,

> farmers did not subdivide their already small plots of land among their children; instead they left the farm to one son and dowered one daughter. Other siblings had to learn a trade, enter the Church, or emigrate. In addition, a son could not marry until his parents retired and turned the farm over to him, but this often did not happen until he was in his 40s or older. These social structures helped make the Irish world-famous for their high rates of celibacy and emigration. By the early 1920s, 43 percent of Irish-born men and women were living abroad. Fertility rates within marriage were high, especially in rural areas ... [T]here is general agreement that from the late nineteenth to the mid-twentieth century, the Irish were the most celibate nation of any country that kept such records.[36]

HOMER'S GHOST

Roy Foster was in little doubt in his 1989 history of modern Ireland that 'Discontent with the de Valera vision can be intuited perhaps most vividly in Patrick Kavanagh's poem about the sterility and frustration of rural life, *The Great Hunger*'.[37] Kavanagh's 'documentary' veracity in his recounting of

twentieth-century Ireland should not be overplayed, as some of the critics considered above and several contributors to the present volume have
variously warned. Literature is never pure transcription of a pre-existing
'reality', but a complex construction of imaginings, most treacherous,
perhaps, when most apparently rooted in 'the real world' of times and
places. James Joyce famously told Frank Budgen that if Dublin were
destroyed it could be rebuilt from his account of it in *Ulysses*. Whether or
not that is the case (and as long ago as Arnold Bennett hostile commentators remarked that Joyce had little sense of urban planning and archi-
tecture, as if *that* were what he meant by 'Dublin'), it is certainly true that
a good fist could be made of reconstructing the Ireland of the middle
decades of the last century from the writings of Patrick Kavanagh. The
reconstruction would not, however, be of an actual place and time, but
of an imagined world, every bit of it infused with the assumptions of
the discursive practice that, for want of a better name, we hail by the
title of 'Patrick Kavanagh'.

Kavanagh clearly had in mind what Joyce had done with 'Homer',
that empty vessel for innumerable reconstructions, projections and fantasies, when, in his most widely quoted poem, 'Epic', he reported that
'Homer's ghost came whispering to my mind' with the claim that 'I
made the Iliad from such / A local row'. But if gods (not poets, note)
'make their own importance', they do so by criteria not subject to the
usual constraints of political history, where the Munich bother rings
loud. Though we know nothing of Homer, and little, though more, of
Bronze Age Troy and Ithaca, we do have two texts, the *Iliad* and the
Odyssey, which, perhaps fortuitously tied to that resonantly empty name,
offer narratives of human endeavour, aspiration, achievement and failure, forever rewritten and redefined in their endless, never-ending
retelling. So, the little local rows of Kavanagh's Ireland, whether disputes
over the literal ownership of a half-rood of rock, or over the shifting
boundaries of British and Irish, free state and occupied territory, city
and country, body and soul, man and woman, will continue to be fought
within that haunted extraterritorial realm we call poetry. There is a key
play on words at the very centre of Kavanagh's fourteen-line sonnet, as
old McCabe is seen in line seven to 'Step the plot defying blue-cast steel'.
For the plot of land, the disputed ground of the last century's often mur-
derous struggles, defiantly marked out by treading the bounds, is, in the

end, also the plot of a story, an imaginative construct, a narrative with all that *poeisis*, the power of the 'maker' to make things, and to make things happen, entails. Or retails. Or retells. And what then, Homer's ghost might ask, what then?

NOTES

1. Mary Kenny, 'Waiting for Ginsberg', *Guardian*, 26 August 1965, p.6.

2. Seamus Heaney, 'The Sense of Place', in *Preoccupations: Selected Prose 1968–78* (London: Faber & Faber, 1980 rpt, 1984), p.137. Less frequently remarked is the other side of Heaney's argument, emphasizing that, in the words he quotes from Kavanagh's *Self-Portrait*, '"A poet is never one of the people"... "He is detached, remote ... He might take part but he could not belong"', ibid, p.138.

3. Peter Fallon and Derek Mahon (eds), 'Introduction', *Penguin Book of Contemporary Irish Poetry* (Harmondsworth: Penguin, 1990), pp.xvii–xviii.

4. Ibid., p.xviii. The original appeared in *Kavanagh's Weekly*, 7 (24 May 1952), p.2. See also Kavanagh, *Collected Pruse* (London: McGibbon & Kee, 1967; Macmillan, 1973). For a discussion of Kavanagh's idea of the parochial, see the unpublished doctoral dissertation by Victoria Ann Davis, 'Restating a Parochial Vision: A Reconsideration of Patrick Kavanagh, Flann O'Brien, and Brendan Behan' (University of Texas at Austin, 2005), ch.1: 'Remapping the Parish: Patrick Kavanagh and the Development of a Parochial Vision', available online at www.lib.utexas.edu/etd/d/2005/davisv 09008/davisv09008.pdf.

5. Paul Durcan, *A Snail in My Prime* (London: Harvill, 1993), p.3. A later poem, 'What Shall I Wear, Darling, to *The Great Hunger*?' (ibid., pp.123–4) contrasts with Durcan's characteristically enigmatic, surreal irony the world Kavanagh addressed in his poem and the glamorous, fashion-chasing ethos of the Dublin glitterati, for whom every historical catastrophe is the opportunity for a performance.

6. Paul Durcan, 'The Drumshanbo Hustler: A celebration of Van Morrison', *Magill* (May 1988), p.56.

7. See Jody Allen-Randolph, 'An Interview with Eavan Boland', in *Irish University Review: Special Issue on Eavan Boland*, ed. Jody Allen-Randolph and Anthony Roche, 23, 1 (Spring/Summer 1993).

8. James Liddy, 'Open Letter to the Young about Patrick Kavanagh', *The Lace Curtain: a magazine of poetry and criticism*, 1 (Winter 1969), pp.55–7. On Liddy's propagation of Kavanagh in the pages of his little magazine *Arena*, see Thomas Dillon Redshaw, '"We Done Our Best When We Were Let": James Liddy's *Arena*, 1963–1965', *The South Carolina Review*, 38, 1 (Fall 2005), pp.97–117; available at www.clemson. edu/caah/ cedp/097-117%20-%20Redshaw%20w%20jpeg%20images.pdf.

9. Michael Smith and Trevor Joyce, 'Editorial', *The Lace Curtain*, 2 (Spring 1970), p.2.

10. Gerald Dawe, *How's the Poetry Going? Literary Politics and Ireland Today* (Belfast: Lagan Press, 1993), pp.30–6.

11. Gerry Smyth, 'The Moment of *Kavanagh's Weekly*', in *Decolonisation and Criticism: The Construction of Irish Literature* (London: Pluto, 1998), pp.103–12.

12. 'The Story of an Editor Who Was Corrupted by Love', *Kavanagh's Weekly*, 13 (5 July 1952), p.1.

13. See Stephen McKinley, 'His Brother's Keeper', *Irish Echo* (New York) (September 2002). Such encomia should be read in the light of Gerald Dawe's minatory comments; as too, perhaps, should the précis the New York weekly offered in 2004, with its Irish-American readership clearly in mind, of Antoinette Quinn's biography: 'Her life of Kavanagh challenge[s] the view long advanced by the younger Kavanagh that his brother was rejected during his lifetime by Ireland's literary establishment – indeed, she said, if her book has a hero aside from its subject, it's Dublin's middle class, who realized it had a "wayward genius" in its midst and supported him in every way it could' (*Irish Echo*, New York, October 2004).

14. Donagh MacDonagh (ed.), *Poems from Ireland* (Dublin: The Irish Times, 1944).

15. Edna Longley, *The Living Stream: Literature and Revisionism in Ireland* (Newcastle upon Tyne: Bloodaxe, 1994), p.20.

16. Seamus Heaney, *Preoccupations: Selected Prose 1968–1978* (London: Faber & Faber, 1980), pp.115–30 and 131–49; and *The Government of the Tongue* (London: Faber & Faber, 1988), pp.3–14, quotation at p.4.

17. Michael Allen, 'Provincialism and Recent Irish Poetry: The Importance of Patrick Kavanagh', in *Two Decades of Irish Writing*, ed. Douglas Dunn (Cheadle Hulme: Carcanet Press, 1975), p.35. Allen's essay is a key early discussion of Kavanagh's thinking on the parochial and the provincial.

18. Stewart finds 'oddly unconvincing' Heaney's reading of the language of the 'Inniskeen Road' sonnet. I feel compelled to add here a reservation of my own, with regard to Heaney's claim, repeated without demur by several critics, that in the poem's opening line, 'The bicycles go by in twos and threes', Kavanagh is departing from 'a more standard English voice', where 'pass by' or 'go past' would be the normative usage (Heaney, *Preoccupations*, p.138). The claim is groundless, and the 'localist' reading based on it chimerical. 'Go by' is a perfectly standard English usage (or it is in parts of South Lancashire, where they speak the best English). For instance, a 1956 pop-song by 'The Four Lads', later revamped by Dean Martin, begins with the reiterated line, 'Standing on the corner, watching all the girls go by.'

19. John Montague, *The Figure in the Cave and Other Essays* (Dublin: Lilliput Press, 1989), pp.8–9.

20. Gerald Dawe, 'Brief Confrontations: The Irish Writer's History', *The Crane Bag*, 7, 2 (1983); rpt in *Against Piety: Essays in Irish Poetry* (Belfast: Lagan Press, 1995), p.27.

21. Longley, *Living Stream*, pp.205–6. Corcoran's comment can be found in Neil Corcoran (ed.), *The Chosen Ground: Essays on the Contemporary Poetry of Northern Ireland* (Bridgend: Seren Books, 1992), p.7.

22. Jonathan Allison, 'Patrick Kavanagh and Antipastoral', in *The Cambridge Companion to Contemporary Irish Poetry*, ed. Matthew Campbell (Cambridge: Cambridge University Press, 2003), pp.42–58 (at p.42).

23. Edward Hirsch, 'The Imaginary Irish Peasant', *PMLA*, 106, 5 (October 1991), pp.1116–33.

24. Ibid., p.1116. For a contemporary response to what Longley calls Kavanagh's 'sniping' at the Revival, see Hubert Butler's 1954 piece, 'Envoy and Mr Kavanagh', reprinted in *Escape from the Anthill* (Mullingar: Lilliput Press, 1985). Chapter 2, 'Patrick Kavanagh and the Perils of the Peasant Poet', of Davis's *Restating a Parochial Vision*, discusses the image of the peasant in Kavanagh's pastoral.

25. A. Norman Jeffares, *Anglo-Irish Literature* (Dublin: Gill & Macmillan, 1982), p.191.

26. Patrick Kavanagh, *Collected Pruse* (London: McGibbon & Kee, 1967), p.16.

27. Kavanagh identified F.R. Higgins as a type of the Literary Revival 'dabbler' in 'The Gallivanting Poet', *Irish Writing*, 3 (November 1947).

28. Seamus Deane, 'Boredom and Apocalypse: A National Paradigm', in *Strange Country: Modernity and Nationhood in Irish Writing Since 1790* (Oxford: Clarendon Press, 1997), p.158.

29. Seamus Deane, *A Short History of Irish Literature* (London: Hutchinson, 1986), p.233.

30. Declan Kiberd, *Inventing Ireland: The Literature of the Modern Nation* (London: Jonathan Cape, 1995), p.492.

31. Richard Kearney, 'Post-Revival Demythologizers', in *Postnationalist Ireland: Politics, Culture, Philosophy* (London: Routledge, 1997), pp.124–6.

32. Antoinette Quinn, *Patrick Kavanagh: Born-Again Romantic* (Dublin: Gill & Macmillan, 1991); *Patrick Kavanagh: A Biography* (Dublin: Gill & Macmillan, 2001; 2nd edn 2003).

33. Marjorie Howes, *Yeats's Nations: Gender, Class, and Irishness* (Cambridge: Cambridge University Press, 1996), p.135.

34. Ibid., p.135, and note, p.212.

35. Terence Brown, *Ireland: A Social and Cultural History 1922–1979* (London: Fontana, 1981), p.187.

36. Howes, *Yeats's Nations*, p.136. Howes's endnote cites Conrad Arensberg, *The Irish Countryman: An Anthropological Study* (New York: Peter Smith, 1950 [1937]), and Conrad Arensberg and Solon T. Kimball, *Family and Community in Ireland* (Gloucester, MA: Peter Smith, 1961). A wide-ranging and now classic survey of the Irish Free State during the interwar years can be found in a collection of essays based on RTE's 1962 Thomas Davis Lectures, published in the year Kavanagh died. See Francis MacManus (ed.), *The Years of the Great Test 1929–39* (Cork: Mercier Press, 1967). The volume also throws some light on the ethos of 1960s Dublin against which the young writers who turned to Kavanagh were rebelling: the essay on 'Social Life in Ireland 1927–1937' by Terence de Vere White, for example, interprets 'social life' to mean the life of high society. Today, the book nevertheless still offers a clear and informative insight into the period it addresses.

37. R.F. Foster, *Modern Ireland 1600–1972* (Harmondsworth: Penguin, 1989), p.539.

CHAPTER TWO

Life and Work:
The Poetics of Sincerity

ELMER KENNEDY-ANDREWS

THE IMPORTANCE OF BEING PATRICK

There is in Patrick Kavanagh's career an uncommonly close link between the life and the work. His writings are primarily focused on himself, his relationship with his surroundings, the forces that have produced him, his personal struggles. For Kavanagh, the purpose of the work is truthful self-expression. Writing in the Irish Times in 1942, he declared:

> Some readers may say that I am being romantic. But the romantic attitude is only another name for old decency. And the romantic is the man who is not afraid to speak his mind in praise or condemnation, whereas the 'scholar' and tourist are always waiting to hear what the other fellow says till they steal it to put in the purse of death with the smelly dust.[1]

This is Kavanagh, the self-appointed crusader against untruth, the champion of the imaginative view of life. It is 'the kink of rectitude',[2] he suggests, that makes a poet. But the poet must be careful not to be distracted by popularity or celebrity from telling the truth that is rooted in the mystique of the common earth: 'O for a country ... / where every arty fraud is jeered / where shines no movie star – / the ancient fields where God is feared / and men are what they are' ('Two Ways').[3] Not for Kavanagh the Yeatsian play with multiple masks nor the modernist cult of impersonality. Truth is personality:

> The trouble with a novel, or any work of art, is that the theme is often nothing. It is the background, the sensibility, which is the

real message. The personality of the writer is the valid part of his theme. It is the ignoring of this fact that the personality is part of a man's statement of truth which invalidates newspaper stories. The journalist is supposed to submerge his own personality and accept amorally the blind facts.[4]

Rereading Kavanagh in this age of 'the death of the author' and the post-modern devaluation of subjectivity, one is recalled to old-fashioned romantic claims of literary sincerity ('sincerity'/'sincere' are favourite Kavanagh words in both his prose and his poetry) as described by Lionel Trilling:

> [Sincerity] derived from the Latin word *sincerus* and first meant exactly what the Latin word means in its literal use – clean, or sound, or pure. An old and merely fanciful etymology, *sine cera*, without wax, had in mind an object of *virtu* which was not patched up and passed off as sound, and serves to remind us that the word in its early use referred primarily not to persons but to things ... One spoke of sincere wine ... simply to mean that it had not been adulterated, or, as was once said, sophisticated ... As used in the early sixteenth century in respect of persons, it is largely metaphorical – a man's life is sincere in the sense of being sound, or pure, or whole; or consistent in its virtuousness.[5]

This idea of sincerity as resistance to 'adulteration' and 'sophistication' strikes a particular chord in the case of Kavanagh, the 'ploughman poet', who sought to preserve his vision of the realities of peasant life against the 'lies' that had been perpetuated by a Revivalist orthodoxy led by Lady Gregory, Yeats and Synge. As John Montague put it, Kavanagh 'liberated us into ignorance',[6] meaning that Kavanagh broke with romantic nationalism and Yeatsian mythologizing to demonstrate the poetic possibilities of the parish, quotidian experience, sensuous life, the miracle of the ordinary. Following his move to Dublin in 1939, Kavanagh was to spend the rest of his life inveighing against what he regarded as the adulteration of Irish public and cultural life, in his journalism and satiric verse laying into those whom he held responsible for the entrenchment of mediocrity, dilettantism, charlatanism, venality, insularity, nationalist hysteria, conventionalism, unreality, begrudgery and creative paralysis in the post-Independence Irish Gehenna.

The idea of sincerity as 'soundness', 'purity' and 'wholeness' is also especially relevant to Kavanagh, whose career was described by one of his earliest commentators, John Nemo, as a 'quest for the self'.[7] Kavanagh's version of sincerity, that is, involves not only honest self-expression, but also the degree of self-realization that makes honesty possible. That integrated state of being, Kavanagh repeatedly tells us, he achieved in the summer of 1955. Following an unsuccessful libel action and a spell of serious illness, he experienced what he characterized as a spiritual rebirth, the attainment of a new kind of sincerity based on a notion of 'not caring' which replaced his earlier commitment to self-understanding and social engagement. 'Not caring' or detachment was a prerequisite of a desired state of repose, a condition of wholeness and integrity imbued by the 'comic spirit': 'There is only one Muse, the Comic Muse. In Tragedy there is always something of a lie. Great poetry is always comic in the profound sense. Comedy is abundance of life.'[8] The reason why he later rejected his masterpiece, The Great Hunger, was that in his view it failed to achieve 'wholeness':

> I'm afraid I'm too involved in The Great Hunger; the poem remains a tragedy because it is not completely born. Tragedy is underdeveloped comedy: tragedy fully explored becomes comedy. We can see it and we are not afraid. Because of these things, I am of the opinion that The Great Hunger ... is a cry, a howl, and cries and howls die in the distances.[9]

Comedy is the 'ultimate sophistication'[10] because it engages all the faculties, fusing the activity of head and heart, the aesthetic and the moral, so that the poems' speakers are identifiable with the poet and capable of giving the effect of directly addressing the reader. 'Comic' sincerity is a serious matter. Since the poet aims to fuse and not oppose style and substance, sincerity may give way to bitterness or didacticism but never irony. Technique, Kavanagh said, is 'a method of being sincere':

> The business of technique [is] to provide us with a means to reveal ourselves truthfully without being silly, mawkish, or in any way to speak that which would make us unhappy. The purpose of technique is to enable us to detach our experience from ourselves and see it as a thing apart.[11]

What also becomes evident is that self-expression is not the expression of personal experience alone. Sincere poetry is poetry that integrates individual feelings with the generalized feelings of humankind. Kavanagh aims to detach himself from personal suffering so that it can be seen as an aspect of the human situation. The individual merges with the universal through an act of romantic faith in their natural interconnectedness, and a durable Catholic vision of life that enabled him to place his personal experience in a larger universal scheme of rebirth and redemption.

FROM MONAGHAN TO THE GRAND CANAL

Kavanagh's formulations of sincerity encourage us not only to view his work as a process of symbolic integration but also to read it as we might read 'confessional' poetry and prose. Kavanagh, that is, invites us to read his life through his work, to piece together an autobiographical narrative, often with identifiable real-life people. *The Green Fool* (1938) and *Tarry Flynn* (1948) are both continuous narratives more or less telling the story of his early life; the poems, not being bound by this narrative pressure, are free to exist as lyrics in their own right, yet contribute to the Kavanagh *Bildungsroman* by isolating and exploring emotionally concentrated and transformative experiences.

Born 21 October 1904 to James, a cobbler and small farmer, and Bridget (née Quinn), in the townland of Mucker, in the parish of Inniskeen, County Monaghan, the fourth child and first son in a family of ultimately ten children (one died while still a baby), Patrick had no formal education beyond Kednaminsha National School, which he left at the age of 12. He was a self-made man, self-educated, a believer in poetry's mystical power, proud of his humble roots. The most complete account of these early years is contained in *The Green Fool*, his first attempt at autobiography. Here, Kavanagh describes his childhood on the family farm, working in the fields, lazing around the headlands, going to school, becoming a small farmer, developing an interest in poetry, and ends with a reference to the publication of his first collection of poems, *Ploughman and Other Poems*, and his current residence in London, where he wrote *The Green Fool*. The book combines an anthropological interest in the lives of a small farming community viewed through the eyes of an insider farmer-narrator and a concern to provide an entertaining, lively, amusing, impressionistic autobiography. The narrative is in fact surprisingly light on specific autobiographical facts, devoting its attention to detailing the Inniskeen social milieu. Distance in time and place from his rural origins may no doubt account for the tendency towards affectionate idealism. The title casts the author-narrator as a kind of Dostoievskian holy fool, his poetry-writing at first making him a figure of fun among his community but gradually earning him recognition and respect. Though in his 'Self-Portrait' of 1964 Kavanagh was to refer to The Green Fool as 'a dreadful stage-Irish, so-called autobiography'[12] tailored to the requirements of the English market, the book in fact reveals, as Antoinette Quinn puts it, 'an unresolved tension between a Revivalist romanticisation of country folk and a comic realist representation'.[13] Reviews in both England and Ireland were favourable, but the book was abruptly pulled from circulation in 1939 following an action for libel taken by Oliver St. John Gogarty, the author and medical doctor, who objected to a remark which implied that he kept a mistress. Kavanagh was taken by surprise for he thought he had protected himself adequately against possible libel action by changing most of the names of real-life people and confining himself to superficial, functional characterization. The experience was not only financially disastrous for Kavanagh, but introduced him to the bitter in-fighting and jockeying for position in Dublin literary circles from which thereafter he was never to be far distant.

His earliest poems appeared in the 'Poet's Corner' of the Irish Weekly Independent between August 1928 and June 1929. In 1929 and 1930 he also managed to place some poems in the Irish Statesman, and began a profitable correspondence with the editor AE (George Russell), his earliest mentor. The Green Fool includes the legendary story of a three-day pilgrimage from Monaghan to Dublin which the 26-year-old poet undertook in 1930, begging food and money along the way, to meet the luminaries of Irish literary life, including AE and Seamus O'Sullivan, the editor of The Dublin Magazine. Kavanagh's first major breakthrough, however, was the London publication of a slim collection of thirty-one poems written between 1930 and 1935, Ploughman and Other Poems (1936). These poems are divided between personal lyrics of self-examination, such as 'Inniskeen Road: July Evening', and more objective studies of rural life, such as 'Peasant Poet', the two strands which together make up the weave of Kavanagh's later poetry, with sometimes the objective vision predominating, as in his explorations of artistic, political and social aspects of modern Irish culture, and sometimes the subjective element to the forefront, as in those poems devoted to the ongoing drama of his poetic soul. These early poems record his sense of loneliness and separation from the rest of the community, but reaffirm a belief in the mystical power of his imagination to divine the pagan beauty of the natural world and transcend his humble lot. With the publication of Ploughman, the legend of Kavanagh the 'peasant poet' with his roots in the soil was ready to take shape.

The reasons for Kavanagh's move away from the family farm, first to London and then, in 1939, to Dublin, are not hard to divine: the lack of encouragement and opportunity to pursue his poetic vocation, the relentlessness and oppressiveness of the routines of farming life, the lack of contact with like-minded people. However, in his 'Self-Portrait', with the benefit of hindsight, he refers to the move as a mistake:

> It was the worst mistake in my life. The Hitler war had started. I had my comfortable little holding of watery hills beside the Border. What was to bate it for a life? And yet I wasted what could have been my four glorious years, begging and scrambling around the streets of malignant Dublin.[14]

Much of his best poetry is written out of this sense of ambivalence towards his native place. He loved the fields and hills but detested rural society and hard work, which destroyed the creative spirit. No bohemian, Kavanagh moved to literary Dublin in search of respectability: 'Part of my poverty-stricken upbringing was my belief in respectability – a steady job, decency. The bohemian rascals living it up in basements and in mountain hideouts horrified me.'[15] As much an outsider in the city as he had been in the country, Kavanagh was to spend the rest of his life – mostly in Dublin – on the margins of respectability, begging and scrambling for work, for money, for a place to live, for recognition.

By the time he arrived in Dublin in 1939 the Revival was on its last legs, though some were still playing at pastoral and trying to be peasants, and ready to hail Kavanagh as the real thing, the authentic Irish peasant. Kavanagh, however, was struggling to discard the stereotype of the literary peasant and to avoid the pressures to turn poetry into a commodity for sale on foreign markets. Earlier writers such as Joyce or Yeats, writing from a colonial or post-colonial standpoint were, not unnaturally, absorbed by the binary opposition between Ireland and England. Kavanagh's great contribution to the development of an Irish poetics was his disregard of the colonial theme and concentration on the universal particular. As he famously put it in *Kavanagh's Weekly* in 1952: 'Parochialism and provincialism are direct opposites. A provincial is always trying to live by other people's loves, but a parochial is self-sufficient.'[16] Nationality, he believed, was an abstraction, of little use to poetry. 'I do not believe', he declared, 'that there is any such thing as "Irish" in literature.' As against the national theme, he asserted the value of the ordinary, the local and the particular – 'The things that really matter are casual, insignificant little things'[17] – and the need for realism instead of sentimentalities to express the life of rural Ireland.

The Great Hunger, the major long poem which he began in 1941, disputes the sentimentalities perpetrated by romantic poets and politicians, and lapped up by cultural tourists and complacent urbanites. If his first collection, *Ploughman and Other Poems*, still betrayed Revivalist Yeatsian influences, *The Great Hunger* marked a definite change of attitude. Yet, despite the oppressiveness of rural life, Kavanagh's love of the land remains. The poem is not written against the land, but against false romantic views of the land. Celtic Twilight Romanticism, he believed, was inherently dishonest. He blamed Protestants: they were the ones who 'had invented Irish Literature as a sort of national religion and they were shy about letting Catholic outsiders in on the jag'.[18] In his 'Self-Portrait', he famously declares that the Irish Literary Movement sponsored by Lady Gregory, Yeats and Synge and purporting to be 'frightfully Irish and racy of the Celtic soil was a thoroughgoing English-bred lie'.[19] Not for Kavanagh the classic themes and methods of the Revivalists: nostalgia for past glories and a lost language, allusions to Celtic mythology, the civilizing influence of the Big House. No less obnoxious to him was the fantasy of rural Ireland propounded by Eamon de Valera, enshrined in the Constitution of 1937 and, ironically, deriving from the racial and cultural ideas of an Englishman, Matthew Arnold. In a landmark (pun intended) 1942 St Patrick's Day broadcast, the Taoiseach de Valera spoke of a countryside 'joyous with sounds of industry, the romping of sturdy children, the contests of athletic youths, the laughter of comely maidens, whose firesides would be the forums of the wisdom of serene old age'. What de Valera chose to overlook was the actual desolation, deprivation and depopulation of the Irish countryside, partly as a result of emigration and migration, partly through late marriage or no marriage. In The Great Hunger, Kavanagh replaces these idealized images of farm life with a vivid portrait of a half-conscious, frustrated, lonely old bachelor farmer, condemned to a daily round of hard labour, stuck with his mother until she dies at 91, and devoid of energy to struggle against his fate. The poem details the forces that have shaped Patrick Maguire's life: the land, the Church and social custom. So controversial was Kavanagh's representation of rural Ireland that when sections of the poem, under its original title The Old Peasant, were first published in 1942 in Cyril Connolly's Horizon magazine, it attracted the attention of the Dublin Vice Squad. At the time, rumours were rife that the poem had been banned under the Censorship of Publications Act, but this turned out not to be true. In 1942, George Yeats's Cuala Press published a limited edition of 250 copies of the entire poem knowing that it was a likely candidate for banning on account of several sexually explicit passages. Only an abridged version was included in A Soul for Sale (1947), but a complete version reprinted in Collected Poems (1964) and in the Complete Poems (1972) managed to escape the depredations of a notoriously philistine and puritanical Irish Censorship Board.

Patrick Maguire is a representative figure, emblematic of the Irish small farmer generally, but also a projection of the figure Kavanagh might have become had he not left Inniskeen. The only solution to the situation portrayed in the poem, it would seem, would be to leave the countryside, and it is the story of departure to which Kavanagh turns in his next major work, the autobiographical novel Tarry Flynn. Like The Green Fool, Tarry Flynn is both a portrait of the artist as a young man and a picture of a small Irish backwater, though with less emphasis on its folkloric interest. While reflecting his childhood experience of 'the usual barbaric life of the Irish country poor',[20] the novel is written in accordance with Kavanagh's evolving notions of comic detachment, in contrast to the socio-critical approach of The Great Hunger, inspired by Sean O'Faolain's often contentious periodical, The Bell. In order to avoid the kind of litigation that attended the publication of The Green Fool, he veils real-life identities more carefully and sets the story in the fictional parish of Dargan in County Cavan in 1935. The characterization of Mrs Flynn is in some measure a tribute to Kavanagh's own mother, who died in 1945, three years before the publication of *Tarry Flynn*. But the character of Mrs Flynn is also adapted to the demands of the novel, in particular, to the contrast that is developed between her practical, down-to-earth devotion to her family and the dreamy, impractical son. Tarry is a version of the poet as described in Kavanagh's 'Self-Portrait': 'The poet is never one of the people. He is detached, remote, and the life of small-time dances and talk about football would not be for him. He might take part but could not belong.'[21] In the end, Tarry makes good his escape from the land, as Kavanagh had done, not with bitterness or resentment, but out of a desire for a larger imaginative experience. The novel registers the pain of departure and ends sentimentally, with a poem which celebrates the beauty of the sacred green world which Tarry is leaving: 'And then I came to the haggard gate, / And I knew as I entered that I had come / Through fields that were no earthly estate'. Though *Tarry Flynn* contains more autobiographical fact than *The Green Fool*, it also tends to romanticize the figure of the author-hero. Having rejected *The Green Fool* for its allegedly Literary Revival romanticism, Kavanagh considered *Tarry Flynn* to be 'not only the best but the only authentic account of life as it was lived in Ireland in this century',[22] a view which has some justification in light of the novel's authentic representation of such rural curiosities as squabbling neighbours, local feuds, parish missioning, local law suits, ritual match-making, the routines of farming life, and the many other richly detailed aspects of the Monaghan *comédie humaine*. A week after its publication by the Pilot Press in London, the book was banned by the Irish Censorship Board on the grounds that it was 'indecent and obscene'. A few weeks later, however, the ban was withdrawn on appeal.

Kavanagh always thought of himself primarily as a poet, but his poetic output is in fact considerably smaller than that of his prose work. On arrival in Dublin, he immediately set about cultivating the attention of the Dublin literati in the hope of securing a job. A naïve 35-year-old 'culchie' (a Dublin insult used to dismiss non-Dubliners as country bumpkins), he was ready to play the part of the peasant poet in order to gain acceptance; but, uncouth and rudely outspoken as he often was, he had a knack for making himself unpopular. His soul was not for sale at any price. Integrity mattered more than success – mostly. Even if he had been willing to compromise, it is doubtful if he would ever have been able to break into the enchanted circle of Dublin literary society, given the influence of the Catholic Church and the few powerful political families who had gained control after 1916. Though not yet an alcohol drinker, he frequented the Palace Bar, a Fleet Street haunt of the literary set, presided over by Bertie Smyllie, editor of the Irish Times, and did manage to persuade both Smyllie and Frank Geary, editor of the Irish Independent, Ireland's biggest daily, to put some book reviewing and special feature writing his way during 1942 and 1943. His first regular journalistic job came in 1942 when, under the pseudonym of 'Piers Ploughman', he began writing a twice-weekly column, 'City Commentary', for the Irish Press. The following year he gained employment on the Catholic weekly, The Standard, to write book reviews for its 'Literary Scene' section. Unable to confine himself to book reviewing, Kavanagh used his column as a platform from which to offer his own views on Irish literary and cultural matters more generally. It was during this time that his first attacks on the Literary Revival appeared. When his Irish Press column came to an end in 1944, he spent more than a year without regular employment, recording his frustration in his poem 'Pegasus', where he compares his soul to an old horse that he is unable to sell to Church or State or meanest trade. With the help of the archbishops of Dublin and Tuam he was eventually taken back on The Standard as editorial and features writer, condemned to the soul-destroying work of reporting on funerals, ordinations, pilgrimages and other religious affairs. In 1946 he was delighted to accept the job of film critic for The Standard, later paying generous tribute to Patrick Curry, the editor, who gave him the opportunity to express himself freely:

> He was the only man who ever gave me a regular job. He was also the only editor who would and did give me the complete freedom to say what I liked without fearing that the remarks of a 'genius' would cause scandal, widespread sinfulness and – worse still – loss of advertising revenue.[23]

It soon became apparent, however, that Kavanagh's main qualification for the job was an undisguised contempt for popular film. Again, he refused to confine himself to his official brief, straying from film criticism to general literary and social criticism. After putting up with Kavanagh's casual attitude for over three years, Curry sacked him in July 1949.

During this time, Kavanagh had also struck up an association with *The Bell*, a monthly literary and cultural journal, founded in 1940 and edited by Sean O'Faolain until 1946, when Peadar O'Donnell took over the job of editor. In 1947 O'Donnell hired Kavanagh as deputy editor. Kavanagh's *Bell* publications included a verse playlet, 'The Wake of the Books', a satire on Irish censorship though, Kavanagh conceded, 'There's much that's insincere in what is banned – / And time if left the corpse would bury it deeper / In ten years than our bitterest conscience-keeper'. O'Faolain and Frank O'Connor had put *The Bell* in the forefront of the attack on the Gaelic revival and romantic conceptions of Ireland. Now, however, Kavanagh turned on both these writers, despite the support they had given him personally in the past. In a highly controversial piece, 'Coloured Balloons' (*The Bell*, December 1947), he charged O'Connor with abandoning his commitment to authenticity and realism for the sake of populist acclaim: 'I have heard O'Connor compared to Chekhov. No two writers could be more unlike. Chekhov's genius is the cutting edge of sincerity ruthlessly piercing through the crust of the ordinary. His courageous poetic mind is never the slave of his audience.'[24] Kavanagh's excoriation of fellow artists and former friends intensified in December 1947 in the pages of *Irish Writing*, which contained his essay on F.R. Higgins, 'The Gallivanting Poet'. Higgins is lambasted for his addiction to the myth and illusion that was 'Ireland', and ridiculed for his Protestant desperation to prove his Irishness: 'All this', says Kavanagh, 'was the essence of insincerity, for sincerity means giving all oneself to one's work, being absolutely real.'[25] Between December 1949 and July 1951, Kavanagh's 'Diary' column for the monthly *Envoy* gave him further opportunity to castigate literary mediocrity and Revival phoniness. When *Envoy* folded in 1951, he persuaded his brother to invest his savings in starting *Kavanagh's Weekly*. This was a small-circulation paper which lasted for thirteen weeks until Peter Kavanagh's financial resources ran out. The paper offered penetrating, witty social and cultural commentary, but such was the offensiveness of Kavanagh's contributions that by the time it collapsed in 1952 he had alienated himself so completely from Irish public life that his journalistic career was all but over. There followed stints writing a weekly column for the *Irish Farmers' Journal*, the *National Observer* (a Fine Gael monthly) and even the *RTV Guide*. His journalism, often aggressive and controversial, was impatient of close analysis and argumentation, devoid of any coherent intellectual system, but marked by the same intensity and concern for sincerity as informed his poetry.

Shortly after completing *The Great Hunger* he began work on another long poem, *Lough Derg*, intended as a sequel to *The Great Hunger*. In *Lough Derg* he continued to explore his relationship with his environment, but he was never satisfied with the poem and it was only published posthumously in 1978. During the 1940s he also wrote a series of verse satires and parodies of fellow poets, in which he expressed his concern about the state of contemporary Irish culture and art. Chief among these poems is 'The Paddiad: Or the Devil as a Patron of Irish Letters', written in 1949 and first published in *Horizon* magazine. Based on Pope's 'Dunciad', 'The Paddiad' ridicules Dublin's literary elite by turning them into Hibernian dunces, hacks concerned more with self-promotion and mutual back-scratching than with artistic excellence. 'Paddy of the Celtic Mist', 'Paddy Connemara West' and 'Chestertonian Paddy Frog' are based loosely on actual writers whom Kavanagh particularly despised: Robert Farran (novelist and poet), M.J. McManus (literary editor of the *Irish Press*) and Austin Clarke. The presiding Devil is a composite of Bertie Smyllie, M.J. McManus and Maurice Walsh (novelist). Kavanagh's general complaint is levelled against those who seek to promote an ethnic Gaelic, Catholic, Revivalist Irish poetic. Kavanagh himself is Paddy Conscience, an amalgam of Joyce, the satirical Yeats and O'Casey. The dishevelled Paddy Conscience is a figure of the vagabond outcast poet who is opposed to the bourgeois mediocrity of the other Paddies.

As well as these public poems, Kavanagh continued to write poems of personal soul-searching in which he returned – with more than a hint of nostalgia – to the wellspring of his creativity in rural Inniskeen. His next collection, *A Soul for Sale* (1947), contains both public and personal poems, among them such Kavanagh classics as 'Stony Grey Soil' and 'Pegasus'. From 1950 there emerged a new kind of personal poetry. In poems such as 'Ante-Natal Dream', 'The Defeated', 'Epic' and 'Auditors In', he engages in an exploratory, confessional poetry of honest self-examination, at times humorously self-critical, pondering the conditions of creativity, reviewing from his urban base the validity of the old pastoral themes and settings, experimenting with a relaxed vernacular:

> The problem that confronts me here
> Is to be eloquent yet sincere;
> Let myself rip and not go phony
> In an inflated testimony. ('Auditors In')

The ending of this poem gestures towards the new-found sense of composure and self-realization that Kavanagh had achieved by this stage in his life: 'I am so glad / To come accidentally upon / My self at the end of the tortuous road'. All this was to be temporarily wrecked by the devastating turn of events to follow.

Shortly after the demise of *Kavanagh's Weekly*, a 'Profile' appeared in *The Leader* in October 1952 picturing Kavanagh as an alcoholic scrounger and opinionated waffler. Kavanagh sued for libel. The case came to court on 4 February 1954. Chief Counsel for the defendants was John A. Costello, who had been Taoiseach from 1948 to 1951, and who was to become so again between 1954 and 1957. Kavanagh lost his case and was ordered to pay all costs. By now in an advanced stage of alcoholism and unable to find a regular job (for three months in 1954 he worked as a spray-painting salesman), he was to suffer even more terribly when he was diagnosed with lung cancer and entered the Rialto Hospital in Dublin in March 1955 to have a lung removed. The *Irish Times* prepared his obituary. Even close friends gave up on his recovery. But recover he did, and during the summer of 1955 underwent his famous 'rebirth' by the banks of the Grand Canal between Baggot and Leeson Street Bridges. With the fires of righteous indignation somewhat abated, his social protest would never again be as virulent as it once was. Returning to the pastoral mode, he found in nature the source of divine revelation. Poetry became religious experience. 'A poet', he said in his 'Self-Portrait', 'is a theologian'.[26] A simple lyricism expressed a new spirit of acceptance, repose and celebration. The new emphasis was on self-realization rather than social criticism. He spoke of departure and return, keen to see a unity between his early and late poetry, sincerity being ever the key concern:

> There are two kinds of simplicity, the simplicity of going away and the simplicity of return. The last is the ultimate in sophistication. In the final simplicity we don't care whether we appear foolish or not. We talk of things that earlier would embarrass. We are satisfied with being ourselves, however small.[27]

The naïve simplicity of the early work has grown into the knowing simplicity of the later poems, which are the work of the pilgrim-seer who
has completed his lonely hegira towards wisdom and love.

In 1958 his brother published a number of his poems in New York
under the title *Recent Poems*, though some of them were not at all recent.
Two years later, Longmans brought out what was to become his most
financially successful collection, *Come Dance with Kitty Stobling and Other
Poems*, a volume which also contained earlier poems going back to the
late 1940s. In 1961 the Dublin publisher McGibbon & Kee offered him
a contract to publish his *Collected Poems*. By 1960 his health was beginning
to decline again, and his work-rate noticeably slackened. He continued
to give a series of extramural lectures at University College Dublin and,
in 1962, wrote 'Self-Portrait' for RTE. Much of 1962 was spent in
Inniskeen, where his sister Annie nursed him. 1965 saw him at
Northwestern University, Chicago, lecturing on Yeats. Setting out to be
deliberately provocative, he declared that Yeats 'wasn't Irish and never
wrote a line that any ordinary Irish person would read', and that 'all this
pretension and bawling lecturology' was 'disastrous and shocking'.[28]
His audience of academic Yeatsian devotees was not impressed. A final
series of country poems was written during extended stays in Inniskeen
between 1959 and 1966, but they testify to progressively depleted personal resources and technical weakness. In 1967 he married Katherine
Barry Moloney, whom he had met seven years previously in London,
and who came from a prominent Republican family, her mother having
been the sister of the legendary Kevin Barry, the young rebel hanged by
the British in 1920. Katherine, along with his sister Annie, tended him
faithfully during these last years. Seven months after his marriage, on 30
November 1967, he died of pneumonia and was buried in Inniskeen.

THE PURE FLAME

Though committed to an ideal of sincerity in both life and art,
Kavanagh, as his biographers and critics frequently point out, conspicu-
ously failed to live up to this ideal himself in his dealings with other
individuals. Problems arise, too, when 'sincerity' is invoked in a literary
context. A glance at the inconsistencies in his 'Self-Portrait' is sufficient
to raise questions about the author's sincerity: one minute he is com-

plaining about his early Monaghan experience ('the usual barbaric life of the Irish country poor'), then, a few paragraphs later, claiming that the biggest mistake he ever made was to leave the family farm. As an account of his career, Antoinette Quinn concludes, 'Self-Portrait' 'is not merely idiosyncratic; it is wilfully misleading'.[29] The situation is even more complicated in the poetry. Kavanagh asks us to take at face value what he seems to be offering, to accept that he is speaking truthfully to us in his poems. But, on close inspection, internal contradictions become apparent.

Take, for example, a Kavanagh standard, 'Stony Grey Soil', in which, we assume, the poet sets out to explain to us as fully and clearly as he can his present state of mind. He is expressing his innermost feelings. But when we examine the poem closely we discover that the very nature of its confession throws into doubt the existence of an autobiographical 'I' that is capable of making such confessions. The speaker's depiction of the situation depends on a series of oppositions: between a 'vision of beauty, love and truth' and its occlusion, between Apollonian eloquence and self-conscious mumbling, between a fresh unadulterated relationship with the natural world and a relationship distorted and degraded by work. And yet, the writing that sets out these oppositions simultaneously undoes them. The speaker wonders if his pen hasn't been poisoned, yet expresses the idea with an artfully controlled balance of bitterness and tenderness. He tells us that his lyric gift has been usurped by a 'peasant's prayer', yet the poem demonstrates, in its rhythmic vitality and sharp, fresh images, that his lyric faculty is alive and well.

In temporal terms, the oppositions of the poem depend upon the word 'still' in the sixth stanza: we are left to wonder whether the speaker has lost youthful lyric vision or whether what he fears has not yet overtaken him, falsifying his claim that 'Wherever I turn I see / In the stony grey soil of Monaghan / Dead loves that were born for me'. When the poet suggests that there is a difference between what he once saw and what he actually sees now, we cannot help asking: how can we be sure that he is telling us what he actually sees now, and not (deliberately or unintentionally) saying what he thinks he should be seeing and feeling?

The oppositions between past and present, between pleasure and anxiety, between original vision and deadening experience, break down at the level of syntax. In the second stanza, 'You clogged the feet of my boyhood' would seem to have a causal relationship with what immediately follows, an expectation heightened by the opposition of 'You' and 'I': 'You clogged the feet of my boyhood / And I believed that my stumble / Had the poise and stride of Apollo / And his voice my thick-tongued mumble'. On this reading, the stumbling of the clogged feet is productive of Apollonian grace and eloquence. However, the 'And' need not signify causality, but could function instead as a loose conversational and associative marker introducing a reference to a pristine condition which actually precedes the clogging effect of Monaghan's stony grey soil. A further twist is that, paradoxically, the state of preliterate innocence is described in terms of classical mythology: the speaker's classical understanding of his situation belongs to the past tense ('I believed'), that is, to that stage in his life prior to the effects of what Trilling calls 'adulteration' or 'sophistication'.

'Stony Grey Soil' rewrites the whole Romantic problematic of self-consciousness. The poem suggests that the poet's wholeness and integrity depend on his oneness with nature, on his unmediated relationship with the divine presence in the world around him. At some point, Kavanagh tells us, he lost this youthful capacity to respond directly and passionately to his world, to speak freely. What followed was a fall into doubt and self-division, a state in which the self (as conscious subject) observes the self (as object). Yet the idyllic state in the past can only be accessed and re-enacted in the present tense of the poem's own self-consciousness. Kavanagh only wants us to see self-consciousness as the bringer of confusion and loss, yet self-consciousness is all there is to offer any hope of self-understanding or self-(re)possession or self-identity.

The poem makes the poet's sincerity difficult to judge – all the more so since other poems written around the same time point to a very different truth or feeling. 'Pegasus', for example, ends by proclaiming the power and victory of the imagination that has enabled the poet to rise above the circumstances that have mired him in frustration and failure. Yet the issue of Kavanagh's sincerity cannot simply be dismissed: to read Kavanagh at all, we have to accept at least the fiction of a truthful or sincere speaker. It is a truism that what a poet says in his poetry is not always what he thinks or claims he says: what is said is always conditioned by the poet's sense of his audience, by social context, by the linguistic structures to which he must more or less conform, by the potentially distorting drive to discover beauty or truth. Given that sincerity is such a notoriously elusive commodity, how is it to be assessed?

The kind of contextual information on social, biographical and literary factors included in this chapter can help to illumine the poetry. But the difficulty with this extra-poetic information is that it belongs to a different order of knowledge and can, in fact, undermine as much as illumine the special form of knowledge contained in the internal circuitry of the poem. The poet's sincerity cannot simply be a matter of checking his poetic statement against the extra-poetic documentary evidence. As Kavanagh put it: 'I am not suggesting that being true to life in a realist way is the highest function of a writer ... the highest function is the pure flame from the material'.[30] Instead of merely equating sincerity with autobiographical disclosure, a more productive approach might be for the reader to look at the way claims of sincerity work creatively in relationship with their inevitable failure, the way the myth of the self is compromised by its own internal contradictions. As seen from 'Stony Grey Soil', sincerity claims can have more of a destabilizing than stabilizing effect in the poetry. A poetic commitment to self-expression can produce unintended consequences, which in turn stimulate a readerly opening-up of the gaps and aporetic junctures at the heart of what is ostensibly sincere self-knowledge. It isn't the degree of a poem's commitment to sincerity that counts, but the subtlety of its engagement with the paradoxes of self-consciousness, its formal handling of the tensions between self-possession and self-doubt.

NOTES

1. 'Mr Belloc Again', *Irish Times* (13 June 1942), p.5.
2. Patrick Kavanagh, 'From Monaghan to the Grand Canal', in Antoinette Quinn (ed.), *A Poet's Country: Selected Prose* (Dublin: Lilliput Press, 2003), p.280.
3. Patrick Kavanagh, 'Two Ways', in Peter Kavanagh (ed.), *The Complete Poems: Patrick Kavanagh, 1904–1967* (Newbridge: Goldsmith Press, 1984); originally published as *The Complete Poems of Patrick Kavanagh* (New York: Peter Kavanagh Hand Press, 1972), p.28. The poem is not included in either Antoinette Quinn (ed.), *Patrick Kavanagh: Collected Poems* (Harmondsworth: Penguin, 2005), or *Patrick Kavanagh: Collected Poems* (London: Martin Brian & O'Keefe, 1972). Available online at www.tcd.ie?English/patrickkavanagh/twowaystaq.html.
4. 'War and Love', *The Standard* (28 January 1949), p.3.

5. Lionel Trilling, *Sincerity and Authenticity* (Oxford: Oxford University Press, 1971), pp.12–13.

6. John Montague, 'Isolation and Cunning: Recent Irish Verse', *Poetry*, 92 (4 July 1959), p.49.

7. John Nemo, *Patrick Kavanagh* (London: George Prior; New York: Twayne, 1979), p.115.

8. 'Poets on Poetry', X, 1 (March 1960), p.156. Quoted in Nemo, *Patrick Kavanagh*, p.124.

9. Patrick Kavanagh, *November Haggard, Uncollected Prose and Verse of Patrick Kavanagh*, ed. Peter Kavanagh (New York: Peter Kavanagh Hand Press, 1971), p.15.

10. Patrick Kavanagh, 'Self-Portrait', in Quinn (ed.), *Poet's Country*, p.306

11. Kavanagh, *November Haggard*, p.73.

12. Kavanagh, 'Self-Portrait', p.306.

13. Antoinette Quinn, *Patrick Kavanagh: A Biography* (Dublin: Gill & Macmillan, 2003), p.97.

14. Kavanagh, 'Self-Portrait', p.307.

15. Ibid., p.308.

16. Kavanagh, 'Parochialism and Provincialism', in Quinn (ed.), *Poet's Country*, p.237.

17. Kavanagh, 'Self-Portrait', p.313.

18. Patrick Kavanagh, *Lapped Furrows*, ed. Peter Kavanagh (New York: Peter Kavanagh Hand Press, 1969), p.46.

19. Kavanagh, 'Self-Portrait', p.306.

20. Ibid., p.307.

21. Ibid., p.308.

22. Ibid., p.306.

23. Quoted in Peter Kavanagh, *Sacred Keeper: A Biography of Patrick Kavanagh* (Newbridge: Goldsmith Press, 1979), p.134.

24. Patrick Kavanagh, 'Coloured Balloons', in Quinn (ed.), *Poet's Country*, p.212.

25. Patrick Kavanagh, 'The Gallivanting Poet', in Quinn (ed.), *Poet's Country*, p.193.

26. Kavanagh, 'Self-Portrait', p.315.

27. Ibid.

28. Quoted in Quinn, *Patrick Kavanagh: A Biography*, p.430.

29. Ibid., pp.409–10.

30. Patrick Kavanagh, 'From Monaghan to the Grand Canal', in Quinn (ed.), *Poet's Country*, p.275.

CHAPTER THREE

Kavanagh's Poetics and Prose:
Against Formulae

ALEX DAVIS

Kavanagh's career as a prose writer is, like so much in his life and work, an untidy affair. From 1936 until shortly before his death in 1967, he devoted a great deal of energy to the production of work for various newspapers, journals and other print outlets. Like the critical and occasional prose of his near-contemporary Austin Clarke, this body of work is of mixed quality. The disastrously organized *Collected Pruse* (1967), put together by Niall Sheridan, is an unfortunate, though perhaps telling, witness to over thirty years of writing fiction, memoirs, articles, essays, columns and reviews. Cobbled together, the volume mangles several of the original texts and pointlessly capitalizes on Kavanagh's notoriety by reprinting newspaper accounts of a failed libel case brought by the author against *The Leader* in 1954.

Kavanagh's forays into autobiography and fiction produced two highly realized books: the autobiographical *The Green Fool* (1938) and the novel *Tarry Flynn* (1948); an engaging if unreliable memoir, *Self-Portrait* (1964); and a number of short stories. Well-received by reviewers, the success of *The Green Fool* was short-lived: it was withdrawn in Ireland and Britain within a year of publication following a successful libel action brought by Oliver St John Gogarty. But Kavanagh's prose writing was dogged by more than, as in this instance, ill luck. *Tarry Flynn* took Kavanagh the best part of the 1940s to write, going through many revisions; and abandoned attempts at sustained fiction litter his writing life during this decade. As a journalist, essayist and reviewer, Kavanagh was far more productive: he wrote columns for, among other organs, the *Irish Press* ('City Commentary', 1942–44), *The Standard* ('The Literary

Scene', February to June 1943, and for which he also wrote film reviews from 1946 to 1949), Envoy ('Diary', 1949 to 1951), and a film page for the Republic of Ireland's television and radio listings magazine, the RTV Guide. With his brother Peter, Kavanagh produced from April to July 1952 a platform for his often scabrous views on literature and politics in the short-lived Kavanagh's Weekly, to which he contributed the majority of articles. He placed articles and other occasional pieces in a wide range of Irish and British journals, including The Bell, Ireland of the Welcomes, Irish Writing, Nimbus and Studies.[1] The quality of this work varies enormously and, it must be said, there is a good deal of indifferent hack-work among it – hardly surprising, given the impecunious Kavanagh's constant need for money. With the exception of the unreliable Collected Pruse, Kavanagh lacked the opportunity to publish a selection of his significant shorter prose pieces; a scholarly edition, A Poet's Country: Selected Prose, edited by Antoinette Quinn, would not appear until 2003.[2]

Given its publishing history, it is unremarkable that Kavanagh's critical prose does not develop a sustained aesthetic. The majority of it engages with the work of other writers, often, though not exclusively, his Irish predecessors and contemporaries. Although Kavanagh's animosity towards many of his subjects leads him into overstatement and, at times, downright contradictory pronouncements, a number of key preoccupations can be discerned in this straggling body of work. Kavanagh's poetic is raised on Romantic foundations, on theories of inspiration and organic form commonplace to post-romantic conceptions of creativity. As a corollary of these assumptions, Kavanagh derides poetry he views as constructed according to lifeless 'formulae', pre-eminent among which is the writing of the Irish Literary Revival, especially that of W.B. Yeats and J.M. Synge. This, in turn, prompts Kavanagh to advocate what is, broadly speaking, a 'realist' approach to the representation of Irish subject matter. Rejecting cultural nationalism, Kavanagh's poetic realism is linked to an intense regionalism or localism, through which, he maintains, 'Universal' themes can be addressed. A late fixation is the centrality of 'comedy' to poetry, a belief held so strongly by Kavanagh that it prompted the rejection of his masterpiece, The Great Hunger (1942), as 'underdeveloped Comedy, not fully born', an image wholly at one with his lifelong organicist assumptions about poetic creativity.[3]

The stillborn literary work is the result of what, in effect, is a

Horatian attentiveness to the craft of poetry; a predetermined approach to composition that, for Kavanagh, can easily slide into adherence to dogmatic formulae. In an appraisal of James Joyce, who admired Horace, Kavanagh claims 'that Joyce had little or none of that ethereal commodity known as inspiration. He is the very clever, cynical man who has found a formula.'[4] Kavanagh was ambivalent about Joyce's achievement: venerating A Portrait, he was uneasy about Ulysses and frankly contemptuous of Finnegans Wake. Troubling Kavanagh is his sense that Joyce's is an artisanal method of writing, whereas Kavanagh clearly shared Keats's belief 'That if Poetry comes not as naturally as the Leaves to a tree it had better not come at all'.[5]

Kavanagh's essentially Romantic faith in inspiration is discernable from his earliest poetry, collected in Ploughman and Other Poems (1936). The majority of the poems in this volume are based, not on his own experience of rural life in County Monaghan, but on his fitful exposure to the English-language poetic canon and, from 1925, to the mysticism of AE (George Russell), in whose Irish Statesman he published several of his early lyrics.[6] AE's aesthetic priorities, as Antoinette Quinn has argued, had been forged in the Celtic twilight of the late nineteenth century, and had stayed there.[7] Lacking even the soporific odour of Decadence, his belated Romanticism permeates the most achieved poem collected in Ploughman and Other Poems, 'Inniskeen Road: July Evening'. Despite prefiguring Kavanagh's subsequent poetry in its emphasis on the quotidian aspects of Irish rural life, the poem portrays the poet as the clear descendant of the Romantic solitary through its hyperbolic identification of the speaker with the real-life model for Daniel Defoe's castaway Robinson Crusoe, Alexander Selkirk.[8] Likewise, the final stanza of a slightly later poem, 'Art McCooey' (1941), might be read as a bathetic reworking of Coleridge's elevated description of the workings of the 'primary imagination' in the thirteenth chapter of Biographia Literaria, 'as a repetition in the finite mind of the eternal act of creation in the infinite I AM':[9]

> Wash out the cart with a bucket of water and a wangel
> Of wheaten straw. Jupiter looks down.
> Unlearnedly and unreasonably poetry is shaped,
> Awkwardly but alive in the unmeasured womb.[10]

This conception of the poem as the offspring of inspiration, in contrast

41

to being the preconceived product of a lifeless 'formula', is central to all Kavanagh's critical essays; *Ulysses*, while *sui generis*, is indicative of modern Irish writing in its prescriptiveness. In the work of the Irish Literary Revival, especially that of Yeats and Synge, Kavanagh detected a far more ominous dogmatism. Repeatedly, Kavanagh rounds on Yeats, accusing him of being 'responsible for the idea of Ireland as a spiritual entity, the idea which gave us so much bogus literature. It was a formula.'[11] Kavanagh's begrudgery with regards to Yeats, it needs to be said, went hand in hand with a grudging admiration for the older poet, particularly his later work: his reaction to him was overstated and confused, but, arguably, essential to finding his own voice.

Kavanagh, as Seamus Deane long ago recognized, saw through the literary myths of the Revival, despising its representation of the so-called 'peasantry'.[12] Writing in *Envoy* in 1950, Kavanagh stated that 'The adulation of Yeats and Joyce has become a menace to the living, for when a dead poet is praised, something is praised that isn't the real thing at all. Death changes the whole position, so that to be on the side of truth one would need to damn dead poets.'[13] The emphasis in this quotation on the need to tell the 'truth' is indicative of a strongly positivist dimension to Kavanagh's poetry and poetics – his overwhelming desire to reflect the 'real thing' that was post-independence Ireland, and which the 'dead poets' of the Revival in particular had distorted and falsified in their work. Synge's drama is a case in point: creating 'an artificial country' and a 'phoney Irish atmosphere', Synge is condemned as 'the originator of the bucklep' – the ultimate put-down in Kavanagh's critical vocabulary.[14] Buckleppin', for Kavanagh, is the kind of stage Irishry that bedevils both the texts of the Literary Revival and permeates much recent Irish writing. In 'The Gallivanting Poet', Kavanagh's specific target is Yeats's friend, F.R. Higgins, whose contribution to the 'bogus literature' produced in the wake of the Irish Literary Revival was to peddle the 'myth and illusion' which is '"Ireland"' by posing as 'a droll, gallivanting "Irishman"', the latter a being whom like Yeats's idealized Fisherman, Kavanagh avers, 'mystically, or poetically, does not exist'.[15]

Kavanagh's antagonism to the 'national myth' recognizes the latter's suasive appeal and its ideological power.[16] In 'Nationalism and Literature' he argues that cultural and political nationalism are 'indestructible', yet, to the writer, 'Ireland as a myth is no use'.[17] That which is, or would be, enabling to the Irish writer is rather a 'parish myth', an intimately felt sense of locality which Kavanagh believes to be the strength of English literature.[18] Kavanagh's realist fidelity to the 'truth' of Irish society and culture at the mid-century is inextricably entwined with his advocating of regionalism, or 'parochialism' as he termed it, and his consequent denigration of nationalism. Central to his thinking about the arts in Ireland is his paradoxical belief that it is through the familiar and the local that one taps into the universal. As he comments in a postscript to his demolition of the buckleppin' Higgins,

> National characteristics are superficial qualities and are not the stuff with which the poet deals. The subject matter of the poet is the Universal and in this he is at one with Catholicism. By a peculiar paradox the pursuit of the Universal and fundamental produces the most exciting local colour as well.[19]

Kavanagh's realism and regionalism find a parallel in the urban localism of Austin Clarke, whose meticulous anatomization of the venality of Irish society at this date is grounded in the environs of Dublin. Yet, wilfully or not, Kavanagh refused to see any connection between his and Clarke's work. Rather, Kavanagh viewed Clarke as a hang-over from the Literary Revival, and numbered him among those lambasted in the 1949 satire, 'The Paddidad':

> In the corner of a Dublin pub
> This party opens – blub-a-blub –
> Paddy Whiskey, Rum and Gin,
> Paddy Three Sheets in the Wind,
> Paddy of the Celtic Mist,
> Paddy Connemara West,
> Chestertonian Paddy Frog
> Croaking nightly in the bog.
> All the Paddies having fun
> Since Yeats handed in his gun.[20]

The work of these Paddies, Kavanagh elsewhere called the 'Irish thing' not the 'real thing', and he viewed it as only suitable for export, particularly to Irish-America.[21] Unquestionably, the identification of Clarke with the Paddies-for-export is erroneous; it is as inaccurate as Samuel

Beckett's cruelly funny depiction of Clarke as Austin Ticklepenny, 'Pot Poet', in *Murphy*. That said, this act of misprision, as Robert F. Garratt notes, allowed Kavanagh to overlook Clarke's 'turn to realism' and thus to foreground the unique significance of his own.[22] More magnanimously, Clarke did see some kind of connection between his work and that of Kavanagh. Kavanagh's mixed response to Joyce echoes Clarke's in that both poets, following Ezra Pound, had little interest in the so-called 'mythical method' T.S. Eliot identified in *Ulysses*; the manner in which Joyce 'manipulat[es] a continuous parallel between contemporaneity and antiquity', between the events of 16 June 1904 that constitute the text's narrative and episodes and characters in Homer's *Odyssey*.[23] For Kavanagh, it is simply a 'mistake' to read such 'deep symbolism' into *Ulysses*, as 'It is almost entirely a transcription of life'.[24] And it is precisely this form of 'transcription' that Clarke, in a 1946 appraisal of 'Poetry in Ireland To-day', perceived in *The Great Hunger*, which he described as 'a realistic study of country life, almost Joycean in its intensity'.[25]

The same conjoining of regionalism and 'Joycean' realism informs the defence of 'parochialism', and the attendant attack on 'provincialism', that Kavanagh mounted in 1952 in the pages of *Kavanagh's Weekly*:

> In Ireland we are provincial not parochial, for it requires a great deal of courage to be parochial. When we do attempt having the courage of our parish we are inclined to go false and to play up to the larger parish on the other side of the Irish Sea. In recent times we have had two great Irish parishioners – James Joyce and George Moore.[26]

The presence of Moore alongside Joyce no doubt stems, in part, from Kavanagh's delight in Moore's deliciously malicious depiction of Yeats in his memoir of the Irish Literary Revival, *Hail and Farewell*.[27] Yet, in the present context, Kavanagh's admiration for Moore's book derives more from his conviction that, as he writes elsewhere, '*Hail and Farewell* is the companion of *Ulysses*, in some ways a better picture of Dublin than Joyce's work'.[28] As 'parishioners' of Dublin, Joyce and Moore oppose the narrow-minded pretensions of provincialism: 'The provincial has no mind of his own; he does not trust what his eyes see until he has heard what the metropolis – towards which his eyes are turned – has to say on any subject. This runs through all activities.' By way of contrast, the parochial writer asserts the primacy of known place for cultural expression: 'The parochial mentality on the other hand is never in any doubt about the social and artistic validity of his parish. All great civilisations are based on parochialism – Greek, Israelite, English.'[29]

As Kavanagh memorably announces in 'Epic', 'I have lived in important places' – in this particular sonnet, a place or parish in which a local squabble over 'half a rood of rock' is granted, through Homeric precedent, as much significance as the contemporary 'Munich bother' of 1938: 'I made the *Iliad* from such / A local row. Gods make their own importance'.[30]

Antoinette Quinn has made the persuasive claim that Kavanagh's powerful reconfiguration of parochialism should be read as a mode of post-colonial writing, in that it rejects any monolithic conception of Irish culture – whether that of the Literary Revivalists or that of Irish Ireland thinking and the rhetoric of Eamon de Valera. A comparison with Austin Clarke is once again instructive. In *Pilgrimage and Other Poems* (1929), Clarke, in Homi Bhabha's terms, 'refigures' or 'restages' the Celtic-Romanesque past in the context of the Irish Free State, forcing the past to confront and critique the post-colonial present: 'Such art does not merely recall the past as social cause or aesthetic precedent; it renews the past, refiguring it as a contingent "in-between" space, that innovates and interrupts the performance of the present.'[31] In Kavanagh's case, his parochialism deconstructs the idea of Ireland having an essential identity, and thus eschews the idea that there should be a national literature that embodies or represents this essence to the people.[32] In short, he is attacking 'ethnicity', though, it should be added, Kavanagh's thinking in this respect has a strong Catholic bias and displays a distinct animosity towards the largely Protestant Revival. Kavanagh, Quinn states, 'countered the syncretic national myth with a "parish myth", challenging unifying symbols, such as the image of Ireland as a woman, by presenting the island as a mosaic of different regions, drawing attention to their cultural diversity, and insisting on the primacy of the local in literature'.[33] In Bhabha's terms, Kavanagh's post-colonialism, regardless of his recurrent sectarianism, emphasizes the *hybrid* or 'in-between' nature of modern Ireland.[34] By turning Ireland into a 'mosaic' of parishes, Kavanagh rejects the idea that there are dominant cultural and political centres and dependent provincial peripheries. Kavanagh's aim in formulating the parochial aesthetic may

well, in small part, have been strategic: John Wilson Foster has suggested that Kavanagh's 'parish myth' is a self-serving construct, that
Kavanagh

> may not have been entirely convinced by his own distinction
> between parochialism and provincialism. It may have been to
> some extent a rationalisation or compensation in the face of the
> nationalist success of the Revival ... For he may after all have
> secretly worshipped the cosmopolitan reputation such as the chief
> Revival writers enjoyed.[35]

Whatever truth resides in this pronouncement, Kavanagh's parochialism
bears comparison with the provincialism courted by Hugh MacDiarmid
and Edwin Muir in Montrose during the 1920s. Like his Scottish contemporaries, Kavanagh's self-imposed eccentricity to the centres of cultural power granted him – as Robert Crawford has noted of MacDiarmid
– 'a sense of empowering marginality', and produced some of his finest
work.[36]

Kavanagh's parochialism paved the way for his late thoughts on poetry:
an aesthetic stance which he disarmingly dubbed, in his late 'Self-
Portrait', as one of 'not caring'.[37] Comedy, not tragedy, is the substance
of poetry; the rendering of one's unique lived experience is the goal of
the poet. Subsequent to a (successful) operation for lung cancer, in 1955
Kavanagh engaged in a rewriting of his life. The great essay, 'From
Monaghan to the Grand Canal', depicts the poet as experiencing a kind
of epiphany as he convalesces on the banks of the Grand Canal, between
Baggot Street and Leeson Street – this is the poet's 'hegira', a departure
that in fact signals a return, an imaginative circling back to his origins
in County Monaghan:[38]

> And now raising my eyes to the horizon I am again looking across
> the small fields of south Monaghan and south Armagh, and won-
> dering did any of the Irish writers who claimed to bring realism
> instead of the old sentimentalities ever express the society that lies
> within my gaze, with the exception of my own small effort in *Tarry
> Flynn*?[39]

It is interesting that, despite sloughing off much of his previous poetry
as dependent on 'old sentimentalities', the essay refuses to shed the

novel, *Tarry Flynn*. 'Self-Portrait' also praises *Tarry Flynn* as 'not only the best but the only authentic account of life as it was lived in Ireland this century'. The 'realism' of *Tarry Flynn* is contrasted in 'Self-Portrait' with the 'stage-Irish lie' that is his earlier extended prose work, the autobiography *The Green Fool*.[40] This is a harsh judgement on a work which was instrumental in Kavanagh's development as a writer, as Antoinette Quinn has rightly argued.[41] *The Green Fool* signals the moment in Kavanagh's early career in which the literary 'realism' he would extol in 'From Monaghan to the Grand Canal' supplants the influence of *Palgrave's Golden Treasury* on his aesthetic. The parochial poetic is unthinkable without the example of this early text.

The Green Fool was a commissioned work for the publisher Constable, and thus reflects the vogue for rural Irish autobiography evinced by the success of such translations from the Irish as Maurice O'Sullivan's *Twenty Years A-Growing* (1933), an account of the author's experiences on the Blasket Islands in the early part of the twentieth century. Perhaps for this reason, Kavanagh implicitly links *The Green Fool* to that phase of his career in which he wrote according to 'that formula for literature which laid all the stress on whether [a work] was Irish or not'.[42] Indeed, the autobiography includes a wealth of observation of Irish rural life that might be viewed as rank provincialism, as 'go[ing] false' and 'play[ing] up to the larger parish on the other side of the Irish Sea', to a British audience hungry for such Irish exotica. At times, the narrator seems little more than an instance of the picaresque protagonist: a 'device', as the Russian Formalists argued, whose motivating function is simply to string together a series of amusing or instructive episodes. As such, the narrator is less important than the narrative events he motivates – here, such episodes as a hiring fair, a rural wedding, country people's attitudes towards death, a pilgrimage to a holy well, etc. – and these events thus lack the strongly causal relationship they would possess in a classic realist novel. In this respect, *The Green Fool* would have appealed to readers familiar with the image of Ireland to be found in, for example, a travelogue such as H.V. Morton's best-selling account of motoring through the Free State, *In Search of Ireland* (1930). However, *The Green Fool* is a local's and not a visitor's narrative, and the text's picaresque dimension is in the service of both a sociological and autobiographical imperative. In the first of a series of articles on Irish rural life written for the *Irish Times*, Kavanagh observed that the 'pursuit of beauty is one of the defects of the tourist's point of view. The tourist is in a hurry; he demands quick returns of the picturesque and the obvious.'[43] The 'point of view' in The Green Fool is that of the aspiring poet; his and the reader's 'return' on the picaresque elements of the text is a sharp sense of the impact of modernity on traditional ways of Irish rural life. The (fictitious) demolishing of the narrator's family's thatched cabin towards the beginning of the text, and its replacement by a slated house, has been read as a metaphor for the autobiography's ambivalent response to the Literary Revival.[44] 'A modern dwelling cut off from the Gaelic tradition', the house, like the work in which it is set, gestures towards Revivalist themes and modes of writing, but is distinct from them.[45] Yet the newly built house is also a metonym for modernity, and is built within a text in which the narrator's insular rural experience is repeatedly punctured by news of the World War and, later and closer to home, civil war. At the end of the text, with the narrator in London, the hawking of the Daily Worker and the Blackshirt serve to remind us that Ireland's turbulent recent history is being played out against an international backdrop: that The Green Fool might be read, in more than just its date, as a 'Thirties' text.

The narrator's development as a writer mirrors the historical changes that press in on his life. Northrop Frye has observed that

> Most autobiographies are inspired by a creative, and therefore fictional, impulse to select only those events and experiences in the writer's life that go to build up an integrated pattern ... We may call this very important form of prose fiction the confession form, following St. Augustine, who appears to have invented it, and Rousseau, who established a modern type of it ... After Rousseau – in fact in Rousseau – the confession flows into the novel, and the mixture produces the fictional autobiography, the Künstlerroman, and kindred types.[46]

As a Künstlerroman, a 'portrait of the artist', The Green Fool's depiction of its narrator's emergence as a poet is necessarily selective of what Kavanagh took to be key moments in his maturation as a man and writer. Of these, a particularly revealing (and amusing) episode occurs with the narrator's visit to Dublin in search of AE. Inquiring about the elder poet's whereabouts in the National Library, the narrator takes the opportunity to ask for a copy of The Waste Land, about which he has heard a good deal but never read: 'The man with the goatee beard wanted to know if it was a book on drainage, and before I could explain was almost on his way to procure one of that type for me.'[47] Desirous of contact with one of the central figures of the Literary Revival, curious about one of the major works of literary modernism, offered a book on the rural environment – all these details add to the 'integrated pattern' of The Green Fool and its author's emerging poetic. The belated Romanticism of AE will be encountered and absorbed, just as, on meeting Russell, Kavanagh has books pressed upon him by a second bearded man; modernism, figuratively speaking, will remain unread; and a 'prosaic', realist representation of Irish rural experience will ensue in the poetry of the 1940s and 1950s.[48]

There is thus continuity between the picaresque realism of The Green Fool and the comic realism of Tarry Flynn, despite Kavanagh's late dismissal of the former text. Written during the course of the 1940s, Tarry Flynn is a humorous counterpart to the 'savage realism', in Terence Brown's apt phrase, of The Great Hunger.[49] The Great Hunger is a profound and moving meditation on a conservative, patriarchal social order; a commentary on the problems caused by late marriage and the sexual difficulties which ensued from this practice; and a fierce exposé of the hardship suffered by those who lived in a relatively unmechanised, underdeveloped rural economy; the novel extends the parochial mode Kavanagh is developing in his poetry at this date into fictional form. Like his long poem, the novel is largely plotless, Kavanagh having decided late in the novel's lengthy composition to omit from his final text a plotline centring on a dance-hall. In this respect, Tarry Flynn might be said to anticipate John McGahern's limpid record of rural life, That They May Face the Rising Sun (2002), a novel which also creates a largely 'story-less' world of human interaction within a small community. Although light-hearted, Tarry Flynn shares the ambition of The Great Hunger in resisting both de Valeran and Revivalist idealizations of Irish country life and practices. What Dillon Johnston says apropos the poem can equally be applied to the fiction: it 'demolishes the monumental image of the peasant', though by means of a credible and sympathetic fictionalization of a region rather than the saeva indignatio of the poem.[50] Recognizing the closeness between Kavanagh's prose and poetry in the 1940s, while acknowledging their tonal difference, brings into focus the extent to which Kavanagh's work at this date sits squarely within a realist mode of writing, as characterized by the fiction of Sean O'Faolain and Frank O'Connor, the latter of whom in 1942 defended both the poem and the as yet unfinished novel in the Irish Times and in Horizon.[51] Tarry Flynn's eponymous protagonist's final months on the family farm are dominated by humorous petty-minded clashes, both intrafamilial and between parishioners. Set in 1935, the novel represents rural existence in a way not unrelated to The Great Hunger: economic misery and sexual frustration are central to the lives of the inhabitants of Dargan, while the church exudes moral superiority and exerts overweening patriarchal authority. In both poem and novel, these events are focalized through a single figure; in The Great Hunger, the narrative voice is omniscient, while in the novel the point of view is that of a character-focalizer. Certain critics have been tempted to read The Great Hunger as taking some of its formal bearings from The Waste Land, a claim that rests on the poem's (in Quinn's word) 'multifaceted' technique, which is said to recall Eliot's, and other modernists', penchant for collage and montage, multiple focus, shifts in tone from irony, to farce, to pathos.[52] Such critics are taking a lead from Clarke's hunch that Kavanagh was (in part) thinking about Eliot's example in composing his own long poem.[53] However, the controlling consciousness of the poem is as determinate as the predominant focalization of Tarry Flynn through its titular protagonist: both works should be considered 'realist' in not only their fidelity to the 'truth' of rural life in the 1930s and early 1940s, but also their 'closed form'. As Augustine Martin has judiciously commented:

> [T]here are beguiling correspondences between Kavanagh's poem and Eliot's ... But The Great Hunger is not really an open form: there is no multiplicity of voices or personae; the controlling consciousness is Kavanagh's, the dominating sensibility his alter ego, Maguire, just as Tarry is the dominanting sensibility of Tarry Flynn.[54]

Though firmly wedded to the preoccupations and style of parochialism, Tarry Flynn in one respect prefigures Kavanagh's final poetic of 'not caring'. For Tarry, the most banal of activities is freighted with meaning: 'Even teeming the pot was very important in his life and in his imagination. Any incident, or any act, can carry within it the energy of the imagination.'[55] Subsequent to the passage from 'From Monaghan to the Grand Canal' quoted above, in which he praises his novel for avoiding 'old sentimentalities' in favour of a robust realism, Kavanagh immediately states: 'I am not suggesting that being true to life in a realist way is the highest function of a writer ... [T]he highest function is the pure flame from the material.'[56] And the nature of that material for the late Kavanagh, as for Tarry, is immaterial: *anything* can produce that 'flame' of poetry. 'Naming things is part of the poet's function', writes Kavanagh in 'Nationalism and Literature', adding 'an unnamed thing has little life in the mind'.[57] Such is the practice of Kavanagh's later sonnets, as in the sestet to 'The Hospital':

> Naming these things is the love act and its pledge;
> For we must record love's mystery without claptrap,
> Snatch out of time the passionate transitory.[58]

Kavanagh's persona in these works in both prose and verse is Adamic, albeit modestly and colloquially so; and fittingly one of these sonnets is entitled 'Leaves of Grass'. It was percipient of AE to thrust Whitman's poems upon the young Kavanagh, on that visit to Dublin recalled in *The Green Fool*.

NOTES

1. For details of Kavanagh's contributions to periodicals, see Peter Kavanagh, *The Garden of the Golden Apples: A Bibliography of Patrick Kavanagh* (New York: Peter Kavanagh Hand Press, 1972); and John Nemo, 'Patrick Kavanagh: A Bibliography of Materials by and about Patrick Kavanagh', *Irish University Review* 3, 1 (Spring 1973), pp.81–106.

2. In 1951 and 1955 Kavanagh compiled selections of his prose. The manuscript of the former has been lost; Antoinette Quinn speculates that the latter is the MS in the Kavanagh Archive at University College Dublin, *Some Evocations of No Importance and other pieces*. In 1956 Kavanagh prepared a collection with the Blakean title, *The Forgiven Plough*, which had been commissioned by the Arts Council of Ireland, but it was never published; see Antoinette Quinn, *Patrick Kavanagh: A Biography*, 2nd edn (Dublin: Gill & Macmillan, 2003), pp.307, 357–8; and Patrick Kavanagh, *A Poet's Country: Selected Prose*, ed. Antoinette Quinn (Dublin: Lilliput Press, 2003), pp.18–20.

3. Kavanagh, *Collected Poems*: Author's Note, *A Poet's Country*, p.303.

4. Kavanagh, 'James Joyce', ibid., p.204.

5. John Keats, 'To John Taylor', 27 February 1818, in *Letters of John Keats*, ed. Robert Gittings (Oxford: Oxford University Press, 1970), p.70.

6. On the overwhelming impact on the post-colonial writer of an 'educational system

... carry[ing] the contours of an English heritage', see Edward Kamau Brathwaite, *History of the Voice: The Development of Nation Language in Anglophone Caribbean Poetry* (Port of Spain: New Beacon Books, 1984), p.8.

7. See Antoinette Quinn, *Patrick Kavanagh: Born-Again Romantic* (Dublin: Gill & Macmillan, 1991), p.11. Although Kavanagh would have been exposed to avant-garde and modernist writing in *The Irish Statesman*, and through his reading of *Poetry* (Chicago), it would appear to have had little imprint on his aesthetic. See my discussion of *The Green Fool* and the relationship between *Tarry Flynn* and *The Great Hunger* below. On Kavanagh's early reading, see Quinn, *Patrick Kavanagh: A Biography*, pp.47–8; and on the lasting influence of AE on Kavanagh's poetic, see ibid., p.55.

8. Patrick Kavanagh, *Collected Poems* ed. Antoinette Quinn (Harmondsworth: Penguin, 2005), p.15.

9. Samuel Taylor Coleridge, *Biographia Literaria; Or, Biographical Sketches of My Literary Life and Opinions*, ed. George Watson (London: Dent, 1956), p.167.

10. Kavanagh, 'Art McCooey', *Collected Poems*, p.43.

11. Kavanagh, 'William Butler Yeats', *A Poet's Country: Selected Prose*, p.181.

12. See Seamus Deane, *Celtic Revivals: Essays in Modern Irish Literature* (London: Faber, 1985), p.37.

13. Patrick Kavanagh, 'Diary', *Envoy* 2, 7 (1950), p.90.

14. Kavanagh, 'Paris in Aran', *A Poet's Country: Selected Prose*, pp.190, 191.

15. Kavanagh, 'The Gallivanting Poet', ibid., p.193.

16. Kavanagh, 'Nationalism and Literature', ibid., p.248.

17. Ibid., p.247.

18. Ibid., p.248.

19. Kavanagh, 'The Gallivanting Poet', ibid., p.201.

20. Kavanagh, 'The Paddidad', *Collected Poems*, pp.150–1.

21. See Patrick Kavanagh, *Lapped Furrows*, ed. Peter Kavanagh (New York: Peter Kavanagh Hand Press, 1969).

22. Robert F. Garratt, 'Tradition and Continuity II: Patrick Kavanagh', in *Modern Irish Poetry: Tradition and Continuity from Yeats to Heaney* (Berkeley, CA: University of California Press, 1986), p.138.

23. T.S. Eliot, 'Ulysses, Order, and Myth', in *Selected Prose*, ed. Frank Kermode (London: Faber, 1975), p.177. Compare Pound's response to the parallels with Homer in *Ulysses*: 'These correspondences are part of Joyce's mediaevalism and are chiefly his own affair, a scaffold, a means of construction, justified by the result, and justifiable by it only.' Ezra Pound, *Pound/Joyce: The Letters of Ezra Pound to James Joyce, with Pound's Essays on Joyce*, ed. Forrest Read (New York: New Directions, 1967) p.197.

24. Kavanagh, 'James Joyce', *A Poet's Country: Selected Prose*, p.202.

25. Austin Clarke, *Reviews and Essays of Austin Clarke*, ed. Gregory A. Schirmer (Gerrards Cross: Colin Smythe, 1995), p.109.

26. Kavanagh, 'Parochialism and Provincialism', *A Poet's Country: Selected Prose*, p.237.

27. On Kavanagh's reaction to Moore's portrayal of Yeats, see 'George Moore's Yeats', ibid., pp.182–5.

28. Kavanagh, 'Sex and Christianity', ibid., p.173.

29. Kavanagh, 'Parochialism and Provincialism', ibid., p.237.

30. Kavanagh, 'Epic', Collected Poems, p.184.

31. Homi K. Bhabha, The Location of Culture (London: Routledge, 1994), p.7.

32. On which topic, see David Lloyd, Nationalism and Minor Literature: James Clarence Mangan and the Emergence of Irish Cultural Nationalism (Berkeley, CA: University of California Press, 1987).

33. Antoinette Quinn, 'Introduction', in Patrick Kavanagh, Selected Poems (Harmondsworth: Penguin, 1996), p.xxii.

34. See Bhabha, Location of Culture, passim.

35. John Wilson Foster, 'The Poetry of Kavanagh: A Reappraisal', in Colonial Consequences: Essays in Irish Literature and Culture (Dublin: Lilliput Press, 1991), p.101.

36. Robert Crawford, 'MacDiarmid in Montrose', in Alex Davis and Lee M. Jenkins, Locations of Literary Modernism: Region and Nation in British and American Modernist Poetry (Cambridge: Cambridge University Press, 2000), p.55. The crucial difference between Kavanagh and his Scottish contemporaries is that the latter's chosen peripheralism was in the service of their full-blooded cultural nationalism.

37. Kavanagh, 'Self-Portrait', A Poet's Country: Selected Prose, p.311.

38. Kavanagh, 'From Monaghan to the Grand Canal', A Poet's Country, p.272.

39. Ibid., p.275.

40. Kavanagh, 'Self-Portrait', ibid., p.306.

41. See Quinn, Patrick Kavanagh: Born-Again Romantic, p.53.

42. Kavanagh, 'From Monaghan to the Grand Canal', A Poet's Country: Selected Prose, p.276.

43. Kavanagh, 'The Poet's Country', ibid., p.29.

44. See Quinn, Patrick Kavanagh: Born-Again Romantic, p.62.

45. Patrick Kavanagh, The Green Fool [1938] (Harmondsworth: Penguin, 1975), p.19.

46. Northrop Frye, Anatomy of Criticism: Four Essays (Princeton, NJ: Princeton University Press, 1957), p.307.

47. Kavanagh, The Green Fool, p.227.

48. In its selection of autobiographical material, The Green Fool may seem to resemble another Irish Künstlerroman, Joyce's A Portrait of the Artist as a Young Man (1916). But Joyce's text is perhaps better glossed by Paul de Man's almost Wildean musings in 'Autobiography as De-Facement': 'But are we so certain that autobiography depends on reference; as a photograph depends on its subject or a (realistic) picture on its model? We assume that life produces the autobiography as an act produces its consequences, but can we not suggest, with equal justice, that the autobiographical project may itself produce and determine the life and that whatever the writer does is in fact governed by the technical demands of self-portraiture and thus determined, in all its aspects, by the resources of the medium?' Paul de Man, The Rhetoric of Romanticism (New York: Columbia University Press, 1984), p.69.

49. Terence Brown, Ireland's Literature: Selected Essays (Mullingar: Lilliput Press, 1988), p.105.

50. Dillon Johnston, Irish Poetry after Joyce (Dublin: Dolmen Press, 1985), p.127. Fierce or savage indignation is a phrase from Jonathan Swift's epitaph, much admired by Yeats;

The Great Hunger is a major work in a tradition of Irish satire in English that can be traced back to Swift's example.

51. See Frank O'Connor, 'The Future of Irish Literature', *Horizon*, 5, 25 (1942), pp.55–63, the notorious 'Irish edition' which included excerpts of *The Great Hunger*; and *Irish Times*, 15 February 1942.

52. Quinn, *Patrick Kavanagh: Born-Again Romantic*, p.143; and see Edna Longley, *The Living Stream: Literature and Revisionism in Ireland* (Newcastle upon Tyne: Bloodaxe, 1994), p.204.

53. See Clarke, *Reviews and Essays*, p.178.

54. Augustine Martin, 'The Apocalypse of Clay: Technique and Vision in *The Great Hunger*', in Peter Kavanagh (ed.), *Patrick Kavanagh: Man and Poet* (Newbridge: Goldsmith's Press, 1987), p.288.

55. Patrick Kavanagh, *Tarry Flynn* [1948] (Harmondsworth: Penguin, 1978), p.21.

56. Kavanagh, 'From Monaghan to the Grand Canal', *A Poet's Country: Selected Prose*, p.275.

57. Kavanagh, 'Nationalism and Literature', ibid., 246.

58. Kavanagh, 'The Hospital', *Collected Poems*, p.217.

CHAPTER FOUR

The Moment of
Kavanagh's Weekly

GERRY SMYTH

The value of the periodical publication has been recognized in Ireland since at least the eighteenth century, although it is only more recently that it has come to function as a major tactical weapon of Irish political and cultural debate.[1] In the century after the first appearance of *The Nation* in 1842, a number of different types of journal appeared which could use the extraordinary success and effectiveness of that publication as a yardstick for their own aspirations. Some, such as Griffith's *The United Irishman*, Pearse's *An Claidheamh Soluis* or Connolly's *The Workers' Republic*, might desire *The Nation's* ability to harness a mass readership and actively intervene in current debates. Some, such as Yeats's *Beltaine* and *Samhain*, might covet the form's potential audience while wishing to maintain their esoteric cultural pursuits. Others, such as the various university and scholarly organs, might consider themselves beyond such populist activities; instead, their work tended to be oriented towards a small initiated readership that would appreciate empirical research and sustained analysis above the polemics and generalized declarations of their more accessible fellows. Some, finally, such as George Russell's *The Irish Statesman* and Sean O'Faolain's *The Bell*, might try to incorporate all the above into a discourse of cultural criticism, attempting to strike an eclectic balance between intervention, reflection and critique. Traces and developments of each of these approaches can be found in all subsequent Irish periodical literature.

These boundaries were extremely flexible, and certain individuals such as Russell could range between the various levels of discourse with ease.[2] Implicit in each, however, was an acknowledgement of the convenience and adaptability of the modern journal form as a means of engaging in up-to-the-minute exchange with colleagues and opponents. Whereas the major historical or literary treatise always risks being rendered *passé* by current events, the essay, the editorial, the work-in-progress and the review are present-oriented discourses, always provisional responses on the part of subjects locatable in time and space. They are *discursive* in the sense that they are recognizable interventions in ongoing debates, responses and interjections and rejoinders which imply other subjects and other points of view. Especially during the volatile years on either side of the revolution, Irish cultural and political opinion was constantly having to react to rapidly changing circumstances. Much in the way that the short story became the dominant literary form of the post-colonial period, the periodical press became at this time a sort of halfway house between the newspaper and the book – neither journalism nor monograph, but incorporating aspects of both – as a means for the Irish intellectual to intervene in the debate over national identity.

The 1950s, says Seamus Deane, 'saw the death of more journals than any other decade before or since'.[3] This is indicative of the constant changes impacting upon cultural debate during this period, as certain points of view crystallized into publishing energy for a while, only to dissipate when that energy came to be regarded as misplaced or irrelevant. The post-Emergency period also witnessed, however, the consolidation of certain forms of periodical literature affiliated to institutional discourses such as Celtic Studies, Theology and specialist scholarship in areas such as Classics and Philosophy. In this flurry of intellectual activity the discourse of literary criticism was widely employed, as it had been since *The Nation* (and before), as a means of analyzing Irish identity. Literary criticism, that is, became established as a major cultural and political preoccupation, as the subject positions and narrative possibilities implied in different ways of reading texts implied different ways of being 'Irish'.

Richard Kearney suggests that the Irish intellectuals of the 1950s accepted and contributed to a formal split in journalistic discourse between, on the one hand, socio-political debate dealing with reality, and on the other, literary debate dealing with imaginative vision.[4] While this is true to a point, it by no means tells the whole story. Such a neat division underplays the subtle negotiations and struggles over disciplinary boundaries that were carried on in the pages of all the Irish journals of the 1950s, as well as the power invested in certain discourses to pronounce on issues of national import. Whether it was a technical journal such as Ériu, founded at the turn of the century by the prestigious Celticist Kuno Meyer as 'The Journal of the School of Irish Learning', or a periodical affiliated to a particular section of Irish society, such as the Jesuit publication, *Studies* (subtitled *An Irish Quarterly Review of Letters, Philosophy and Science*), or a 'little magazine' like John Ryan's *Envoy*, or whether it was a self-consciously intellectual undertaking with openly interventionist and internationalist pretensions such as *The Bell*, each was aimed resolutely at the heart of the present in as much as all were actively attempting to define (and thus to capture) contemporary Irish identity. This was the milieu – subtle, finely nuanced and highly sensitive – into which *Kavanagh's Weekly* barged in April 1952 with the characteristic blend of belligerence and insouciance for which its co-editor and main contributor became so infamous.[5]

It is important to recall the wider context of the period. According to both contemporary accounts and subsequent historiography, the 1950s was a disappointing, not to say miserable, time in modern Irish history, economically, politically, socially and culturally.[6] The malaise manifested itself in a number of ways. First, the effects of the 'Emergency' (as the war years were referred to in official terminology) were felt well into the following decade, and the standard of living in the part of the country not affiliated to Great Britain continued to lag behind most of Europe, despite the influx of millions of Marshall Aid dollars. Neither Fianna Fail nor two Coalitions, neither de Valera nor Costello nor MacBride in four rapid changes of government within ten years, managed to halt the economic decline and the social and cultural stagnation which accompanied it. Two decades of sterile debate on corporatism, vocationalism, state regulation and other economic philosophies had produced a situation which saw Ireland possessing, in the words of Joseph Lee, 'the lowest living standards, the highest emigration rates, the worst unemployment rates, and the most intellectually stultifying society in northern Europe'.[7]

Kavanagh's Weekly appeared in thirteen issues between 12 April and 5 July 1952 – which is to say, at the heart of the economic and cultural malaise that was post-Emergency Ireland.[8] As one critic puts it, '*Kavanagh's Weekly* captures the *Zeitgeist* of a particularly depressing period in Irish history. The country's economic boom was over and its spirits, like its finances, slumped. The atmosphere of apathy and pessimism was almost palpable.'[9]

The journal was financed by Kavanagh's brother Peter, who had recently returned from working in America with a sizeable amount of money. He found Patrick living in poverty and squalor in his Pembroke Road flat with no outlet for his writings since the demise of Envoy for which a monthly 'Diary' column had provided a regular, if modest, income. The journal was founded as a vehicle for the two brothers' critique of contemporary Ireland, and with just a few contributions from other writers they produced over the next three months about 9,000 words each week. In a sustained onslaught against what they considered to be the faults of both nation and state, virtually no one and nothing, past or present, was spared. During their short run the Kavanaghs succeeded in offending large sections of the population as well as a number of powerful and sensitive individuals.

Patrick Kavanagh was 47 years old in April 1952 and already an established poet and man-of-letters around Dublin. He had been 'found', as he said himself,[10] by George Russell (AE) in the 1930s, a primitive young country poet who had walked to Dublin from his birthplace, Mucker in Monaghan, on his first trip to the capital because he believed it to be in keeping with the peasant persona he liked to adopt in his poetry of that time.[11] His reputation was made with the long anti-pastoral epic The Great Hunger published in 1942, and in the following decade he came to be regarded along with Austin Clarke as one of the major Irish poets since Yeats.

Like many other writers during the Emergency years and after, Kavanagh encountered a dearth of outlets for cultural discourse in Irish civil society, and his work suffered as a consequence. After The Great Hunger there were only two other 'creative' publications before 1958, when the poems that would eventually comprise the volume Come Dance with Kitty Stobling (1960) were published as Recent Poems, once again by his brother Peter on his own printing press in New York. These publications were A Soul for Sale (1947), a collection of poems which contained an expurgated version of The Great Hunger, and a novel, Tarry Flynn (1948). This was the context in which Kavanagh's Weekly emerged. The lack of a public for literature became one of the many indications in Kavanagh's Weekly of the failure of the new Ireland:

The death which has overtaken Irish life in other fields has descended on the field of literature ... There is no use in concealing the fact that there is practically no literary public in this country and there has never been a literary tradition ... If a writer appeals to the few who count he may get all sorts of commissions. But it can be taken as a fact that no sincere writer can make a living by his creative writing. (3:7)

Kavanagh immediately establishes a link between 'life' and 'literature', but then goes on to criticize the way this link has developed in post-colonial Ireland. A society as 'thin' as Ireland could not morally sustain the narrative complexities of literature, nor indeed support financially the individuals who might wish to write that literature. Instead, the post-colonial intellectual was absorbed by various state or semi-state institutions, such as Radio Éireann, the Abbey Theatre, the universities, the Dublin Institute for Advanced Studies or the Cultural Relations Committee. The alternative was to scrape a precarious existence on the hack work available at home or, if one was as famous as Seán O'Faoláin or Frank O'Connor, on occasional commissions from the journals and publishing houses of London and New York. For a sincere creative writer like Kavanagh, recourse to state-institutional outlets for his work was demeaning, at least while *Kavanagh's Weekly* was still a viable concern; and although he accepted a temporary lectureship at University College, Dublin a few years later, the point about the difficulty of making a living through imaginative writing was well taken by the Irish poets, playwrights and novelists of the 1940s and 1950s.

Although *A Soul for Sale* and *Tarry Flynn* were reasonably successful, by far the greater energy at this time was expended by Kavanagh on journalism, reviewing and, when *Envoy* came along, that mixture of subjective pronouncement and literary assassination that was to become so familiar to readers of *Kavanagh's Weekly*. The following is an early example:

The play at the Olympia, *The Land is Bright*, is about as malignant a tumour as has ever been grafted on to Irish village life. It is almost more indecent in its idiocy than a L.A.G. Strong job ... The play is definitely a tragedy – for the audience. It is not to be wondered that the author preferred to remain anonymous, a fact which should be considered as it shows that he is not so devoid of sensibility as might at first be thought ... I often wonder if Ireland isn't utterly inferior, an exhibitionistic society whose natural gods are actors. (2:8)

In such a highly litigious society as post-independence Ireland, Kavanagh's 'honest' critical style was dangerous and exciting, and had already earned him a reputation as an unsafe journalist.[12] No one was protected from the relentless search for 'truth', and neither delicacy of expression nor subtlety of opinion were required by one who was known 'to treat all literary allegiances, friendships or truces as temporary'.[13] His reasons for disliking The Land is Bright probably had to do with authenticity of representation and his general dislike of the Dublin theatre scene, but no attempt is made to analyze the play in any depth or to defend his evaluation of it. Instead, the pejorative cultural judgement is immediately linked to a comment on Irish society. Cultural and political failures are thus mutually implicated.

Indeed, throughout Kavanagh's Weekly this implicit relationship between cultural and more general social and political concerns is stressed. Like his literary foster-father AE, during this stage of his career Kavanagh took all Irish experience as his province, and throughout the thirteen issues of the journal he ranged freely over a wide variety of discourses, including economics, politics, popular culture, sociology, philosophy and psychology. The full title of the publication is Kavanagh's Weekly: A Journal of Literature and Politics. Although the cultural and political aspects are formally separated into articles and editorials, however, the search for truth and falsehood in all their forms remains constant throughout. The poor state of Irish literature is never far away in an editorial about the state of the nation, while there is always a link, sometimes stated, sometimes implied, between politico-economic performance and cultural vitality. And this is as true of the old Gaelic society as it is of the modern Irish one:

> The Irish tradition regarding the poet was not a good one; it constantly and persistently encouraged the poet into undignified ways. The real trouble is that perhaps there was no civilised tradition ... The Gaelic poets hardly deserve the name of poets for they lacked the one quality of a poet – leadership. A poet draws the people's attention to the obvious that they otherwise do not see: he gives

them courage, the courage to be themselves – the only kind of
courage that is worth having. (10:7)

The contradictions between community and personality that were to
dominate Kavanagh's thought and work for the rest of his life are already
apparent here, and his first tentative attempts to achieve a resolution of
these categories will be analyzed shortly. Also worth noting, however, is,
firstly, his harnessing of poetic and social ('civilized') traditions, often
collapsed into the abstract quality of 'Life' – as he wrote: 'Art is never art.
What is called art is merely life' (6:7); and secondly, the implicit truth
that the writer-critic is the individual in society best qualified to diag-
nose this relationship. Like other post-Revival writers such as O'Faoláin,
O'Connor and Clarke, Kavanagh coveted the kind of affective aura possessed by a Yeats or an AE. However, in an age of increasing specialization and professionalism, the day of what Antonio Gramsci called the
'traditional intellectual' was nearing its end, and the kind of amateur,
interventionist power desired by many of the intellectuals of the 1950s
was no longer available.[14]

Kavanagh's enterprise was unusual, then, in that unlike most critics
in the twentieth century, he had little experience of formal academic
discourse, and it was not until the mid-1950s that his critical work
received any institutional patronage.[15] His affiliations were always with
literature first and then with that section of the population he believed
had been criminally misrepresented by the writers and ideologues of the
Revival and the revolution – the small farmers, agricultural labourers and
village dwellers of rural Ireland. *Tarry Flynn* he claimed to be 'not only the
best but the only authentic account of life as it was lived in Ireland this
century'.[16] These affiliations – cosmopolitan and sophisticated on the one
hand, local and simple on the other – gave a curious contradictory tone
to many of his pronouncements on Irish life and literature; indeed, it is
the ambiguity of his stance that makes Kavanagh such an interesting figure in terms of his critical engagement with the post-colonial state. The
targets of his attacks were invariably those official Church- and State-
sponsored institutions and those individuals (especially de Valera and
Austin Clarke) whom he believed guilty of perpetuating disabling myths
about Ireland's present and recent past. Editorial control allowed
Kavanagh the freedom to vent the anger he felt at the role of the poor

neglected poet to which modern Ireland had condemned him, and to attack those institutions and individuals he believed to be responsible for this fate. At the same time, it was also a forum where he could begin to formulate an aesthetic with which to negotiate the particular set of circumstances in which he found himself. Like many other post-independence intellectuals, Kavanagh experienced the tension between alienation from and commitment to the new Ireland, and this split between destructive political iconoclasm and constructive cultural utopianism is clearly visible in the pages of Kavanagh's Weekly.

The destructive element is founded on Kavanagh's belief in his own ability to recognize the reasons for Ireland's failure and his willingness to inform as many people as often and as honestly as possible what those reasons were. Interestingly, Kavanagh formulated this capacity as 'the critical mind':

> Readers unused to the critical mind may think us destructive but this is because they are accustomed only to the flabby unthinking world of the popular newspaper.
>
> Our hope is to create in a few thousand people the power to think critically before it is too late. In life there needs to be a constant battle to recover losses. Even to hold your place you have to fight. Hence what looks like destructiveness is merely the critical mind. (3:1)

Again, those members of society more sensitive to 'life' were more likely to be in possession of 'the critical mind' than others, hence the embattled, missionary tone of much of the writing in Kavanagh's Weekly. But what is also interesting is the fact that 'the critical mind' can be brought to bear on both cultural and political phenomena. It is a transposable faculty that can allow the initiated to see beneath the false mask worn by modern Ireland. Literary criticism, then, must be consistent with cultural, political and social criticism, as in each case it involves the same cross-fertilization of 'the critical mind' with 'life'. And as all the above extracts indicate, modern Ireland was characterized for Kavanagh by a shameful lack of either of these qualities.

Kavanagh's negative criticism often threatened to dominate his personality and work, leaving him, as Antoinette Quinn writes, '[a] man flailing between two faded worlds, the country he had left and the literary Dublin he never found'.[17] Kavanagh's solution to the aesthetic and personal dilemma caused by modern Ireland was based, famously, on his discovery of the concept of parochialism and its use as a metaphor for gaining access to poetic and social truth. 'The job', he wrote, 'is to find some substitute for the national loyalty, some system to take the place of the enslaving State' (10:1). Writers and critics need not look abroad, or even at the larger community, for their subjects, he claimed, but only at the things which directly impinge on their own experiences:

> Parochialism and provincialism are opposites. The provincial has no mind of his own; he does not trust what his eyes see until he has heard what the metropolis – towards which his eyes are turned – has to say on any subject. This runs through all activities.
>
> The parochial mentality on the other hand is never in any doubt about the social and artistic validity of his parish. All great civilisations are based on parochialism – Greek, Israelite, English ...
>
> In Ireland we are provincial not parochial, for it requires a great deal of courage to be parochial. When we do attempt having the courage of our parish we are inclined to go false and to play up to the larger parish on the other side of the Irish Sea. In recent times we have had two great Irish parishioners – James Joyce and George Moore. (7:2)

Here, Joyce rather than Yeats is the touchstone of authentic Irish art, because the work of the former is thoroughly informed with the local, with 'life' as it could still be experienced on the familiar streets of Dublin. 'Yeats, protected to some extent by the Nationalistic movement, wrote out of a somewhat protected world and so his work does not touch life deeply. Joyce on the other hand got all that Ireland had to give and his reaction to it made him great' (6:7). More than any writer or critic since the Revival, Kavanagh managed to breathe life into what in the 1950s was threatening to become an exhausted opposition between nationalism and cosmopolitanism, on the way creating 'something new, authentic and liberating'.[18] For Kavanagh, parochialism did not connote insularity or essentialism, as did the version of nationalist ideology dominant since independence; instead it signified a capacity to hold the local and the universal in fructifying tension. For example, *Kavanagh's*

Weekly's blatantly anglophilic stance was not only a goad to 'buckleppin" nationalists (for which term see below), but also a genuine wish to bring empire and parish into mutually enlightening confrontation. The seemingly contradictory desire of the Irish intellectual for what Seamus Deane has called 'the risks of modern individuality and the consolations of traditional community'[19] was not, for Kavanagh, a limit for either himself or Ireland, but a potentially emancipatory displacement of categories which had traditionally shored up dominant nationalist discourse. This acknowledgement of the universal in the local, the specific in the general, allowed Kavanagh to maintain a subversively ironic attitude towards life and literature as he experienced them in post-colonial Ireland. As such, the concept of parochialism developed by him represents one of the first major attempts by an Irish intellectual since Joyce to introduce a qualifying perspective into the narrative of decolonization.

Parochialism, as well as indicating a lifestyle, also demanded a literary style that would be capable of articulating the local community and the role of the poet, and it was at this time, in part through his journalistic work, that Kavanagh began to develop the aesthetic that would later emerge as the relaxed, conversational tone of the *Kitty Stobling* verses.[20] In attempting to maintain a consistent persona throughout his political, critical and poetic writings Kavanagh developed a highly present-oriented style founded on personality and immediacy. Whether the subject be the state of the economy, gambling on horses or an anthology of Irish poetry, the commenting voice should remain the same, always searching for and exposing the 'truth' behind the various forms of lies on which modern Irish life was built. That voice could float in and out of 'poetic' and 'prosaic' registers without warning, as in this 'analysis' of schoolbook poetry:

> For me, when I read Eugene Aram, I am back in my native place, aged about sixteen with all my dreams sealed in the bud ... There I am walking down a lane peeping through the privet hedge into the field of turnips. The mood and atmosphere of the time comes alive in my mind. The comfortable worry of the summer fields is upon me. All the bits and pieces that furnish Imagination's house come up by magic ... I am walking through a field called

Lurgankeel away down towards a shaded corner; it is an October evening and all around me is the protecting fog of family life. How shall I live when the fog is blown away and I am left alone, naked? (5:8)

The sentimental, interrogative tone of the above is at odds with the realistic, assertive style of most of the writing in *Kavanagh's Weekly*. It thus unsettles the reader's expectations about the appropriateness of certain kinds of writing to certain subjects, defamiliarizing (at the textual level) social and cultural norms. Equally, the temporal location of the critical voice in *Kavanagh's Weekly* is always problematic, with the present circumstances constantly threatening to impinge on the discourse, thereby giving all the pronouncements a provisional, spontaneous air. For example, an article on the contribution of George Moore to modern Irish literature digresses into something out of a Myles na gCopaleen 'Cruiskeen Lawn' column:

I started off to write about George Moore. Perhaps I should forget about him and concentrate on the train of thought that his name provokes ...
— A casual passer-by: What about George Moore?
— Forget about George Moore, there's another week. (7:7)

Or in speculating on the influence of Boswell on Joyce, Kavanagh quotes similar diary entries from *Boswell in Holland* and *A Portrait of the Artist as a Young Man*, then adds the following:

March 21. Thought this in bed last night but was too lazy to add to it. Boswell was twenty-two, the same age as Stephen, at the time of the writing. Feel odd similarity. Had Joyce seen Boswell's diary? No. Couldn't have. Considering above wonder if it adds anything to our knowledge of anything or anybody. Probably not. (5:8)

The ironic, *ad hoc* and playful nature of these last two extracts is indicative of much of what passes for literary criticism in the pages of *Kavanagh's Weekly*, and it is clear that the critical style to which the philosophy of parochialism gave rise would be of a highly idiosyncratic kind, having little to do with scholarship, explication or analysis, but much to do with subjective response and evaluative assertion. By unsettling the borders

between his cultural and literary discourse, Kavanagh attempted to avoid
the all too real danger for the post-colonial Irish writer of letting a political conscience smother an artistic impulse (on which issue, see Maurice
Harmon's analysis in *Seán O'Faoláin: A Critical Introduction* of the life and
work of Kavanagh's contemporary Seán O'Faoláin).[21]

The first editorial, entitled 'Victory of Mediocrity', is a good example of the general style and approach of *Kavanagh's Weekly*. It is a belliger-
ent revisionist interpretation of the achievements of the revolution,
going on to attack openly the individuals and institutions responsible
for perpetuating the lies on which the thin society of post-colonial
Ireland eked out its miserable social, economic and cultural life:

> Thirty odd years ago the southern section of this country won
> what was called freedom. Yet from that Independence Day there
> has been a decline in vitality throughout the country. It is possible
> that political liberty is a superficial thing and that it always pro-
> duces the apotheosis of the mediocrity. For thirty years thinking
> has been more and more looked upon as wickedness – in a quiet
> way of course.
>
> All the mouthpieces of public opinion are controlled by men
> whose only qualification is their inability to think.
>
> Being stupid and illiterate is the mark of respectability and
> responsibility. (1:1)

Already the reader is introduced to what were to become some of the
keywords of *Kavanagh's Weekly*: vitality, mediocrity, responsibility. The style
is straightforward and accessible, the tone assertive and angry, the persona oscillating between that of the informed social/political commentator and the plain man of the people, telling it as he sees it. Kavanagh
never patronizes, panders or condescends to his readers; farmer and
academic, peasant and politician, all are equally addressed and implicated
in contemporary Ireland's dilemma. What it also demonstrates at this
early stage is a willingness to question all the images and narratives
which had emerged in Irish cultural discourse during the process of
decolonization. Later in the same editorial Kavanagh refers to the liberty
that was won by the previous generation as 'the liberty of the graveyard',
and throughout the thirteen issues of *Kavanagh's Weekly* a highly ironic
attitude towards all the national shibboleths is maintained.

Each week brought a literary critical article in which Kavanagh raged against what he considered to be the depressing state of contemporary Irish letters. His main targets were the 'buckleppers' – enemies of the creative imagination who made a living from selling false images of Irish life. The grandfather of all 'buckleppin'' literature was Synge, but it was his modern-day disciples who week after week bore the brunt of Kavanagh's ire – writers such as F.R. Higgins, W.R. Rodgers, Walter Macken, Mary Lavin and Austin Clarke. In a piece entitled 'Paris in Aran', after accusing Synge of transposing cosmopolitan attitudes into the rural environment of the West of Ireland, he continues:

> What is the dominant note in Synge? I would say bitterly non-Irish. It all came from the basic insincerity upon which he built ... Synge never asked himself the fundamental question: where do I stand in relation to these people? Whether or not Synge portrayed the people of the West truly is not of much importance; as I say, it is the lie in his own heart that matters ... His peasants are picturesque conventions; the language he invented for them did a disservice to letters in this country by drawing our attention away from the common speech whose delightfulness comes from its very ordinariness. (9:7)

In an argument that goes some way along the road mapped by Daniel Corkery twenty years earlier, Kavanagh sees Synge's major flaws as his distrust of ordinary Irish life and language, and his inability to gain access to authentic Irish experience. Moreover, the insincerity of representation that resulted in Synge's work was being compounded in modern Ireland by 'buckleppers' such as the Irish branch of PEN,[22] whose anthology of Irish poetry, entitled Concord of Harps (from which he was excluded), Kavanagh reviewed as 'a piece of satire that couldn't be equalled by a man trying to satirise', and 'the funiest [sic] book I have read for years' (4:7). Where Kavanagh parted company with Corkery (and with most other social commentators of the previous and present generations) was in his understanding of 'authentic Irish experience', which, as we have already seen, he characterized as an unstable compound of life, personality and parish.

Against the Synge-inspired buckleppers, Kavanagh set what in one article he called 'saints of the imagination' (2:7) – Joyce, and to a lesser extent Yeats. 'One phrase of Joyce', he claimed, 'is worth all Synge as far as giving us the cadence of Irish speech' (9:7), while he considered *Ulysses* one of the two greatest works (along with *Moby Dick*) in English prose fiction (12:7). The 'Joyce' of his pantheon, however, would have been unrecognizable either to those who relied on ethnicity as a critical criterion or to the scholars, exegetes and theorists who at this time were embarking on the international institutionalization of Joyce's work. *Ulysses* was not a career for Kavanagh but a striking example of parochialism-in-action, a book impregnated with Dublin but at the same time 'only incidentally about Dublin and fundamentally the history of a soul' (12:7). He valued (and desired), in other words, Joyce's local interventionist potential and his ability to bring parish and personality to life in his art. Kavanagh's admiration of Joyce was not that of the critic for the subject, but the writer-critic's acknowledgement of the power of another writer.[23]

Seldom does Kavanagh sustain a line of argument throughout a whole article. Instead he digresses rapidly from pseudo-analysis to pseudo-theory to evaluation and back again in the course of a few hundred words. The effect is more like a pub monologue than a reasoned textual response – rambling, anecdotal, impulsive and occasional. It is by making his critical discourse into a spontaneous, situated event rather than a timeless, voiceless text that Kavanagh attempts to insinuate a role and a power for himself in a society which, turning increasingly towards professionalism and institutionalism, was rapidly doing away with the very notion of the holistic writer-critic towards which he aspired.[24]

Neither as business enterprise nor as cultural intervention was *Kavanagh's Weekly* a success.[25] Writing large portions of each issue by himself and maintaining the same tone and style throughout each page of each copy, while strategically subversive and progressive, was tactically counter-productive for Kavanagh in that the journal was very one-dimensional, its note sounding in a 'shrill monotone'[26] rather than the melodic counterpoint with which the periodical form works best.[27] However, with the development of the concept of parochialism, the attempt to expose the partial vision on which dominant nationalist ideology was constructed, and the resistance offered to the hegemony of specialization in the realm of literature, *Kavanagh's Weekly* represents an important moment in the narrative of modern Irish decolonization as mediated by the discourse of literary criticism.

NOTES

The following journals have been consulted in the preparation of this chapter:

The Bell: A Literary Magazine, ed. Sean O'Faolain and Peadar O'Donnell (Dublin, 1940–48, 1950–54).

Ériu: Founded as the Journal of the School of Irish Learning Devoted to Irish Philology and Literature (Dublin, 1904–).

Envoy: An Irish Review of Literature and Art, ed. John Ryan and Valentin Iremonger (Dublin, 1949–51).

Kavanagh's Weekly: A Journal of Literature and Politics, ed. Patrick and Peter Kavanagh; nos.1–13 (Dublin, 12 April–5 July 1952).

Studies: An Irish Quarterly Review of Letters, Philosophy and Science (Dublin, 1912–).

1. Richard Kearney, *Transitions: Narratives in Modern Irish Culture* (Manchester: Manchester University Press, 1988), pp.250–68.

2. Liam O'Dowd, 'Intellectuals in Twentieth-Century Ireland: And the Case of George Russell (AE)', *The Crane Bag*, 9, 1 (1985), pp. 6–25.

3. Seamus Deane, *A Short History of Irish Literature* (London: Hutchinson 1986), p.229.

4. In his essay 'Between Politics and Literature: The Irish Cultural Journal' (1988), pp.250–68, Richard Kearney locates the roots of this split in the dualistic nature of the journal form itself, which tends on the one hand towards subjective vision and on the other towards objective accuracy.

5. Terence Brown has suggested (in personal correspondence) that its lack of influence diminishes any theory based upon an analysis of *Kavanagh's Weekly*. It is the very marginality of this publication when compared with a (relatively) successful publication such as *The Leader* (an important source for Brown's *Ireland: A Social and Cultural History 1922–1985* [London: Fontana, 1985]), however, that I find interesting here. I have no doubt as to the importance of *The Leader* in Irish cultural politics of the period, or, in the words of J.J. Lee, that it 'reached an exceptional level of intellectual sophistication on both national and international affairs' (*Ireland 1912–1985: Politics and Society* [Cambridge: Cambridge University Press, 1989], p.606). But the economy of 'importance' and 'marginality' is precisely the issue; the question of 'major' and 'minor' criticisms engages with the same kinds of decolonizing issues explored by David Lloyd in his analysis of 'major' and 'minor' literatures in *Nationalism and Minor Literature: James Clarence Mangan and the Emergence of Irish Cultural Nationalism* (Berkeley, CA: University of California Press, 1987).

6. Brown, *Ireland*, pp.211–38; Anthony Cronin, 'Patrick Kavanagh', in *Dead as Doornails: A Chronicle of Life* (Dublin: Dolmen Press, 1976); Lee, *Ireland 1912–1985*, pp.271–328; John Ryan, *Remembering How We Stood: Bohemian Dublin at Mid-Century* (Dublin: Gill & Macmillan, 1975).

7. J.J. Lee (ed.), *Ireland 1945–70* (Dublin: Gill & Macmillan, 1979), p.24.

8. *Kavanagh's Weekly: A Journal of Literature and Politics*, vol.1, nos.1–13 (12 April–5 July 1952). All future journal references in this essay will cite volume and date (where relevant), number and page number – for example, *Kavanagh's Weekly* number 3, page 5, will appear as 3:5.

9. Antoinette Quinn, *Patrick Kavanagh: Born-Again Romantic* (Dublin: Gill & Macmillan, 1991), pp.279–80.

10. From 'The Bellman (Larry Morrow): Meet Patrick Kavanagh' (18 April 1948), republished in Peter Kavanagh (ed.), *Patrick Kavanagh: Man and Poet* [1973] (Newbridge: Goldsmith Press, 1987), pp.117–22 (p.120).

11. Quinn, *Patrick Kavanagh*, p.13.

12. Kavanagh already had experience of Irish libel law, having being involved in a suit brought against his book *The Green Fool* by Oliver St John Gogarty in 1939. Shortly after the demise of *Kavanagh's Weekly* he was to experience it again, this time as plaintiff against what he considered a derogatory article published in *The Leader* in October 1952.

13. Quinn, *Patrick Kavanagh*, p.459.

14. O'Dowd, 'Intellectuals in Twentieth-Century Ireland'; Liam O'Dowd, 'Neglecting the Material Dimension: Irish Intellectuals and the Problem of Identity', *The Irish Review*, 3 (1988), pp.8–17.

15. In 'The Social Role of the Literary Critic', Judith R. Kramer writes: 'The established critics of the twentieth century in both England and America are virtually all faculty members of universities. Their primary source of income is their academic salaries, although many of them are also editors of the critical quarterlies published at the universities. As a faculty member of a university, the critic is no longer a "free lance" intellectual, but rather, a salaried employee of an academic bureaucracy ... In essence, this amounts to a new form of "institutional" patronage.' In M.C. Albrecht, J.H. Barnett and M. Griff (eds), *The Sociology of Art and Literature: A Reader* (London: Duckworth, 1970), p.442.

16. Kavanagh (ed.), *Patrick Kavanagh: Man and Poet*, p.394.

17. Quinn, *Patrick Kavanagh*, p.283.

18. Seamus Heaney, *Preoccupations: Selected Prose 1968–1978* (London: Faber & Faber, 1980), p.116.

19. Deane, *Short History of Irish Literature*, p.213.

20. Quinn writes: 'Prose and poetry mingled casually and unselfconsciously in this urban journalism. Not only did several of Kavanagh's poems make their first appearance in an opinion column; on occasion, they substituted for an article or book review. The demarcation between his creative and his critical writings diminished as the same preoccupations and attitudes, the same words, and above all, the same speaking voice were encountered in both' (Quinn, *Patrick Kavanagh*, pp.254–5). See also Heaney's two essays – 'From Monaghan to the Grand Canal: The Poetry of Patrick Kavanagh' and 'The Sense of Place' (Heaney, *Preoccupations*, pp.115–30 and pp. 131–49) – for an analysis of Kavanagh's poetic style which, he claimed, 'has a spoken rather than a written note' (p.116).

21. Maurice Harmon, *Sean O'Faolain: A Critical Introduction* (Dublin: Wolfhound Press, 1984).

22. International PEN: Promoting literature, defending freedom of expression: http://www.internationalpen.org.uk/internationalpen/; http://www.englishpen.org.

23. As part of his contribution to the *Envoy* special number dedicated to Joyce, Kavanagh submitted the poem 'Who Killed James Joyce', containing the lines: 'Who killed James Joyce? / I, said the commentator, / I killed James Joyce / For my graduation. What weapon was used / To slay the mighty Ulysses? The weapon that was used / Was a Harvard thesis. / How did you bury Joyce? / In a broadcast Symposium. / That's how we buried Joyce / To a tuneful encomium. / And did you get high marks, / The Ph.D? / I got the B.Litt / And my master's degree.'

24. In his essay 'Swift's Tory Anarchy', in *The World, The Text, and The Critic* [1983] (London: Vintage, 1991), pp.54–71, Edward Said develops a similar argument with regard to the work of Jonathan Swift in the early eighteenth century.

25. I have been unable to discover circulation figures for *Kavanagh's Weekly*, although its lack of sponsorship and Anthony Cronin's remarks (Cronin, *Dead as Doornails*) on the number of unsold copies which ended up as firing in the Pembroke Road flat indicate the journal's lack of commercial success.

26. Quinn, *Patrick Kavanagh*, p.284.

27. In 'A Note on the Journal Genre' (in *Transitions*, pp.250–68) Richard Kearney writes: 'Its aim was to invite the reader to participate in the multiple interpretations of events represented by the different essays. Indeed the very term "essay" is perhaps significant here, for it acknowledges that the various contributions printed in a single issue of a journal are no more than a variety of *attempts* (French, *essais*) to reach a consensus. The essays of a magazine are parts in search of a whole, diverse perspective which require the reflective response of the reader if they are to achieve any sort of overall synthesis' (p.268). *Kavanagh's Weekly* lacks this sense of diversity, sacrificing variety for a consistent confrontational tone which demands only assent or dissent, but never synthesis.

CHAPTER FIVE

Kavanagh and the Irish Pastoral Tradition

OONA FRAWLEY

The representation of place and nature in Irish writing, particularly during the period of Patrick Kavanagh's lifetime, frequently correlates to conceptions of Irish identity. During the period of the Revival that pre-ceded Kavanagh's own writing, place, nature and landscape were, in fact, explicitly tied to conceptions of national identity, as the nation-to-be took textual, and then palpable, shape, constructing for itself ideals of Irishness based in the rural. Kavanagh openly reviled the link between nationalism and literature entrenched in much Revival writing. In 'Nationalism and Literature' for example, he lamented that Ireland lacked what he called 'parish myth': 'Instead we have this national thing which is no use to any-one'.[1] Nevertheless, his work, by so frequently emphasizing nature, place and landscape, engages with notions of identity in Ireland even if simply because of the politicized nature of earlier writing on these themes. Kavanagh's writing, in its concern with nature, place and landscape, also mirrors the identity shifts taking place in Ireland in the years following the period of both the Revival and independence. In this sense the Monaghan poet can be seen to have contributed to what I call an Irish pastoral form.

Critically, this might seem a strange point at which to begin, since Kavanagh's reputation has rested in no small part on the interpretation of his work as fiercely anti-pastoral. Responding to the spectre that was for him the Irish Literary Revival, Kavanagh attempted to redeem his poetry from what he thought of as the impertinence of a romanticized view of rural Ireland through an emphasis on what he called the 'parochial'. In one of the most cited passages from his prose, Kavanagh defines this key term, which has determined much of the reading of his work:

Parochialism and provincialism are opposites. The provincial has no mind of his own; he does not trust what his eyes see until he has heard what the metropolis – towards which his eyes are turned – has to say on any subject. This runs through all activities.

The parochial mentality on the other hand is never in any doubt about the social and artistic validity of his parish. All great civilizations are based on parochialism – Greek, Israelite, English ...

In Ireland we are inclined to be provincial not parochial, for it requires a great deal of courage to be parochial. When we do attempt having the courage of our parish we are inclined to go false and to play up to the larger parish on the other side of the Irish Sea ...

Parochialism is universal; it deals with the fundamentals.[2]

The frequent focus of Kavanagh's work on the parish of his birth has been ascribed to this parochial approach to writing. And, since Kavanagh's birthplace as well as much of his subject matter can be loosely described as 'rural' – in its concern with farm life, landscape, detail of the natural world and with the mentalities developing from the deprivations of Irish rural living at the time – the 'parochial', in relation to Kavanagh's own work, has tended to be thought of not simply as regional or macrocosmic writing, but as a specific kind of local Irish writing that is 'rural'. This emphasis in Kavanagh criticism, on parochial writing as rural writing is surprising, in that the only two examples of 'parishioners' Kavanagh provides in 'The Parish and the Universe' are George Moore and James Joyce.

In this sense, the 'parochial' in Kavanagh's writing has been associated with what has been thought of as his brand of anti-pastoral, which has a strain of realism in it that Kavanagh believed absent from other Irish writing that addressed itself to the countryside. This anti-pastoral, 'parochial' aesthetic is considered to be in resolute revolt against representations of the natural world that 'go false', with the suggestion that 'provincial' writing produced by those like Kavanagh's Revival predecessors 'plays up' notions of the natural world exaggerated or romanticized by metropolitan perspectives on 'the country'.

This approach to Kavanagh allows for the drawing of some useful distinctions between his literary representation of the rural and that of

Revival writers, and particularly, to Kavanagh's own mind, Yeats and Synge. It certainly highlights the difference between Kavanagh's experience of nature as a farmer and Synge's and Yeats's more distant relationships with nature by virtue of relative financial privilege; by comparison to theirs, Kavanagh's early view was, perhaps, more literally of the parish than of the province. Since this approach emphasizes differences between Kavanagh's aesthetic and those of others, however, it prevents us from situating Kavanagh's representations of nature, landscape and place within a larger canon of Irish literature that also consistently engages with these themes. An overemphasis on Kavanagh as a parochial, anti-pastoral poet has thus meant that little attention has been paid to the fact that, as Declan Kiberd has pointed out, 'antipastoral is, for all its nay-saying, still a version of the mode'.[3] Kavanagh's poetry and prose can be seen, in fact, as employing not merely a version of the pastoral, but as partaking of an Irish pastoral tradition that develops in slightly different ways to the English pastoral model. Seen as an inheritor of this type of pastoral, which frequently represents nature in all of its harshness as well as its beauty, and in which land and landscape are more politicized than in other pastoral traditions, Kavanagh is not as easily separated from Yeats and Synge or, indeed, an Irish literary heritage: by engaging – even if not self-consciously in the manner of many Revival authors – with a tradition of Irish writing that dates from the eighth century, Kavanagh, like Yeats and Synge, contributes to the shaping of a national literature that relies heavily on nature, landscape and local place, and, in this key way, also contributes to the conscientious shaping of Irish identity in the twentieth century.

Rather infamously, Kavanagh wrote that 'there has never been a tradition of poetry in Ireland'[4] and claimed that 'in a thousand years Ireland has not produced a major poet or, indeed, a good minor one'.[5] However untrue the first statement and however inflammatory the second, these proclamations should not deter us from considering Kavanagh's place within a tradition of Irish writing, since his work reveals a rather remarkable commitment to thematics that have underwritten Irish literature for over a millennium. The majority of criticism on Kavanagh, however, has not only failed to recognize this continuity with Irish tradition, but has read his work based largely on statements like those cited above. When it comes to nature and place, Kavanagh's work has too often been read, in other words, under his own critical guidance. This seems to be a mistake of a rather fundamental kind, deserving prompt correction. While Kavanagh's journalism, essays and miscellaneous prose provide insight into the writer's development and shifting ideologies, they cannot be relied upon as maps by which his poetry, fiction and drama can be read. Indeed, critical circumstances in Ireland have changed radically enough for the persistence of readings of Kavanagh's poetry predicated on this prose to be surprising. Declan Kiberd has observed that academic research in Ireland was, until recently, impeded by the very kind of what he dubs 'auto-criticism' and 'self-commentary' that Kavanagh affected:

> Irish writing ... seemed to contain within itself its own auto-criticism, its own essential self-commentary. This was as true of *Ulysses* as of the poetry of Yeats, of *At Swim-Two-Birds* as of Kavanagh, and it left many scrupulous critics wondering just how much of value could be added. Yet these acts of auto-criticism were individual occasions and even when taken together would hardly amount to a national critical methodology.[6]

At a time when Irish criticism has bloomed, it seems appropriate to reconsider Kavanagh without a reliance on such self-interpretations. However much he set himself in opposition to any Irish tradition of writing, and particularly to those like Yeats and Synge, whom he believed to have propounded what he called 'a thoroughgoing English-bred lie'[7] about Ireland and Irishness during the Revival, Kavanagh's work engages, through his frequent focus on the natural world and on ideas of place, with some of the major preoccupations of Irish writing.

While Kavanagh publicly scorned Irish literary production with the implication that his own writing was to be seen as innovative and repre-senting an absolute break with the past, his work can, in fact, be seen as a specific incarnation of a tradition of Irish pastoral writing that was farther from new than he would have cared to admit. Edna Longley has noted that critics have often applied theory about pastoral writing rather haphazardly to Ireland, 'as when the Literary Revival is held solely responsible for rus-tic stereotypes';[8] in fact, as Longley seems to imply, the tradition of the pastoral in an Irish context derives from a period much earlier than the Revival. From its eighth-century beginnings, Irish literature demonstrates a marked preoccupation with nature, landscape and place, witnessed in literature ranging from the 'hermit poetry' composed by monastic scholars between approximately the eighth and eleventh centuries to the corpus of bardic literature, and, in Kavanagh's own time, from the poetry of Yeats to the incomparable treatment of Irish place in Joyce's *Finnegans Wake*. So strong is the tradition of Irish writing on these themes that a form of pastoral develops that can be described as Irish, with characteristics that, while they draw upon other pastoral traditions, are distinct from the classical or English pastoral mode.

In the classical pastoral tradition deriving from the work of Theocritus and Virgil, the natural world is often idealized and perfected, frequently devoid of the kind of realistic detail that might mar a scene. As a result of the implied dialectic between the simple rural life represented in the text and the complicated urban one from which the author often writes, the pastoral becomes imbued with a nostalgia for the lost ideal or paradise being depicted. And, as many critics have noted since William Empson's pioneering study,[9] it can come to function as a politicized mode of writing critical of a contemporary society far from perfect in the way that the imagined, textual society is shown to be.

While the earliest Irish writing to address itself to nature and place tends to do so within the lines of this classical pastoral, a shift occurs in approximately the thirteenth century, at a time when cultural upheavals (such as the Norman invasion and the consolidation of power by the Catholic Church) seem to have moved the Irish literary tradition in a slightly different direction. At this point, that rather faint nostalgia for a simple life is heightened as nature itself becomes a site for nostalgia, a place from which to lament the passing or loss or changing of culture: Irish pastoral of the medieval period mourns the loss of a cultural world, and does so from the position of the natural world of which other traditions mourn for the passing.[10] While this literature recognizes nature's beauties, the realities of nature – harsh weather, the difficulties in finding sustenance, the vagaries of living in a wilderness with little shelter and little cultural or social support – are also present, so that the natural world is not idealized in the same manner as it is in, say, Virgil's *Eclogues* or, indeed, in earlier Irish literature. Medieval Irish literature moves towards a pastoral form that is at once realistic and acknowledging of beauty while containing a coded reading of cultural change. This shift is a vital one in the context of much later Irish literature and has as we will see, implications, for the ways in which we read Kavanagh's poetry and prose.

If it would be difficult to separate the strands of Irish and English history after the end of the sixteenth century, it would be equally difficult from this point on to segregate the Irish pastoral tradition from the English one. Nonetheless, some key differences appear to remain in place. Rather than engaging with a trope of nostalgia – literally, 'homesickness' – for an idealized, vanished world that was *imagined*, Irish authors who employed the pastoral mode were often expressing a quite literal homesickness. For a colonized people and, subsequently, for a post-colonial nation, the pastoral form must, I suggest, be fundamentally different in this crucial way: the homesickness explicit in pastoral nostalgia does not function merely as a literary device, but as a political tool, a way of commenting on social circumstance. For a culture subject to numerous invasions, major political upheavals and an eventual colonial rule lasting centuries, it is unsurprising that the natural world became a potent repository for meaning in literature: a representation of stability – while all else changed, place and geography remained constant – landscape and place also attested to the shifts taking place within the culture at different times, as, for instance, place-names changed, migrations took place, and tangible alterations such as the felling of trees occurred under colonial occupation. While the pastoral mode arguably always functions as a politicized mode of writing, in Ireland that politicization was exaggerated and heightened by historical circumstance, and particularly by colonialism. Nostalgia, in its heightened presence in the Irish pastoral mode, provided a way of stabilizing an uncertain present by connecting it to the past.

It would appear to be in part for these reasons that, as the movement known as the Irish Literary Revival got under way, the land, nature and place of Ireland were important aesthetic themes, subject to a nostalgia that drew not only on medieval Irish pastoral traditions newly rediscovered in translation but also on English pastoral forms and Romantic ideals of nature. In describing the process of decolonization, Edward Said has emphasized the importance of imaginatively – as well as physically and governmentally – reclaiming a landscape.[11] The Revival's imaginative reclamation of a 'real Ireland' was informed by nostalgia for culture perceived as elided or veiled by colonialism, and this culture was thought to reside, quite literally, beyond the Pale. The period's focus on the west of the country as the site of an Ireland otherwise vanished – the site of that posited 'real Ireland' – negotiates the territory of imaginative, nostalgic reclamation, as does the construction of the peasant as representing an authentic Irishness. In setting out to self-consciously construct a body of national literature, participants in the Revival, from its scattered beginnings, emphasized the beauty of Ireland's countryside, suggesting that the rural was somehow 'more Irish' than urban areas, which were often seen to be the centres of colonial administration. Ironically, of course, most Revival participants were urban dwellers, and many of the movements of the period were based in Dublin. Influential writers such as Standish James O'Grady, drawing on Irish tradition and on Romanticism, promoted an idea of an Irish civilization that was ancient and based in nature.[12] The result was that Irish identity was rapidly confirmed as something intimately connected to nature, to land and to rural life.

The form of the pastoral that prevailed during the Revival thus seemed initially to revert to more classical and English traditions of the pastoral that idealized nature and kept at bay the strain of realism from the medieval Irish pastoral tradition, while drawing on that tradition's heightened nostalgia for a lost culture. To assume, however, that a fetishization of the peasantry and of the rustic and rural persisted unchallenged throughout the period of the Revival by its major authors would be to go along with Kavanagh's too easy assessments. The most prominent writers of the movement, Yeats and Synge, were often targeted by Kavanagh for their perceived part in the creation of 'peasant' drama as well as stereotypes of Irish rurality, but both came to critique their early nostalgia for a lost, imagined, pre-colonial Ireland and moved away from simple idealizations of the natural world. While both writers initially created idyllic pastoral dream-worlds in which nature remained vague and romantic, such idealizations are unsurprising, seen as a stage in the decolonizing process described by Said. What is surprising, perhaps, is how quickly Yeats and Synge moved to critique their own nostalgias for an originary Ireland that stressed a simplistic, idealized rurality. By the close of The Aran Islands, Synge recognizes his construction of a 'primitive' ideal at the start of his visits, and begins to see other aspects of island existence: the relentlessness of nature, the islanders' absolute reliance on its vagaries for their livelihoods, and his own acute distance from such a way of life. On recognizing his removal from the islanders' experience and his construction of a particular way of seeing their lives, Synge becomes critical of his earlier idealizations, with the result that The Aran Islands remains not simply a pseudo-anthropological record of the Revival's interest in the west of Ireland and in the Irish language, but a valuable reflection of the movement of the Revival towards more critical representations of Ireland, as seen in the work of Synge that followed.

Yeats also shifts away from classical and English pastoral forms to a more critical, reflective Irish pastoral that includes the disappointments and hard realities if not of the natural world then of his own romanticizations of it. 'Innisfree' remains a strong example of that early idealization: in a classical pastoral stance, the poem is constructed from the point of view of a man in the city, dreaming of a lost rural idyll that the poem's diction suggests is still achievable – the poet, after all, 'will arise and go now'. In later years, Yeats recognizes that that idyll was never to be retrieved and, indeed, perhaps never existed in the first place; and the mature poet came to lament the persistent popularity of this and other poems that he later deemed to have an 'element of sentimentality'.[13] In fact, by 1925, Yeats recited 'The Lake Isle of Innisfree' only reluctantly because of popular expectation, and 'with an air of suppressed loathing'.[14] The poetry that Yeats composed in his later years was as far removed from his early idealizations as possible, full of a self-reflection and self-critique that recognized the role nostalgia had played in the construction of those idealizations. Musing on his childhood recollections of Ben Bulben and his yearning to reach it again, Yeats comes to see that 'my finger could but have touched / Cold stone and water' ('Towards Break of Day', lines 13–14): the younger poet's attempts to imbue nature with something magical and mystical had failed, and the mature poet has moved closer to a realism informed by the needs of a different age. By the end of his poetic life, Yeats had moved far beyond the construction of simple nostalgias and towards the construction of unlived, unexperienced ideals that, as in 'Byzantium', are purely imaginative and, curiously enough, based in the urban.

In the sense that neither Synge nor Yeats persisted in executing work centring on simplistic idealizations of rural Ireland, Kavanagh has been read against an idea of the Revival that has itself been outdated and only recently challenged.[15] Kavanagh's own representations of nature, place and landscape seem, in fact, to beat a path similar to that of Synge and particularly to Yeats. There is a move from simple idealizations of nature towards a middle phase (when *The Great Hunger* is composed) in which he assaults literary idealizations of nature in the manner of the medieval Irish pastoral tradition, and, finally, into a third phase in which the pastoral form relies on imaginative reconstructions of place as a locus of individual consciousness. Kavanagh's career also follows another example of Yeats's, as Dillon Johnston has astutely pointed out: 'Yeats demonstrated that a poet could testify to his personal experience – psychological, intellectual, perceptual – while actively playing a public role.'[16] Despite his fervour against the Revival, it is clear that the movement provided Kavanagh with useful models, both in terms of literary production and an example – even if it was one to be rebelled against – for the public role of the poet.

Kavanagh's earliest work, coincident with the tail end of the Revival and composed while Yeats was still alive, is full of rather predictable idealizations. While Kavanagh's youth goes some way to explaining his early idealizing exercises, it does not explain his swift rise to popularity (and, of course, notoriety as well). Critics have argued that Kavanagh's early reputation was, in fact, formed primarily by concepts of Irishness and Irish writing shaped by the early period of the Revival. Thus Antoinette Quinn, in her 2001 biography of the poet, can write that

By 1936 Kavanagh had achieved a literary reputation in Dublin far in excess of his slender output or his slight, underdeveloped talent. This reputation, which preceded and anticipated his later achievement, was based on the vogue for peasantry in the wake of the Literary Revival. In the 1930s he was perceived as an incarnation of a Literary Revival ideal, a peasant poet, a singer of the bogs and, as such, a remarkable phenomenon. Ironically, in view of Daniel Corkery's classification of the ascendancy greats, Yeats, Synge and Lady Gregory, as 'exotic' rather than indigenous writers, Kavanagh, on Corkery's definition, the quintessentially indigenous writer – small farmer, Mass-goer, football player – was to urban eyes an exotic. Though various peasant stereotypes were common in literary circles, those were confined to the page or the stage, and an actual, living poetic peasant was a curiosity.[17]

According to D. O'Brien,

> The Literary Renaissance was petering out, but many were still anxious to be peasants and to play the Gael. Kavanagh was the real thing, or rather, his existence mocked mendacious, sentimental images of the true Ireland as manufactured by people with smooth hands and voices.[18]

Robert F. Garratt, writing about tradition and continuity from Yeats to Heaney, affirms in a similar vein that Kavanagh 'was held up as the genuine article of a Revival fiction, the peasant-poet from the bog, capable of stirring poetic utterances yet simple to the core'.[19]

According to these readings, Kavanagh's arrival in Dublin was taken as a confirmation of stereotypes of rurality. Evidently not a 'manufactured' rural character, he appeared as a kind of 'peasant-poet', a 'quintessential' type of Irishman, 'real' and 'genuine'. However, far from being placed in a role by a public demanding the personification of popular stereotypes of rural Irishness, Kavanagh *voluntarily* played this part. On the occasion of his first trip to Dublin to meet AE, who had published several of his poems and offered encouragement to the young poet, Kavanagh, Quinn reports, donned the costume appropriate to his assumed poetic role:

> Lest the sage doubt his rural authenticity or need for patronage, he decided to wear his shabby old work clothes for the visit instead of dressing up in his Sunday suit. Since his appearance was quite unmistakably countrified, his adoption of the guise of a Syngean tramp was, as he later realised, quite unnecessary. To exaggerate his peasant persona still further, Kavanagh decided to walk the sixty-odd miles to Dublin, rather than travel by train or bicycle, though it was the depths of winter and the journey took the best part of three days ... He was deliberately acting the part.[20]

If Kavanagh was 'exaggerating his peasant persona', it is curious that analysis and criticism have tended to focus not on the role-playing attested to by Kavanagh's biographer, but on Kavanagh as a 'real' manifestation of Irishness and Irish identity. Such critiques disturbingly confirm the notion of the peasant as the 'genuine' Irishman, and imply that Kavanagh's work, when it concerns the rural, is somehow also more 'genuine' because of his country origins, less likely to be the result of a guise or persona than if he had been a more 'urban' or 'metropolitan' poet – which, ironically enough, he was to become.

This view of Kavanagh as 'real' peasant-poet is immensely problematic, because it focuses Irish identity on stereotypes and encourages us to see 'Kavanagh' as a performance of those stereotypes. Kavanagh, of course, did much to encourage the image of himself as a more 'genuine' writer of the rural than others. In 'Self Portrait', he describes *Tarry Flynn* as 'the only *authentic* account of life as it was lived in Ireland this century';[21] but he was also at pains to deny, in later years, his part in shaping his reputation as a 'peasant poet':

> In those days in Dublin the big thing besides being Irish was the peasant quality. They were all trying to be peasants. They had been at it for years but I hadn't heard. And I was installed as the authentic peasant, and what an idea that was among rascals pretending to have an interest in poetry. Although the literal idea of the peasant is of a farm labouring person, in fact a peasant is that mass of mankind which lives below a certain level of consciousness. They live in the dark cave of the unconscious and they scream when they see the light.[22]

Kavanagh's rhetoric here is fascinating: he denies having known about a vogue for peasantry ('I hadn't heard'), which implies, in turn, a denial of knowledge of the Revival and its themes. This claim is, of course, contradicted by what we know about that first journey to Dublin and his conscious decision to play up his rural roots. Kavanagh thus attempts to create a double-persona, denying the plausibility of the 'authentic peasant' as poet, whom he derides here for living 'unconsciously', while allowing himself to be 'installed' as one, a situation that, of course, becomes self-reflexive and even postmodern in its complications: in displaying a consciousness of what he believes actual peasant life to be, by his own definition he removes himself from the very role he has adopted.

Nonetheless, Kavanagh continued to emphasize his 'authenticity' in order, it would seem, to differentiate himself from Revival writers that he perceived as 'false'. Kavanagh's sense of 'falseness' in Irish literature was the result of what one critic calls that literature's 'contrived pastoralism'.[23] Such an analysis, however, like Kavanagh's reflections about his own role-playing, misses the point that all pastoral writing is constructed and so contrived, Kavanagh's versions no less than others. Critical writing on Kavanagh, following the precedent set by Kavanagh himself, has fallen into the trap of attempting to distinguish his work from the work of Revival poets at a high cost. That cost is, ultimately, a failure fully to grasp how the pastoral has fulfilled a key function in the process of building a canon of national literature in Ireland. It has also led to the absence of a clear understanding of how Kavanagh might be seen to be not merely performing a *volte-face* in reaction to such canon-building, but as contributing to the crucial consideration of Irish identity in its changing relations to the idea of the rural, and to the actual rural world.

By engaging with the themes of landscape, place and nature, Kavanagh, I am suggesting, consciously engages too with this question of a national literature, and does so, I would argue, largely because the Revival had existed to show him how, and because an Irish tradition of pastoral writing was long in place. Like Yeats, Kavanagh recognized the need to establish masks and personae, and, newly arrived in Dublin and attempting to make a name for himself, he employed a 'peasant' mask in part because he was astute enough to realize that his rural Irishness could be used to establish his reputation as a writer at a time when 'peasantry' was equated with Irishness. That he knew the countryside so well was a tremendous help, and one that he was capable of taking advantage of in many guises and forms: not only to promote his poetry, but also simply to make a living as, for instance, a columnist who provided a rural perspective on the big city.[24]

Since the Revival had been so concerned with defining a body of national literature, it makes sense that Kavanagh, following in its wake, would be concerned with the ways in which such a canon accommodated his own experience and personae. Finding that there was a space in which the ideal could contain the real, Kavanagh proceeded quite consciously to employ personae and masks inspired by Revival imagery. The deliberateness of this is attested to by Quinn, who points out that

'Throughout the 1930s Kavanagh tended to market any verse with Irish place-names or content in Irish journals and to send more neutral material to English editors'.[25] Among other things that it had changed, the Revival had expanded the marketplace for Irish writing. In using popular imagery and choosing to work in that marketplace, Kavanagh thus at an early stage illustrated a certain savvy about the construction of his career and personae. While it was useful, he would shape and allow himself to be shaped as 'an unschooled rustic', as he wrote in 'Poet'. He would be one who declares himself, as the poem 'Peasant' observes, 'the representative of those / Clay-faced sucklers of spade-handles'.[26] To this end, in his early poetry Kavanagh's poetic persona often laments – in the way of more traditional pastoral modes that he is not often credited with engaging – the loss of a 'wise innocence' he had 'Ere Dublin taught him to be wise' ('To A Child'). In the same register, the knowledge that travel and experience have brought was not always welcomed, as 'To Knowledge' reported:

> Before you came I knew the speech
> Of mountains, I could pray
> With stone and water.[27]

The poet has lost a primal ability to commune with nature, it would appear, an ability that he once had, naturally, as by birthright. This loss – and the implicit longing that hovers behind it – has been brought about by the experience of the city, and by knowledge that has shaken the 'peasant poet' out of his unconscious existence. Interestingly, Kavanagh could argue elsewhere – in the essay 'Nationalism in Literature' – while complaining that the peasantry live in an unconscious fog, that 'Once we stop to think the illusion is gone. In the case of a poet's mythology the all-embracing fog must remain impenetrable. We must not escape from it.'[28] In this early work, Kavanagh does not so much display strong anti-pastoral tendencies as, in fact, exhibit a canny employment of pastoral devices that resemble classical, English and early Irish literary Revival modes of the pastoral. The rural is idealized in its simplicity and innocence, and is set against the urban experience of the writer's persona. In a poem like 'The Rustic', the poet claims that

Simple love warm and kind
In the country I'll find
A daughter of nature young and sweet
Who has never learned city deceit.
A child of the unsullied muse
Who has never stood in cinema queues,
Who has never read the books that make
Women motherhood forsake.

Within this positing of the ideal rural lass is, of course, the strong suggestion of satire; Kavanagh at once employs the stereotype and undercuts it through a process of diminishment, disrupting his pastoral daydream with atypical images like 'cinema queues'. While indicative of his later poetry, this is, however, unusual in his early work, which generally tends to present images of rural Ireland that will fulfil the requirements of what he believes to be the popular taste and which, as a result, bear strong resemblance to traditional, and Romanticized, pastoral modes.

That Kavanagh left rural Ireland for Dublin as well as London for a period meant that, like the predecessors he purported to despise and like many who had written pastorals before him, he was writing about the country from a distance, from within the space of the city. In his early phase, this gap meant that the writing was often imbued with a nostalgia and sentimental longing for the simple beauties of Monaghan, of his native townland, of specific fields and ditches. While Kavanagh's urban existence should have revealed him as an astute poet capable of manufacturing a variety of pastoral forms, that urban position in fact appears to have helped in the establishment of his reputation as the peasant-poet in the city, since his life mirrored migratory patterns in post-independence Ireland: his personal migration, as John Goodby writes, 'acquired national significance because it coincided with a general movement from the land to the town'.[29] If at the start of the century most of the population of Ireland had lived in farming communities, that was rapidly changing, as more and more people migrated to Dublin, in flight from the rural hinterland. Kavanagh's early poetic sentimentality thus expressed not only his own experience, but captured the mood of a generation that was shifting the population centres of Ireland and then experiencing, ironically enough, forms of nostalgia that early Revival authors had felt for rural, even pastoral lives that they had often not themselves lived. A poem such as 'Christmas Eve Remembered' reveals this kind of nostalgia, as well as Kavanagh's awareness of his romanticization of it, as he recollects those attending Mass in 'a parish in Monaghan. / Poor parish! And yet memory does weave / For me about those folk / A romantic cloak'.

Kavanagh came to feel uncomfortable about an early writing that he sensed was full of sentimentality, at one time proclaiming thanks to God that he retained copyright of material he was not keen to see reprinted. He complained that what had been admired about that early poetry was only 'the Irishness of the thing. Irishness is a form of anti-art. A way of posing as a poet without actually being one.'[30] This refutation of his early work as sentimental and somehow 'too Irish' echoes Yeats's response to requests to read early poems; Kavanagh, like Yeats, had begun to move away from the role he had initially chosen to fulfil.

The atmosphere in which Kavanagh moved in this early period was, though, very different to that of the Revival. If the years of the Revival's heyday were characterized by optimistic fervour, the post-independence years were stamped by the dismaying after-effects of the civil war, as the emergent republic struggled with the divisions of its foundation and the poverty that the new nation found it had inherited – a poverty worsened by European events and a looming Second World War. As a result, Kavanagh's work can be read as

> the product of a very low, dispirited period in Irish life and literature, the sort of psychological slump that most nations emerging from colonial rule experience after the revival of the past fails and people become aware that they have to make do with the rubble left behind by the departed conqueror.[31]

Part of this 'psychological slump', as it appears in the literature of the period is, I would suggest, the realization that the land and landscape so long yearned and longed for has undergone a symbolic shift, and can no longer retain its place as the idyll. The fevered romanticism that had fuelled nationalist writing and rhetoric was being tempered by the realities of the life of many in the country, realities that independence and outright national possession of the land had not altered. Conditions continued to propel immigration and the movement away from those rural areas where poverty, educational disadvantage and land-ownership patterns meant that many were destined to live out their lives with little advancement or the easing of economic and social burdens. Under these circumstances, it was becoming increasingly difficult to maintain a symbol of the rural landscapes of Ireland as in some way paradisal. While writers like Yeats had foreseen this shift away from idealizing fantasies and begun to address it, the shift did not appear to make itself more broadly felt in literature until Kavanagh's time – and, arguably, the shift was not forcibly realized until the publication of *The Great Hunger*, which marks Kavanagh's move into the second phase of his representation of nature and place, in a poem which is fuelled, as Goodby notes, by a 'mixture of realism and nostalgia'[32] redolent of earlier Irish pastoral conventions.

Kavanagh's best-known poem (which, like his early work, he later repudiated) contains echoes and traces of the medieval Irish pastoral form described earlier: while Patrick Maguire sometimes sees beauty in that which is about him, he cannot limit his experience of the natural world to the aesthetic, and the poem is often overwhelmed by the realities of a life dependent on nature. From the poem's famous beginning, which reverberates with biblical language, Kavanagh immediately disavows the stereotypes and ideals that he had been dealing in, declaring the scene of his poem a 'tragedy' and emphasizing the distance between the reader – and, indeed, the writer – and the figure of Maguire, whom we are repeatedly urged to 'watch'. While 'sometimes ... the sun comes through a gap' and there are 'half-moments of paradise' that grace the landscape in ways familiar to readers of other pastoral traditions and even to readers of Kavanagh's own earlier work, the Irish pastoral tradition returned to so forcefully here tends to undercut the longing and poignancy of such moments, forcing a break with the idealizing habits of classical pastoral and early Revivalism. Unlike the symbolically simple and innocent shepherd of Virgil's creation, Maguire, Kavanagh's narrator, insists, 'means nothing. / Not a damn thing': Kavanagh empties peasant ideals of any symbolic function, and resorts to a representation of the thing-in-itself, trying to capture a realism in the natural world instead. And it is this move that allies Kavanagh's greatest poem with an Irish tradition of the pastoral that dates to the thirteenth century.

Kavanagh is so intent on deconstructing ideals that, at times, the poem itself seems to be under threat of destruction, of seizing up, almost seeming to skip like a record: 'Sitting on a wooden gate, / Sitting on a wooden gate, / Sitting on a wooden gate / He didn't give a damn'. Classical and English pastoral forms do not stretch to this kind of detailing, but the Irish pastoral tradition allows for Maguire's very boredom and anxiety; like the figures of medieval Irish literature, Maguire, so intrinsically involved in the cycles of the natural world, lives on the margins and experiences a nearly constant psychological displacement while, ironically, seeming to belong so entirely to the place he inhabits. Living a life that in terms of classical and English pastoral tradition would be seen as ideal, Maguire is shown as a diminished, languishing figure, repeatedly humbled by the dictates of that supposedly ideal life.

The Great Hunger reveals, too, another level of displacement, reflecting the shifts that marked Irish life in the second half of the twentieth century: migration patterns away from the rural were, by this time, well established. While Maguire's textual life challenges an ideal, that life, in all its loneliness and emotional poverty, is in retreat. He has no heir, and there will be no one to take over the farm, just as in Kavanagh's own family there was eventually no one to take over the family property. While the poem could not be seen in the simple light of a pastoral elegy – there is too much resentment in it at Maguire's lot – there is nonetheless an elegiac element to it, in that the way of life it depicts, harsh though it is, is on the wane. If we are witnessing, in the poem, the shattering of an idealized image of Irish country life, we are also witnessing the end of an age, the end of that way of life, and looking ahead to the terrible displacement experienced by many who would find the only way of life they had known changing beyond recognition.

Embedded in the poem's outlook on rural living is the suggestion that creative force can come out of nature itself but, like Maguire, rarely has the opportunity to find expression: 'Nobody will ever know how much tortured poetry the pulled weeds on the ridge wrote / Before they withered in the July sun'. Kavanagh allows a glimpse into that poetry in such formulations, but undercuts it before it has gotten underway with the ominous 'nobody will ever know'. There is a sense in which the classical or English pastoral form cannot contain the possibility of that 'tortured poetry'. This is a fascinating crux, as it reveals Kavanagh's awareness that traditional pastoral modes cannot function in this particular Irish context. His resolution is to create a pastoral form that does accommodate the divide between aesthetic appreciation and the realities of nature. This is forcefully confronted in Part XIII, where Kavanagh examines the mythologies of peasant life that he believes the country still clings to and which he recognizes are increasingly part of a touristic impulse, a gaze at a distance at rural society. Even those who had an intimate experience of farming and of rural living in general, like Kavanagh himself, were still capable of this 'gap[ing] over the green bank into [Maguire's] fields'. There is a sense in which, as Ireland moved towards independence, it had become the consumer of its own idealizations. And that consumption resulted in the strangeness of looking at one's homeland as a tourist, at one remove. Kavanagh, having so removed himself from the space of the rural, had written at the close of *Tarry Flynn* that 'The best way to love a country like this is from a range of not less than three hundred miles'.[33] Again, he had written to his brother Peter that 'The country is awful except to write about'.[34] He was thus well aware of the ironies of this development, and his poem forces us to examine the process by which this consumptive, silently observing gaze has been constituted. The gap between the observer and the observed has initiated a crisis of meaning in Kavanagh's vision of rural Ireland, in which the ideal silently breaks down under the weight of pastoral realities. The poem is, of course, itself a breaking of this silence, and ends with 'The hungry fiend / Scream[ing] the apocalypse of clay / In every corner of this land'.

Kavanagh's language and form here are startlingly removed not only from the early poetry of the Revival but from his own earlier work. He has purged his poetry of a type of sentimentality and has, seemingly unknowingly, returned to an Irish pastoral form that, many centuries earlier, admitted into its discourse the very realities of nature that *The Great Hunger* insists upon. Kavanagh's major achievement is thus not an utter repudiation of Revival literature or the development of an anti-pastoral poetic, but the modernizing of a long tradition of pastoral writing in Ireland that grants space to both the aesthetic admiration of nature and the recognition of the idealizing process that such admiration entails, set alongside a more realistic, direct confrontation with the actualities of the natural world. *The Great Hunger* must also be credited for its role in raising consciousness about the plight of many rural inhabitants, and for reshaping the way in which rural Ireland was viewed. If

Irish identity was engaged with rurality and country life, then Kavanagh's poem disallowed the possibility of idealizing that existence, and, instead, forced a recognition of the oppressive conditions under which many people actually lived.

Following *The Great Hunger*, Kavanagh experimented further with an Irish pastoral mode, once more adapting it to reflect contemporary Irish experience and the shifts occurring in conceptions of Irish identity. Despite writing predominantly from Dublin for most of his career, it is only at a certain point that Dublin becomes the subject of his pastoral writing. In moving towards urban pastoral in the justly praised Canal Bank sonnets, Kavanagh took the pastoral form one step further, like Yeats forcing the reader to recognize that that kind of idyll, far from depending on a particular rural space or any other specific location, existed only in the imagination.[35] As he gave lectures and radio addresses and wrote for some of the major papers of the day, Kavanagh had become an urban, metropolitan poet, far removed from the peasant role he had initially adopted. The shift from the earliest work, which focused on his remembrances and recollections of life in Inniskeen, to the latest work that offered lush, evocative descriptions of his new parish on the banks of Dublin's canal, is one that reflects major trends in Irish culture in the twentieth century, trends with important implications for notions of Irish identity. Primary among these trends was, of course, the movement from rural to urban centres. When Kavanagh began writing at his Monaghan family home, he was representative of the majority of an Irish population based in the countryside. This has changed so quickly that, in the present day, the Irish government is concerned enough about rural degeneration to fund community projects to repopulate what are, in some cases, almost literally deserted villages. In its transposition from country to city, Kavanagh's later work represents the tendency to idealize the natural among the new urban generations, foreshadowing in this the poetry of such later writers as Seamus Heaney.

Far from being a simply anti-pastoral poet, Patrick Kavanagh is, in fact, representative of major shifts in Irish identity and in Irish literature over the course of the twentieth century. In providing a way to reintroduce a strain of realism into the Irish pastoral form, Kavanagh forged a necessary link between Yeats and Heaney that allows for the re-establishment of representations of rurality that avoid naïvety and are conscious of the way in which ideal images are both constructed and deconstructed. Strangely enough, in a far more urban-centred contemporary Ireland, Kavanagh's poetry, even texts like *The Great Hunger* that have received the label of 'anti-pastoral', is often romanticized as celebrating a 'real', and increasingly rare, Irish rural experience. Kavanagh's early experience of the natural world has become foreign enough to contemporary Ireland that, as schoolchildren learn his poems in class, we have begun to turn Kavanagh into the kind of pastoral poet that he himself believed Yeats to be. As Irishness has been increasingly linked to the urban and sophisticated, to the Celtic tiger, the property boom, the European Union, to the international exports of everything from U2 to computer software design, Kavanagh's poetry serves as a reminder of the process by which that shift in identities took place, leading us from a farm without electricity to the bright lights of Dublin town, and from the simple idealizations of pastoral poesy to the more nuanced urban pastoral forms of his final poems, in which he 'think[s] a world into existence', perhaps glimpsing the 'colourful country' ('Come Dance With Kitty Stobling'[36]) that Ireland has become.

NOTES

1. Patrick Kavanagh, 'Nationalism and Literature', in *Collected Prose* (London: MacGibbon & Kee, 1967), p.270.

2. Patrick Kavanagh, 'The Parish and the Universe', in *Collected Prose*, pp.282–3.

3. Declan Kiberd, *Inventing Ireland: The Literature of the Modern Nation* (London: Jonathan Cape, 1995), p.489.

4. Patrick Kavanagh, 'From Monaghan to the Grand Canal', in *Collected Prose*, p.226.

5. Patrick Kavanagh, 'The Irish Tradition', in *Collected Prose*, p.233.

6. Declan Kiberd, 'Joyce's Ellmann, Ellmann's Joyce', in *The Irish Writer and the World* (Cambridge: Cambridge University Press, 2005), p.243.

7. Patrick Kavanagh, 'Self Portrait', in *Collected Prose*, p.13.

8. Edna Longley, *Poetry and Posterity* (Newcastle Upon Tyne: Bloodaxe, 2000), p.94.

9. See William Empson, *Some Versions of Pastoral* [1948] (New York: New Directions, 1991); Harold E. Toliver, *Pastoral Forms and Attitudes* (Berkeley, CA: University of California Press, 1984); and Raymond Williams, *The Country and the City* (Oxford: Oxford University Press, 1973).

10. For an extended version of this argument, see Oona Frawley, *Irish Pastoral: Nostalgia and Twentieth-Century Irish Literature* (Dublin: Irish Academic Press, 2005).

11. See Edward Said, 'Yeats and Decolonialism', in *Nationalism, Colonialism, and Literature*

(Minneapolis, MN: University of Minnesota Press, 1990).

12. See O'Grady's *History of Ireland: Critical and Philosophical Vol. 1* (London: Sampson, Low, & Co., 1881 [Dublin: E. Ponsonby]).

13. Cited in R.F. Foster, *W.B. Yeats: A Life, vol. 2, The Arch-Poet 1915–1939* (Oxford: Oxford University Press, 2003), p.179.

14. Ibid., p.303.

15. See, for instance, P.J. Mathews's *Revival: The Abbey Theatre, Sinn Féin, The Gaelic League and the Co-operative Movement* (Cork: Cork University Press, 2003).

16. D. Johnston, *Irish Poetry After Joyce* (Notre Dame, IN: Notre Dame University Press, 1985), p.21.

17. Antoinette Quinn, *Patrick Kavanagh: A Biography* (Dublin: Gill & Macmillan, 2001), p.82.

18. D. O'Brien, *Patrick Kavanagh* (Lewisberg, PA: Bucknell University Press, 1975), p.16.

19. R.F. Garratt, *Modern Irish Poetry: Tradition and Continuity from Yeats to Heaney* (Berkeley, CA: University of California Press, 1986), p.141.

20. Quinn, *Patrick Kavanagh*, p.70.

21. Kavanagh, *Collected Pruse*, p.13.

22. Ibid., p.19.

23. Garratt, *Modern Irish Poetry*, p.142.

24. Interestingly, of course, Kavanagh's columns 'revealed a lively interest in his city milieu' (Quinn, *Patrick Kavanagh*, p.209).

25. Ibid., p.103.

26. Patrick Kavanagh, *Collected Poems*, ed. Antoinette Quinn (Harmondsworth: Penguin Books, 2005).

27. Ibid.

28. Kavanagh, 'Nationalism in Literature', in *Collected Pruse*, p.269.

29. John Goodby, *Irish Poetry Since 1950: From Stillness into History* (Manchester: Manchester University Press, 2000), p.33.

30. Kavanagh, 'Self Portrait', in *Collected Pruse*, p.16.

31. O'Brien, *Patrick Kavanagh*, p.18.

32. Goodby, *Irish Poetry Since 1950*, p.34.

33. Patrick Kavanagh, *Tarry Flynn* (London: Martin Brian & O'Keeffe, 1972), p.251.

34. Cited in Quinn, *Patrick Kavanagh*, p.273.

35. See Kavanagh, 'From Monaghan to the Grand Canal', in *Collected Pruse*, pp.223–31.

36. Kavanagh, *Collected Poems*, ed. Antoinette Quinn.

CHAPTER SIX

The Great Hunger
and Mother Ireland

EDWARD LARRISSY

A HUNGER OF THE SPIRIT

Those who come to Patrick Kavanagh's work for the first time often assume that the title of *The Great Hunger* (1942) refers to the great Irish famine of the 1840s. But as Kavanagh's editor, Antoinette Quinn, observes, it is hard to find a use of the phrase to refer to the famine before Cecil Woodham-Smith made it the title of his well-known book on that subject (1962): indeed, Kavanagh maintained that Woodham-Smith stole his title.[1] Yet as Quinn points out, 'the poem's recurrent imagery of potato harvesting does appear to allude to the great famine' (CP, 268). The obvious conclusion, namely that Kavanagh wished to identify and describe a spiritual hunger whose effects were at least as deleterious as a physical one is, surely, the right one. It is also worth considering the idea that he was attempting to mark, in this ironic way, the century that had passed since the famine. And there is an obvious irony in such a despairing condition being widespread, as Kavanagh takes pains to suggest that it is, in an Ireland supposedly freed from British domination and indifference with the establishment of the Irish Free State in 1922.

Kavanagh's picture of Patrick Maguire, hanging on as an old bachelor on his mother's small farm, is meant to exhibit a mode of existence distinctive of Ireland in the years both before and since that date. High birth-rates, the inheritance of farms by one sibling, and a meagre standard of living, did much to ensure that emigration remained a salient part of the picture. The combined effects of female emigration and the sexual Puritanism encouraged by the Catholic Church promoted the 'ould bachelor' phenomenon. Added to this, by the 1930s and 1940s the growing availability of knowledge about life in modern cities – including Dublin – led to increased dissatisfaction with the limitations of rural existence.[2] These are the chief elements in the background to Kavanagh's picture of the continued dominance of the potato as a food-crop, of an overpowering sense of frustration and failure, and to his brief biography of Maguire at the beginning of section II of the poem:

> He stayed with his mother till she died
> At the age of ninety-one.
> She stayed too long,
> Wife and mother in one.
> When she died
> The knuckle-bones were cutting the skin of her son's backside
> And he was sixty-five. (CP, 66)

As Terence Brown says, 'If there is a case for viewing a major work of art as an antenna that sensitively detects the shifts of consciousness that determine a people's future, The Great Hunger is that work.'[3] This remark identifies a change of attitude, but this change had to contend with a dominant idealization of Irish rural life, as epitomized, for instance, in the short stories of Liam O'Flaherty, whose 'Spring Sowing' offers an intensely romantic picture of a young farmer and his wife going out on a spring dawn to sow potato seeds together.[4] It is also to be found in the frequent pronouncements on the subject by Eamon de Valera, whose republican-minded and strongly nationalist Fianna Fáil party had won power in 1932.[5]

Kavanagh's idea of the elements that go to make up the spiritual hunger of Ireland transcends any superficial critique of ideology. Yet when grasped, it sheds light on the whole of his work. There are a few memorable references to spiritual insight in The Great Hunger, though only one, perhaps, is sufficiently definitive and sufficiently unalloyed by irony to make one feel that this is a state a peasant like Maguire could frequently achieve:

> Yet sometimes when the sun comes through a gap
> These men know God the Father in a tree:
> The Holy Spirit is the rising sap,
> And Christ will be the green leaves that will come
> At Easter from the sealed and guarded tomb. (CP, 68)

Despite the references to Christianity, the spiritual sterility of Irish life, to which the whole poem attests, calls into question the extent to which Irish Roman Catholicism was capable of fostering or nurturing such insight. Of course, as in this example, Christianity, and in particular Roman Catholicism, provides the only vehicle the Irish peasant has for a spiritual life, and Kavanagh acknowledges this, as when he evokes the power of the Mass over the rural congregation, when 'the candle-lit Altar and the flowers / And the pregnant Tabernacle lifted a moment to Prophecy / Out of the clayey hours' (CP, 69). Other insights are equally fleeting, but more equivocal about the role of the Church: 'Sometimes they did laugh and see the sunlight, / A narrow slice of divine instruction' (CP, 76). Unexpectedly, this passage goes on to suggest, without actually stating, that the divine, open-air instruction is actually to 'jump in love though death bait the hook'. And there are elements in the Christian story, which, on an antinomian interpretation (such as that of Blake) might point in that direction, though they will not have been interpreted in that way by any priest.

A particular link to 'love' is provided by those elements in the Christian story which themselves sound like a fertility myth. These are emphasized by the alignment of the Church's calendar with the cycle of fertility: birth, death and renewal. As Kavanagh remarks, suggesting the perception of the farmer: 'And Christ will be the green leaves that will come / At Easter from the sealed and guarded tomb' (CP, 68). Kavanagh leaves implicit a similar point which could be made about the Christmas story of the Saviour being born as a harbinger of light at the darkest time of the year. More straightforwardly, the Church's calendar, of which the fundamental unit is the year, provides high points which the farmer may associate with those of his own calendar, and the latter is by definition bound up with the cycle of fertility. It is sometimes said that The Great Hunger recalls Eliot's The Waste Land (CP, xviii). Like that poem, it identifies a malaise both spiritual and sexual with reference to the cycle of fertility and to sacred symbols which are framed in terms of imagery associated with that cycle. As in that poem, hints of hope are few, though some are tentatively proffered.

Kavanagh does not look to images of the sacred outside the Christian tradition. But he does suggest a remaking of that tradition which would preserve a sense of the miraculousness of life and a reverence for it, as the 'slice of divine instruction' indicates. Another indication is perhaps more striking and unexpected: Seamus Heaney notes perceptively, in relation to *Ploughman and Other Poems* (1936), that although he had seen the book described as Georgian, 'the lyrics are closer to Blake's *Songs of Innocence* than to any such attending to natural surfaces'.[6] This is a remark full of useful insight for the whole of Kavanagh's work, for Blake's sense of visionary radiance, combined with a gift for lyrical panache, does suggest the parallel Heaney evokes. The point, however, only becomes truly persuasive when it is extended to cover the possibility that Blake's Experience, as well as his Innocence, is an influence, with its trenchant bitterness, and its suggestion that pain and corruption are the near neighbours of spiritual potential. In other words, this is not the esoteric Blake of whom Yeats was the best-known advocate, but the frank, pithy and subversive Blake who was an influence on the works of the young Auden, a poet much admired by Kavanagh.[7] At any rate, there are at least three direct references to Blake in *The Great Hunger*. The most straightforward of these references clinches the authority of the other two: in section IX, the speaker imagines passers-by speculating on the experience of the peasant and asking themselves, 'Where is his silver bowl of knowledge hung?' (CP, 76). This is a reference to 'Thel's Motto', Blake's epigraph to *The Book of Thel* (1789), which itself draws on *Ecclesiastes*: 'Can Wisdom be put in a silver rod? / Or Love in a golden bowl?'[8] The change from 'Wisdom' to 'knowledge', and from gold to silver, suggests that Kavanagh is doubtful of the wisdom of Maguire's timorous existence, or of the knowledge gained from his experience. 'Experience' occurs in another of the references to Blake, where we are told of how he imagines himself having come 'free from every net spread / In the gaps of experience'. One should put this together with the exclamation at the end of section III: 'O to be wise / As Respectability that knows the price of all things / And marks God's truth in pounds and pence and farthings' (CP, 68–9). There appear to be at least two passages from Blake at the back of Kavanagh's mind. One is from *The Four Zoas*, Night the Second:

> What is the price of Experience do men buy it for a song
> Or wisdom for a dance in the street? No it is bought with the price
> Of all that a man hath his house, his wife his children
> Wisdom is sold in the desolate market where none come to buy
> And in the witherd field where the farmer plows for bread in vain.
> (MS p.35, ll.11–15)[9]

The other passage is from *Visions of the Daughters of Albion*: 'With what sense does the parson claim the labour of the farmer? / What are his nets & gins & traps' (Plate 5, ll.17–18).[10] This is in no way to deny the influence of Joyce on the idea of 'nets' in *The Great Hunger*: in *Collected Pruse* Kavanagh recommends that we should 'cut down the nets which mediocrity flings to hold back the soul from flight' (*Pruse*, 30). This is advice which Tarry Flynn heeds in the novel that bears his name (1948), when he finally departs from the townland of Drumnay.

The Blakean references, which work alongside those to Joyce and Eliot, suggest that Maguire has not learnt the true price either of experience or of wisdom, and that, though his fields may be fertile, the spiritual hunger which he lacks the courage to do something about ensures misery, come rain or shine.

WOMAN AND THE POETIC MIND

It is worth trying to be clearer about the spiritual life of things as Kavanagh sees it. Even as he leaves Drumnay, Tarry Flynn is conscious of the townland's great beauty and of 'the beauty that lived in stones and all common things'.[11] At the very moment of his departure, he is composing a song in celebration of the little world he is leaving: 'And then I came to the haggard gate, / And I knew as I entered that I had come / Through fields that were part of no earthly estate' (*Tarry Flynn*, 256; the poem was collected as 'Threshing Morning', CP, 112–13). It is the mean fields of his birth that are the fields of paradise. Kavanagh attempts to give a less exalted, but more developed, account of the beauty of the local in his most famous essay 'The Parish and the Universe'. The contrast outlined in this essay, between 'parochialism' and 'provincialism', makes the former the positive term for the courage to find the universal in one's own locality – which is as much as to say, one's own experience. 'Provincialism', by contrast, may look like 'parochialism', but only to the superficial eye: it is always looking over its shoulder to see how things are done in the metropolis. Thus it loses the only true vision a person can ever have: one's own world seen with one's own eyes. It also therefore loses authenticity of form and understanding. To find the 'universal' in the particular in this way, in one's own potato patch, is, of course, a post-Romantic imperative, exemplars of which are to be found in

Wordsworth and Keats; nor would Kavanagh have disavowed such ancestry. (His admiration for Keats was touched on briefly during the trial of the libel case he brought against *The Leader* – *Pruse*, 179.) One of the reasons why the idea achieves such radiant expression in Kavanagh's verse can be revealed simply by drawing out the full implications of finding the universal in the particular: namely, that all meanings about the world may be found there in a form that is actually assimilable by any person with the courage to trust in and explore their own experience.

Kavanagh's next move in his essay is unexpected but deeply instructive about his vision. He evokes the picture of the Irish émigré in London buying his Irish local paper: 'I rushed to buy my *Dundalk Democrat*, and reading it I was back in my native fields' (*Pruse*, 283). He asks: 'Why do we always need to go back?' One might have thought that he had already explained this by reference to finding the universal in the particular: with such intensity, why should one not wish to go back? But Kavanagh offers another, and deeper, explanation:

> What is it we want to return to? Freud says, the womb, and there is something in it too. We are never happy from the moment we leave the womb. The Mother is the roots. The Mother is the thing which gives us a world of our own. The Mother is the basis of romantic love. (*Pruse*, 283)

At first sight, this seems like a different kind of explanation of the power of the parish from that which had been offered earlier. And indeed, the link between the Mother and the capacity to integrate the universal and the particular is not all that easy to reconstruct. One needs to turn to another essay, 'The Irish Tradition', to glimpse what Kavanagh has in mind. He is illustrating 'the nature of the poet', as he puts it, by reference to E.V. Rieu's introduction to his translation of the Four Gospels. According to Rieu, Luke 'knew how to distil truth from fact', and he refers to Luke's 'poetic insight into reality'. Kavanagh chooses to emphasize Rieu's claim that Luke realized 'the part played by Woman in the revelation of the Divine Idea', and concludes that 'That is the poetic mind' (*Pruse*, 233).

Kavanagh certainly believes in distilling truth from fact, and the fact and the truth must be one's own and nobody else's. But distillation is not possible without the assistance of Woman, and the Mother is essential to the early nurturing of 'the poetic mind'. Kavanagh's conception can be illustrated from *Tarry Flynn*, a novel that has often been compared with *The Great Hunger* in point of its unsparing depiction of the hard life of Irish small farmers, its unillusioned estimate of their petty-minded rivalries and squabbles, and its truthful portrait of a harsh-tongued and unsentimental mother. Yet there are crucial differences. The depiction of townland life has far more of the sense of beauty about it, though admittedly this is self-consciously presented as belonging to Tarry's perception. This very fact is connected to another difference: the mother may be harsh-tongued and unsentimental, but for all that she loves her son tenderly and passionately, and he knows it: 'She loved that son more than any mother ever loved a son. She hardly knew why. There was something so natural about him, so real and so innocent and which yet looked like badness' (*Tarry Flynn*, 13). By contrast, there is little sense of a mother's love in *The Great Hunger* to soften the picture of Maguire's mother, 'tall, hard as a Protestant spire', with her 'venomous drawl' (CP, 67):

His mother's voice grew thinner like a rust-worn knife
But it cut more venomously as it thinned,
It cut him up the middle till he became more woman than man,
And it cut through to his mind before the end. (CP, 78)

Tarry Flynn's mother condones her son's peculiar nature, which is that of a poet, although she cannot put it in those terms, protecting him from the jibes of his sisters when he expresses contempt for *The Messenger of the Sacred Heart* (*Tarry Flynn*, 42). She feels an instinctive preference for her son and his ways over the priests: 'Not that she loved the priests – like a true mother she'd cut the Pope's throat for the sake of her son – but she felt the power of the priests and she didn't want to have their ill-will' (CP, 14).

By contrast, Maguire's mother tells him: 'Now go to Mass and pray, and confess your sins / And you'll have all the luck' (CP, 73). She listens, Kavanagh explains, 'to the lie that is a woman's screen / Around a conscience when soft thighs are spread' (CP, 73). It is not that she fully believes this line, for it is explained that, nevertheless, 'She trusted in Nature that never deceives'. But she does not have sufficient faith in Nature to convey to her son the unspoken qualification her instincts enter against the power of the Church. Thus, while Tarry Flynn is assured of his mother's love and her loyalty to Nature, Maguire is left to realize, on occasion, that 'his own heart is calling his mother a liar' (CP, 66).

So loyal to Nature is Tarry Flynn's mother that it is clear to him that she sides with the power of sexuality: 'As far as Tarry could gather from his mother's talk about the Mission, she had hopes that the Missioner's condemnation of sex would have the effect of drawing attention to it' (CP, 39). This is the reason why, unlike Maguire, Tarry is unashamed in his fantasizing about women; and his mother's love is the reason why he actually begins to feel the stirrings of what Kavanagh calls 'romantic love' towards Mary Reilly:

> She was dressed in a light blue cotton dress and her long black hair hung loose over her shoulders. He had seen this girl many times before, but this was the first time she was revealed to him …
>
> But here was someone who was made to break hearts.
>
> Tarry's mind was paralysed by the sight of her …
>
> She was only about nineteen, nearly ten years younger than he was, but she carried within her what Tarry knew was a terrible power of which she was as yet unconscious. (*Tarry Flynn*, 78–9)

Maguire is incapable of such feelings because his mother has abrogated the role of being the basis of 'romantic love'.

This vision of woman is reminiscent of that to be found in certain *aisling* poems, such as Egan O'Rahilly's 'Gile na Gile' ('Brightness of Brightness'), with its reference to meeting a beautiful woman with bright, flowing ringlets. The *aisling* poem is a tradition in which the apparition of a woman, usually, though not always, beautiful and young, is understood to be a personification of Ireland. There were two English versions of this poem by James Clarence Mangan, whose works had been known to Kavanagh from boyhood.[12] In his essay on 'Nationalism and Literature', Kavanagh remarks that 'I suppose that judged in the cruel light of top-class literary criticism, a poet like Mangan comes out pretty badly. But to those involved with the local sentiment Mangan made a profound appeal. At one time Mangan immensely moved me' (*Prose*, 271). Striking encounters with women make occasional appearances in Kavanagh's poems, most memorably perhaps in 'On Raglan Road': 'On Raglan Road on an autumn day I met her first and knew / That her dark hair would weave a snare that I might one day rue' (CP, 130). As we have seen, there is a connection between this kind of moment, the influence of the Mother, and the love of one's particular parish. It is in 'Spraying the Potatoes' (CP, 36–7) that Kavanagh seeks to bring together in more than a mere juxtaposition the themes of the parish and of romantic love. The flowers to which it refers are identified with 'young girls'. An old man approaches the speaker to wish him well with his work, but with apparent inconsequentiality we are reminded that 'The old man dies in the young girl's frown'. There is a time, a natural season, for love and sexuality, and the old man has outlived it. This implication chimes with a similar point made about Maguire's lost chances in The Great Hunger. The final stanza of 'Spraying the Potatoes', like the final paragraphs of 'The Parish and the Universe', evokes a speaker who is exiled from his native fields:

> And poet lost to potato-fields,
> Remembering the lime and copper smell
> Of the spraying barrels he is not lost
> Or till blossomed stalks cannot weave a spell.

Remembering that smell is a direct way back into the lost townland, not entirely in a different category from buying the Dundalk Democrat in Highgate. But the spell woven by 'blossomed stalks' is the same as that exerted by Woman: or, to be precise, it represents the equation between the spell of Woman and the spell of Nature. In Kavanagh's terms, the phrase can be broken down still further, to equate with 'or till you lose the poetic mind'.

Not that the poetic mind is the pure product of Woman. In a passage from Kavanagh's Weekly which is excerpted in his account of the libel trial under the heading 'Women', Kavanagh opines thus:

> I ... discovered that the better-looking women are, the wiser they are. There is probably a reason for this: women are magnets which draw wisdom, and they draw their wisdom through men, so it follows that the more attractive a woman is the more she is likely to draw wisdom; for in the first place she can afford to be selective and have as male friends only fairly intelligent ones. (Pruse, 193)

A major problem with Maguire's mother is that she transmits the 'wisdom' of the most powerful males of her community, the priests, even though deep down she does not believe it, and this becomes his 'wisdom' (a word which is repeated several times in the poem). By contrast,

Tarry Flynn's mother believes in the poetic wisdom of her son, and Mary Reilly, who admires his poem in the local paper, and listens with awe to his disquisition on English Literature, is cast in the same mould. If this is not the dynamic of the relationship between men and women, then the powers of the poetic mind may be impaired or nullified. As Kavanagh puts it at the end of 'On Raglan Road': 'I had wooed not as I should a creature made of clay – / When the angel woos the clay he'd lose his wings at the dawn of day' (CP, 130).

Ireland, an Ireland that had been able to organize its own affairs since 1922, was conniving in the destruction of the poetic mind. Maguire's mother is Kavanagh's portrait of the real Mother Ireland, and the implication is that Irish culture is nurturing a psychological and cultural malaise and impoverishment at its very heart. For the Ireland of his time, the ideal of what Kavanagh called 'romantic love' must have seemed comically out of reach. Crudely sexual attitudes, of men to women in particular, were the alternative, but even acting upon these was almost impossible: 'that metaphysical land, / Where flesh was a thought more spiritual than music, / Among the stars – out of reach of the peasant's hand' (CP, 73). Maguire is afraid of young women: 'He was suspicious in his youth as a rat near strange bread / When girls laughed' (CP, 65). Later in life, he even entertains the notion that a schoolgirl might be more amenable to his advances: 'He had an idea. Schoolgirls of thirteen / Would see no political intrigue in an old man's friendship' (CP, 79). But 'That notion passed too – there was the danger of talk / And jails are narrower than the five-sod ridge'. What is left is masturbation: 'He sinned over the warm ashes again'.

Kavanagh blamed the Catholic Church, or at least what it had made of itself in Ireland, for all this. Reflecting on the work of George Moore, he remarked:

> [I]t does seem to me that somewhere in the nineteenth century, or maybe earlier (or maybe it is somewhere in Irish religion, rather than chronology) an anti-life heresy entered religion. Priests became infected with a heresy that as good as denied that they themselves were born of woman. (Pruse, 257)

The attempt by the new Irish state to foster a society in which this kind of Catholicism had a leading role was epitomized by the ideology and speeches of Eamon de Valera, of whom Kavanagh remarked: 'Though nobody more so than de Valera has preached the Spirit of Ireland, few men who have ever become leaders of this nation have been less in touch with whatever is vital in that spirit' (*Prose*, 153). One of the supposed nurses of that spirit, a feature of the iconography of Irish nationalism, Mother Ireland, is found by Kavanagh to be sick and a spreader of sickness.[13]

NATURE IN THE GREAT HUNGER AND 'LOUGH DERG'

Alienation from Nature does not mean the absence of Nature from *The Great Hunger*. For a start the poem is full of striking observations which we may well attribute to Maguire, or at any rate believe that he would recognize: 'The dragging step of a ploughman going home through the guttery / Headlands under an April-watery moon' (CP, 70); 'Night in the elms, night in the grass' (CP, 71). Of course, Maguire's life is structured by the farmer's relationship with Nature, and apart from the mere fulfilment of the expected tasks, there is also the fact that many of those tasks are organized by the natural cycle. The poem insistently refers to months and their attributes: their weather, the tasks belonging to them. It is, indeed, tempting to try to model the progress of the poem onto the progress of the months, but its structure is not quite as simple as that. Nevertheless, it begins and ends in October, the same October in which we see the ageing and regretful Maguire, who has wasted his months and years, and by this means the poem alludes to the idea of a circle, if only to imply that he was always destined to end in this inglorious because half-numb despair. Much of the poem is devoted to the months from March to July, as if to remind us of the time of life's opportunity. This idea is almost crudely proposed to us in section VIII, where Maguire is 'sitting on a wooden gate / Sometime in July', and he actually 'cursed the ascetic brotherhood / Without knowing why' (CP, 75). Maguire is aware of his existence as making a circle:

> He would have changed the circle if he could,
> The circle that was the grass track where he ran.
> Twenty times a day he ran round the field. (CP, 70)

While still young enough to be confident of changing his life, he 'gave himself another year, / Something was bound to happen before then – / The circle would break down / And he would curve the new one to his own will' (CP, 75). But in fact, 'the peasant in his little acres is tied / To a mother's womb by the wind-toughened navel-cord / Like a goat tethered to the stump of a tree – / He circles around and around wondering why it should be' (CP, 86). Effectively, the cycle of nature, which should be seen as full of possibility and capable of rebirth has been turned into a trap where each repetition is a deeper confirmation of sterility and failure. While it might seem at first glance as if, in these lines, it was the mother's influence in itself that was to blame, the imagery when properly assessed reveals an unnaturalness which Kavanagh probably thought of as a kind of perversion. The mother's navel cord is 'wind-toughened', her womb a 'stump'.

The true contrast with this closed circle is hinted at by a long poem, 'Lough Derg', composed in 1942, at about the same time as *The Great Hunger*. The lough is the site of an island, anciently known as St Patrick's Purgatory, which had been a place of pilgrimage since the Middle Ages. Kavanagh's poem describes contemporary pilgrims who come from places very similar to Maguire's farm: 'From all the thin-faced parishes where hills / Are perished noses running peaty water, / They come to Lough Derg to fast and pray and beg' (CP, 90). The traumas of a sexually repressed society are evoked early on in the poem: 'The girl who had won / A lover and the girl who had none / Were both in trouble' (CP, 91). Guilt and thwarted sexual longing figure prominently in the poem: an 'ex-monk from Dublin' had 'fallen once and secretly, no shame / Tainted the young girl's name' (CP, 94). Yet Kavanagh's attitude to the self-denying ordinances of the pilgrims is subtly but noticeably sceptical and undermining: '"I renounce the World", a young woman cried. / Her breasts stood high in the pagan sun' (CP, 93). One of the most touching moments in the poem occurs when Robert, an unworldly young philosopher who talks to girls 'as a pedant professor', speaks to Aggie, who does not understand: 'She only knew that she could hold his hand / If he stood closer' (CP, 99). A simple but straightforward fact about the pilgrimage ensures its value for Kavanagh: it brings men and women together. In conformity with this fact, he obtrudes a reminder that the image of woman participates in the sacred:

St. Brigid and the Blessed Virgin flanked
Ireland's national apostle

On the south-west of the island on the gravel-path
Opposite the men's hostel. (CP, 93)

Another simple fact to remember about the pilgrimage is its occurring amid the wildness of nature, as we are reminded throughout the poem.

The cycle of nature, of which sexuality is a part, is evoked by the fact that the pilgrims have to go around certain 'stations'. The circuit they thus describe is antithetical to what I have described as 'the closed circle'. It succeeds in assisting a spiritual rebirth occasioned by an attitude of love and forgiveness which Kavanagh sees as antithetical to the puritanical Jansenism he believes to be dominant in the Catholic Church in Ireland: 'The sharp knife of Jansen / Cuts all the green branches' (CP, 108).[14] But at Lough Derg the humble reverence of humanity miraculously sends the pilgrims in the opposite direction: 'But now the green tree / Of humanity / Was leafing again'. It seems that for Kavanagh life can describe only two kinds of circle: the circle of life redeemed by a faith in nature and love, celebrating the variety of life's seasons; or the same circle turned into dead repetition.

As a logical consequence, in Kavanagh's work the life redeemed by poetic vision and that which is not can look very much alike, especially as the former can often be interrupted by hardship and the latter can, as in The Great Hunger, be occasionally illuminated by glimpses of beauty. Kavanagh's versification is instructive on this point. Irregular in metre and rhyme, it bespeaks hard honesty and the avoidance of romantic illusion. Occasionally it verges on doggerel. It is no less than the truth to say that this is appropriate to the tone and subject matter of the poem, for even the doggerel may seem fitting for a description of the life of a sad anti-hero such as Maguire. Yet it would be hard to prove that a more hopeful poem of this period, such as 'Lough Derg' itself, was radically different in style. Kavanagh is painfully aware of the narrow gap that may exist between joy and despair. Nevertheless, we need the idea, or at least the intuition, of the benign circle, which corresponds to a spiritually intense vision of nature, of which, at its best, the Church can offer a glimpse. This circle should have at its heart the right relationship of man and woman, as for so many modern writers. To mid-century Ireland, however, belongs the dubious honour of having institutionalized a philosophy of anti-life for which the appropriate emblem is a poi-

sonous version of Mother Ireland. That Kavanagh wishes to impugn the
whole development of Irish society is obvious from the bitter final lines
of The Great Hunger, with their echoes of the ending of Joyce's equally
damning story 'The Dead': 'The hungry fiend / Screams the apocalypse
of clay / In every corner of this land'.

NOTES

1. Patrick Kavanagh, Collected Poems, ed. Antoinette Quinn (London: Allen Lane, 2004),
p.268. Further references to this work are given in the body of the text as CP, followed by page number.

2. Terence Brown, Ireland: A Social and Cultural History 1922–1979 (London: Fontana,
1981), p.187; R.F. Foster, Modern Ireland 1600–1972 (London: Allen Lane, 1988),
p.539.

3. Brown, Ireland, p.187.

4. Liam O'Flaherty, 'Spring Sowing', in Spring Sowing, 2nd edn (London: Jonathan Cape,
1927 1st edn 1924), pp.9–19.

5. Foster, Modern Ireland, p.538.

6. Seamus Heaney, Preoccupations: Selected Prose 1968–1978 (London: Faber & Faber, 1980),
p.119.

7. For Blake and Auden, see Edward Larrissy, Blake and Modern Literature (Basingstoke:
Palgrave Macmillan, 2006), pp.45–51; for Kavanagh on Auden, see Patrick Kavanagh,
'Auden and the Creative Mind', in Collected Pruse (London: MacGibbon & Kee, 1967),
pp.247–53. Further references to this work are given in the body of the text as Pruse
followed by page number.

8. David V. Erdman (ed.), The Complete Poetry and Prose of William Blake, 2nd edn (New York:
Doubleday, 1988), plate I, p.3.

9. Ibid., p.325.

10. Ibid., p.49.

11. Patrick Kavanagh, Tarry Flynn [1948], 2nd edn (London: MacGibbon & Kee, 1965),
p.248. Further references to this work are given in the body of the text as Tarry Flynn,
followed by page number.

12. Jacques Chuto, Rudolf Patrick Holzapfel and Peter van de Kamp (eds), Selected Poems of
James Clarence Mangan (Dublin: Irish Academic Press, 2003), pp.320–4, 336–7.

13. For a discussion of the image of Mother Ireland, see C.L. Innes, Woman and Nation in
Irish Literature and Society 1880–1935 (Hemel Hempstead: Harvester Wheatsheaf, 1993),
pp.9–42.

14. Cornelius Jansen (1585–1638) attempted an austere reformation of the Roman
Catholic Church from within, with the aid of the teachings of St Augustine, whose
writings had been so influential on Calvin.

CHAPTER SEVEN

An 'Unmeasured Womb':
A Soul for Sale and
the 1937 Irish Constitution

MICHAEL MURPHY

What is it men in women do require? The lineaments of Gratified Desire.
What is it women do in men require? The lineaments of Gratified Desire.
William Blake, Notebook of 1793

Almost all the poems Kavanagh gathered together in *A Soul for Sale and Other Poems* (1947) were written during the Second World War. But with a few exceptions ('The years that pass / Like tired soldiers', 'A poplar leaf was spiked upon a thorn / Above the hedge like a flag of surrender', 'the flaggers in the swamp were the reserves'[1]), the conflagration that had devoured the rest of the world was absent from his poetry. The reasons for this are at least twofold: the Irish State remained neutral during the war; and Kavanagh was much preoccupied with discovering and sustaining a life for himself in Dublin, having finally given up in 1939 the family farm in Inniskeen, his 'comfortable little holding of watery hills beside the Border'.[2] War and a permanent residency in Dublin as a struggling poet and novelist were inextricably linked, for though he may initially have looked upon Dublin as a temporary address before heading onward to London, this was suddenly made impossible. Ironically, wartime Dublin must in part have resembled the landscape he had left behind in Inniskeen with, as Antoinette Quinn says, trenches being dug in parks and turf stacked in the Phoenix Park.[3]

Kavanagh later regretted the move to Dublin; even more so the part he came to feel his writing played in the continuation of the Irish Literary Revival 'as invented and patented by Yeats, Lady Gregory and

Synge' (*A Poet's Country*, p.307). War only exacerbated such feelings of alienation. In an article published in *The Irish Times* in October 1939, Kavanagh wrote of himself as doubly estranged: it is wartime in Europe and he is in Ireland; a farmer born and bred, he is living in a city: 'Being an Irishman I should be abnormal if I didn't dream, think and write of far-past peace and quiet in pastoral fields when everybody else is thinking in terms of war' (*A Poet's Country*, p.39). Such thoughts dominate the poetry he was to write over the coming five years.

Prior to his removal to Dublin Kavanagh was blunter-speaking, as epitomized in a poem such as 'My People', a parody of Yeats's poetic dialogues first published in January 1937. In the poem, a Stranger – a kind of spiritual census-taker or, like the Yeats of 'Among School Children', a visitation from an urban Anglo-Irish elite – inquires 'What kind your people are / I would wish to know'. He has arrived with expectations that are one part the product of industrialization ('Great-shouldered men like rolling stock') and two parts cant (he imagines farming men as 'Great in despair, / Simple in prayer') (CP, p.19). Any such ideas of Ireland as a Land of Saints are firmly rebuffed by the Poet, like Kavanagh at the time a professional farmer who speaks of harsher realities and impoverished expectations: 'They till their fields and scrape among the stones / Because they cannot be schoolmasters'. The urbane Stranger is shocked:

> Poet be fair,
> You surely must have seen
> Beneath these rags of care
> Hearts that were not mean
> And beggarly and faint.

The Poet, though, like Kavanagh's prose description of himself 'standing apart from the light-of-heart and -foot … engaged in a very high-brow argument with an old man who "nearly knows as much as a schoolmaster"' (*A Poet's Country*, p.46), is having none of it: 'why / Should poet seek to prove / the spirit of a Saint?' What he rather offers is to 'fill the flask / Of your curiosity with bitterings' (CP, p.20). The Stranger is not prepared to listen, and turns tail back to the town from whence he came, promising neither to inquire further into the life of rural Ireland or to report what he has heard: 'may Christ condemn / My name if I tell / The dream of your folk / That arose as you speak'.

The Stranger's silence meant that the often harsh reality of Irish rural life went generally unreported. What replaced the Poet's plain speaking was the myth of a pastoral idyll idealized not only in much contemporary literature, but in the speeches and writing of the Taoiseach, Eamon de Valera. Kavanagh was no supporter of de Valera, describing Fianna Fáil as a 'great wet blanket' and de Valera's Republic as a 'mediocrity' (see the introduction to *A Poet's Country*, p.15). And yet his precarious livelihood in wartime Dublin made any stronger resistance to the status quo extremely difficult. Perhaps, too, he enjoyed and was flattered by the minor celebrity his authentic 'peasant' background afforded him. Certainly his later rebuttal of poets who seek a public voice would fit in with a rejection of his own role during these years.

When he could no longer keep silent, he may have suspected that some form of divine retribution similar to that threatened at the close of 'My People' would be visited upon him. In 'Christmas in the Country', published in December 1939, he was probably imputing a link between the newly established Emergency Powers Act, hurried onto the statute book with the outbreak of war in September 1939, and the more long-standing Censorship of Publications Act of 1929, in recounting a conversation between himself and another farmer in which, on being asked 'What do you think of the German now?', they both began to talk under their breaths, 'because of the censorship laws' (*A Poet's Country*, p.54). He was correct to fear as much. Following the publication, in 1942, of parts I and III and the first twenty-six lines from part IV of 'The Great Hunger' under the title of 'The Old Peasant', the edition of *Horizon* in which the poem appeared was seized by Garda acting under the Emergency Powers legislation. Kavanagh was questioned by the police but no action was taken, though we might wonder whether during the interview he was reminded of 'My People' and the Stranger's rebuttal of the Poet's words as 'Your vitriol of Hell'. Kavanagh later referred to the incident in an author's note to the first *Collected Poems*,[4] observing that 'There is something wrong with a work of art, some kinetic vulgarity in it when it is visible to policemen' (CP, p.292). When 'The Great Hunger' was republished – first in an expensive edition of 250 by Dublin's Cuala Press in April and later in *A Soul for Sale* – Kavanagh tempered his vitriol and amended those lines that had led to him being briefly detained by the police.

What could not be altered was a vision of rural Ireland profoundly at odds with the official version. Maguire is, Antoinette Quinn writes, 'timid, cautious, passive, a victim of the small-farm ethos embodied by his mother, in which success in life is measured in terms of high crop-yields, pre-marital chastity and regular attendance at Mass and confession' (CP, p.xix). Precisely such an admixture of self-reliance and passivity, however, defines the prayer of thanksgiving that headed the 1937 Constitution:

> In the Name of the Most Holy Trinity, from Whom is all authority and to Whom, as our final end, all actions both of men and States must be referred,
> We, the people of Éire,
> Humbly acknowledging all our obligations to our Divine Lord, Jesus Christ, Who sustained our fathers through centuries of trial,
> Gratefully remembering their heroic and unremitting struggle to regain the rightful independence of our Nation,
> And seeking to promote the common good, with due observance of Prudence, Justice and Charity, so that the dignity and freedom of the individual may be assured, true social order attained, the unity of our country restored, and concord established with other nations,
> Do hereby adopt, enact, and give to ourselves this Constitution.[5]

Irish self-determination was premised on an act of obeisance, with the 'dignity and freedom of the individual' and 'true social order' reliant on humility, obligation, gratitude and observance. The British Empire had merely been exchanged for one whose seat of power was in Rome. Such language is powerfully countered in 'The Great Hunger' by the realities of a rural Ireland already in crisis, not least because of the mortifications of the flesh, the debt owed by the younger generations to the sacrifices of the Father that had resulted in despair and depopulation. De Valera's institutionalization of a powerful Catholic ethos, as R.F. Foster has commented, is enshrined in the Constitution.[6] We might add that in seeking to make the Kingdom of Heaven incarnate in a rural Ireland distinguished by frugality, industry, Gaelicism and anti-materialism, de Valera was turning his back not only on history but also on contemporary reports such as the Folklore Commission (1935), which (unlike the Stranger of Kavanagh's poem) made clear that the Eden imagined by de Valera was in its last throes.[7] This much is apparent from the resounding and defiant 'vitriol' that characterizes the poem's opening lines, with its bitter parody of Christ's incarnation and its vision of farming men not as locomotives – the 'rolling stock' of 'My People' – but as men of straw, hollow men:

> Clay is the word and clay is the flesh
> Where the potato-gatherers like mechanized scare-crows move
> Along the side-fall of the hill ... (CP, p.63)

If the Holy Trinity was appealed to as the alpha and omega of all human concerns, then its representative on earth and the cornerstone of the Constitution was the family: 'the natural primary and fundamental unit group of Society'. Article 41 of the Constitution describes the family in terms barely distinguishable from the Trinity, existing in a state outside both history and human narratives: 'antecedent and superior to all positive law'. Given the centrality of the family to the emerging Ireland, we might wonder whether the prayer of thanksgiving to the Trinity that headed the published text of the Constitution was aimed at the Dominion of God the Father, God the Son and God the Holy Spirit, 'the Most Holy Trinity, from Whom is all authority and to Whom, as our final end, all actions both of men and States must be referred', or the Holy Family of Mary, Joseph and Jesus. It is to the latter that Maguire turns: 'Jesus, Mary and Joseph pray for us / Now and at the hour' (CP, p.69). Though it is debatable whether he is appealing for spiritual succour, or a permanent release from a life that Kavanagh deliberately associates with Eliot's vision of atrophied urban living in The Waste Land ('April, and no one able to calculate / How far it is to harvest. They put down / The seeds blindly with sensuous groping fingers, / And sensuous sleep dreams subtly underground'). Further nuances accrue if we consider the triumvirate of rights nationhood was to bestow upon the Irish people: sovereignty, independence and democracy. The problem, as 'The Great Hunger' makes clear, was that the family was being subjected to very real and persistent pressures – not least a steady decline in the number of   individuals   getting married. Among them, of course, is Maguire, who, 'faithful to death', follows his mother's counsel and does not marry. In doing so, we might say that the mother is undermining the Constitution where it says: 'The State pledges itself to guard with special care the institution of Marriage, on which the Family is founded, and to protect it against attack'. Her antagonism towards other women makes her 'Wife and mother in one' (CP, p.66), with the resulting Oedipal disturbances reminiscent of Joyce's exposé in *Finnegans Wake* of the deep traumas resulting from the *Trauben* underlying familial life.

Along with all the poems he wrote at this time, Kavanagh came to disavow 'The Great Hunger', calling it 'that tragic thing'. As Declan Kiberd says, such use of the word 'tragic' in a pejorative sense suggests the view that 'in tragedy there is also something of a lie, a refusal to believe in the benevolence of an ever-watching God, who will set the human comedy to rights in the end'.[8] *A Soul for Sale*, however, is a collection that from the beginning struggles to reconcile Kavanagh's redemptive trust that 'God is in the bits and pieces of Everyday – / A kiss here and a laugh again, and sometimes tears, / A pearl necklace round the neck of poverty' (CP, p.72). Repeatedly he turns to images of the Trinity and the Holy Family in order to figure the struggle, in the life of the individual and the nation, to reconcile the foundational myths that lie at the heart of the Constitution. In 'Father Mat', for example, the eponymous priest 'Stare[s] through gaps at ancient Ireland sweeping / In again with all its unbaptized beauty' (CP, p.124). The upholder and celebrant of a sacrament, marriage, that he is himself forbidden, Father Mat sees writ across Ireland that fatal division between 'The domestic Virgin and Her Child / Or Venus with her ecstasy' (CP, p.128). And while Yeats in his joint role as poet and statesman could demand, rhetorically, 'How can we know the dancer from the dance?', the rural reality was one where primal desires and civilized obeisance were fundamentally, and divisively, at odds. Listening to his parishioners during confession, Father Mat imagines nature as a balm: '"They confess to the fields", he mused, / "They confess to the fields and the air and the sky," / And forgiveness was the soft grass of his meadow by the river' (CP, p.127). He is himself divided: for while his 'human lips' reassure and promise salvation to the rural poor ('"Those down / Can creep in the low door / On to Heaven's floor"' [CP, pp.127–8]), another voice rises within him:

> The dancer that dances in the hearts of men
> Tempted him again:
> 'Look! I have shown you this before;
> From the mountain top I have tempted Christ
> With what you see now
> Of beauty [...]
> I took with me all the answers to every prayer
> That young men and girls pray for: love, happiness, riches −'
> (CP, p.128)

Father Mat's *imitatio Christi* comes at the expense of an instinctual self. This is not to say that Kavanagh wasn't prepared to engage with selfhood in terms similar to Samuel Beckett's critique, in 1934, of those Revivalist poets whose celebration of an idealized, moralistic life underwrote the misery of whole swathes of the rural population.[9] Father Mat is hardly alone in his solitary life. Even when celebrating physical love, Kavanagh imagines it as taking place at some deferred point in the future. 'There will be bluebells growing under the big trees / And you will be there and I will be there in May' (CP, p.119), he says in 'Bluebells for Love', a poem which can only imagine love in the future tense. The present reality, as the poem makes clear in its final line, is that the poet and his intended are headed in different directions, 'As you and I walked slowly to the station' (CP, p.120). This sense of love long anticipated but hopelessly deferred is hardly surprising given the incidence of Irish men marrying later and later. The census figures for 1936 (made public in 1938) showed that migration was still leading country people to head for the urban centres or abroad, and that Ireland had the highest incidence in the world of unmarried men and women. Such trends were exacerbated in rural areas. The reasons, as Kiberd elaborates, were as much economic as moral:

> The habit of late marriage was widespread: the accompanying ethic of sexual continence was rooted less in the Puritanism of the Catholic Church than in the need to avoid further subdivision of family farms to the point where they might be unviable. Accordingly, older inheriting sons remained 'boys' until their ageing parents agreed to make way for a young bride who might start a new family with them on the homestead. Many such 'boys' were

still waiting in their late forties.[10]

Hence the reference in 'The Long Garden' to old buckets being used as drums 'when old men married wives' (CP, p.43). 'Art McCooey', meanwhile, describes the frustration of those 'boys' yet to reach their majority:

> We wove our disappointments and successes
> To patterns of a town-bred logic:
> 'She might have been sick ...' 'No, never before,
> A mystery, Pat, and they all appear so modest.'
>
> We exchanged our fool advices back and forth:
> 'It easily could be their cow was calving,
> And sure the rain was desperate that night ...' (CP, p.43)

The association of the sound of a woman making illicit love with that of a cow giving birth not only reminds us of the description in 'The Great Hunger' of Maguire's sister 'grunt[ing] in bed, / The sound of a sow taking up a new position' (CP, p.72); it also reminds us of the utter *otherness* of every expression of gratified human sexuality to a rural population taught to venerate simultaneously the Virgin and the Mother as the mainstays of family and national life. As a result, the poem offers a mocking riposte to the inflated rhetoric of de Valera's St. Patrick's Day broadcast in 1943, in which the Taoiseach celebrated an Ireland 'joyous with the sounds of industry ... the contests of athletic youths, the laughter of comely maidens'.[11] The otherness of sexuality is further figured at the conclusion of the poem 'Art McCooey' in an image that elides the mysteries of artistic and biological conception: 'Unlearnedly and unreasonably poetry is shaped, / Awkwardly but alive in the unmeasured womb' (CP, p.43). Such mysteries – both sacred and profane – come together in the sequence of poems that movingly celebrate and commemorate Christmas.

What is clear is that Christmas was seen by the adult Kavanagh as both a locus of lost innocence and a time in the Christian calendar that necessitated the expiation of guilt. So 'Christmas Eve Remembered' begins 'I see them going to the chapel / To confess their sins' (CP, p.34), while 'Advent' describes the middle-aged poet and his lover together, not in some deferred future tense, as in 'Bluebells for Love', but in Dublin: 'here in this Advent-darkened room / Where the dry black bread and sugarless tea / Of penance will charm back the luxury / Of a child's soul' (CP, p.110). In recent decades the emphasis on Advent as a period of penitence and fasting has undergone a shift in emphasis. To Kavanagh's generation, however, the season pointed to the connection between Christ's birth and death, with the incarnation inseparable from the crucifixion. So it is in 'The Great Hunger', with its great, resonant opening lines parodying the sacred mystery of Christ, the Logos, assuming human form, in the Gospel of St. John: 'Clay is the word and clay is the flesh'. 'Advent', however, is saved from such nihilism because the Word has become housed not in the spiritless drudgery of drilling potatoes but in the poet's ability to bear witness to the Word as it manifests itself in the quotidian: 'We'll hear it in the whispered argument of a churning / Or in the streets where the village boys are lurching' (CP, p.111). Though the opening lines of the poem clearly associate adult experience with some diminution of the limitless potential of the 'unmeasured womb' – 'We have tested and tasted too much, lover – / Through a chink too wide there comes in no wonder' (CP, p.110) – in stark contrast to 'The Great Hunger', the poem does not entirely cede ground to the tragic. Rather, it uses Christ's Incarnation as a means of reclaiming a childlike sense of wonder at the potential of the everyday, 'the newness that was in every stale thing / When we looked at it as children: the spirit-shocking Wonder' (CP, p.111).

A Soul for Sale contains a number of such 'womblike' or 'vaginal' spaces through which access is gained to the metaphysical: there is Father Mat 'stopping to / Stare through the gaps at ancient Ireland' (CP, p.124); the poet and his anticipated lover who 'will not let [the bluebells] guess / That we are watching them or they will pose / A mere façade' (CP, p.120); 'A Christmas Childhood' recalls that 'The light between the ricks of hay and straw / Was a hole in Heaven's gable' (CP, p.39); 'The Long Garden' describes how 'We dipped our fingers in the pockets of God' and 'We looked at [the clothes-line] through fingers crossed to riddle / In evening sunlight miracles for men' (CP, p.43); and the epigrammatic 'Sanctity' closes with 'The agonizing pincer-jaws of heaven' (CP, p.17). When such spaces are closed or measured, they appear like the nets from which Stephen Dedalus struggles to free himself: 'When the soul of a man is born in this country there are nets flung at it to hold it back from flight. You talk to me of nationality, language, religion. I shall try to fly

by those nets.'[12] Joyce knew little (and perhaps cared less) of rural
Ireland, or of the specific ways in which it looked to hold back the new-
born soul. Kavanagh knew it all too well, and in 'Temptation in Harvest'
describes as in a nightmare how the land rose up to stop him leaving for
the city to become a poet:

> Earth, earth! I dragged my feet off the ground.
> Labourers, animals armed with farm tools,
> Ringed me. The one open gap had larch poles
> Across it now by memory secured and bound.
> The flaggers in the swamp were the reserves
> Waiting to lift their dim nostalgic arms
> The moment I would move. (CP, p.123)

Such 'rents' in the fabric of the world can be read as Kavanagh's way of
realizing what Seamus Deane calls 'an internal schism that bears within
itself an interpretation of Irish literary history'. The schism, Deane continues, is 'between fantasy and realism [and] duplicates the Free State's
battle with the Irish Renaissance',[13] and it marks Kavanagh as seeking to
free himself from the celebration of the rural (what in Murphy Samuel
Beckett scathingly called an 'Elysium of the roofless') in order to inhabit
a literal and metaphorical ground:

> the Free State, the little world that succeeded to the extravagant
> rhetoric of the Revival and the Rising and the War of Independence
> and the Civil War. It is a world that has lost faith in the heroic con-
> sciousness of the heroic individual and has replaced it by the
> unheroic consciousness of the ordinary, of the Plain People of
> Ireland.[14]

If this 'celebration' of the unheroic marks an element of Kavanagh's lifelong
argument with Yeats, so too does it distinguish him from Joyce (whom he
nevertheless revered), preferring as he did to play the Holy Fool to Yeats's
Lear or Joyce's Hamlet. If the choices he made backed him into corners
such as he describes in 'Temptation in Harvest', and led him to adopt pos-
tures that John Wilson Foster calls 'tactics of reaction, some wise, some perverse', yet they were, as Foster concludes, 'all understandable'.[15]

That Kavanagh came to dismiss the poems of A Soul for Sale as 'thin
romantic stuff not worth a damn'[16] alerts us to how difficult it was for

him, as a Catholic and a one-time farmer, to find an appropriate voice and role as poet in de Valera's Ireland. If 'The Great Hunger' was to be rejected as 'underdeveloped Comedy, not fully born' (it was nevertheless in good company: Kavanagh waved aside Dante's *Commedia* for similar reasons), and the lyrical impulse of much of *A Soul for Sale* was to be dismissed for being 'thin', we can only wonder what kind of poetry Kavanagh thought himself fitted for. One answer is contained in the author's note to *Collected Poems*: 'I lost my Messianic impulse. I sat on the bank of the Grand Canal in the summer of 1955 and let the water lap idly on the shores of my mind. My purpose in life was to have no purpose' (CP, p.292). In the decade following the Irish Constitution, however, a 'Messianic impulse' was wholly understandable as a means of resisting the binding Catholic sentiments of a Constitution that fed a national obsession by idealizing the bitter realities of rural life.

In Kavanagh's Christmas poems it is always Advent or Christmas Eve, never Christmas morning. This to many is how Ireland must still have seemed after the Passion of the Rising and the Civil War. The rural reality was less 'Emerald Isle' than 'A green stone lying sideways in a ditch' (CP, p.40). Yet in adopting the role of Holy Fool or, as Foster calls him, scapegoat, Kavanagh was deliberately casting himself as a kind of Messiah, one who refused to allow the country to accept for itself the deadening cultural and sexual famine that is the real hunger gnawing away in Kavanagh's poetry at this time. As a result, Kavanagh can be seen as attempting to bring within the compass of the restricted practices of de Valera's Catholicism a landscape that, as Seamus Heaney writes, is 'hallowed by associations that come from growing up and thinking oneself in and back into the place'.[17] These are liminal or provisional places: the 'unmeasured womb' in which poetry quietly grows. The association with the Virgin Mary is, of course, impossible to ignore. Indeed 'A Christmas Childhood' concludes with Kavanagh presenting the budding poet as having 'a prayer like a white rose pinned / On the Virgin Mary's blouse' (CP, p.41). There is, however, a subtle but powerful undercutting of the cult of Mariolatry which determined and limited the roles of women in Ireland. The slant rhymes of the second section of the poem mean that the Virgin's 'blouse' rhymes with 'cows', returning us to 'Art McCooey' and the 'bovine' sound of a woman reaching orgasm. Indeed, the rhyme all but challenges us to unbutton the blouse. What we might imagine seeing contained within the blouse but spilling from it would be not the chaste bosom of a Renaissance Madonna but a figure like Dorothy Cross's remarkable sculpture *Virgin Shroud* (1993) – a life-size cowl made using cow hide and her grandmother's wedding trail from 1914, its crown formed by four udders – or *Amazon* (1992), in which a cow hide (including udder) is fitted to a dressmaker's dummy.

That Kavanagh deliberately used rhyme in this way – to undermine too serious an approach to things – was something he was explicit about. Acknowledging in 1959 his debt to the modernizing influence of W.H. Auden, whose poems he discovered in 1941, Kavanagh writes:

> I discovered that the important thing above all was to avoid taking oneself seriously. One of the good ways of getting out of this respectability is the judicious use of slang and of outrageous rhyming. Auden in a radio lecture a year or so ago mentioned this and made a special reference to Byron's Don Juan. The new and outrageous rhymes are not to be confused with the slickeries of Ogden Nash. (*A Poet's Country*, p. 279)

Apropos of Cross's cow sculptures, Tessa Jackson has written of how 'The udder with its own identification of nurturing and suckling immediately opens up the parallels with the breast. Freud was convinced that "the mother's breast is the starting point of the whole sexual life, the un-matched prototype of every later sexual satisfaction to which fantasy often recurs in times of need"'.[18] The Constitution, meanwhile, enshrined the ideal that a woman provided 'by her life within the home ... a support without which the common good cannot be achieved'. So valuable a moral and economic contribution was this that certain 'restrictive practices' were put in place to protect women's labour: 'The State shall, therefore, endeavour to ensure that mothers shall not be obliged by economic necessity to engage in labour to the neglect of their duties in the home.'

Put at its crudest, a women's role was to work without payment, pro-duce babies and yet remain an idealized Virgin. Kavanagh's poetry seems on the surface to fit in with this schema. Except, as we have seen, that without a woman's sexual life being frankly considered the State was in danger of withering on the vine. If Advent and the lowly stable prepare the way for Easter and Mount Calvary, they are joined by the 'unmeasured' spaces of womb and tomb from which the Word is born and resurrected. Kavanagh may bemoan the loss of childhood innocence – 'We have tested and tasted too much, lover' – yet the poem's second sonnet resoundingly concludes by joining sexual experience with a promise of rebirth. And this time it is not half rhyme but full rhyme to which he turns:

> We have thrown into the dust-bin the clay-minted wages
> Of pleasure, knowledge and the conscious hour –
> And Christ comes with a January flower. (CP, p.111)

Here, as in the couplet at the end of the first sonnet, time is redeemed through the abject, each example of which, the fool's open mouth, bog-holes, cart tracks and the old stable, provide further evidence of Kavanagh's unmeasured rents in time and space:

> ... the tedious talking
> Of an old fool, will awake for us and bring
> You and me to the yard gate to watch the whins
> And the bog-holes, cart-tracks, old stables where Time begins.

As in 'A Christmas Childhood' where 'My child poet picked out the letters / On the grey stone' (CP, p.40), the mingling of 'fantasy' and realism is integral to the rhythms and music of poetry: the father's playing the melodeon joins with the rhythm of the mother milking the cows to become a son's (veiled) image of the Virgin's breasts. This ability to configure the Female as both (Freudian) fantasy and realism is important. For if, as Irene Gilsenan Nordin argues in her account of contemporary Irish poetry's reconfiguring of the body as a force for political, social and spiritual empowerment, 'the trope of the Virgin Mary ... has fixed women's bodies into desexualised images of womanhood', then Kavanagh engages in some degree of resexualization, a return to a Celtic, pre-Christian tradition 'where the body and the spiritual were recognised as vital components of existence', thereby casting the body as 'a liminal space between self and world'.[19] This is the vision that Father Mat is granted but constrained from acting on when he sees 'ancient Ireland sweeping / In again with all its unbaptized beauty: / ... / The smell from ditches that were not Christian' (CP, p.124). It would take several future generations and further amendments to the Constitution for Ireland to follow its instincts.

NOTES

1. Patrick Kavanagh, *Collected Poems*, ed. Antoinette Quinn (Harmondsworth: Penguin, 2005), pp.31, 121, 123. Hereafter CP.
2. Patrick Kavanagh, 'Self-Portrait' (1964), in *A Poet's Country: Selected Prose*, ed. Antoinette Quinn (Dublin: Lilliput Press, 2003), p.307. Hereafter *A Poet's Country*.
3. Antoinette Quinn, *Patrick Kavanagh: A Biography* (Dublin: Gill & MacMillan, 2001, 2nd edn 2003), p.121.
4. Patrick Kavanagh, *Collected Poems* (London: MacGibbon & Kee, 1964), pp.xii–xiv.
5. http://www.constitution.ie/constitution-of-ireland/default.asp?UserLang=EN accessed 24 December 2006.
6. R.F. Foster, *Modern Ireland: 1600–1972* (Harmondsworth: Penguin, 1989), p.537.
7. Ibid., p.538.
8. Declan Kiberd, *Inventing Ireland: The Literature of the Modern Nation* (London: Vintage, 1996), p.477.
9. Ibid., pp.464, 478.
10. Ibid., p.477.
11. Quinn, *Kavanagh*, p.181.
12. James Joyce, *A Portrait of the Artist as a Young Man* [1916], ed. and with an introduction and notes by Jeri Johnson (Oxford: Oxford University Press, 2000), p.171.
13. Seamus Deane, 'Boredom and Apocalypse: A National Paradigm', in *Strange Country: Modernity and Nationhood in Irish Writing Since 1790* (Oxford: Clarendon Press, 1997), p.158.
14. Ibid., p.162.
15. John Wilson Foster, 'The Poetry of Patrick Kavanagh: A Reappraisal', in *Colonial Consequences: Essays in Irish Literature and Culture* (Dublin: Lilliput Press, 1991), p.102.
16. Patrick Kavanagh, *Lapped Furrows: Correspondence 1933–1967 Between Patrick Kavanagh and Peter Kavanagh with Other Documents*, ed. Peter Kavanagh (New York: Peter Kavanagh Hand Press, 1969), p.197.
17. Seamus Heaney, *Preoccupations: Selected Prose 1968–1978* (London: Faber & Faber, 1980), p.145.
18. See Tessa Jackson, 'Earlier Work', in *Even: Recent Work by Dorothy Cross* (Bristol: Arnolfini, 1996), p.8.
19. Irene Gilsenan Nordin, 'Re-Mapping the Landscape: The Body as Agent of Political, Social and Spiritual Empowerment in Contemporary Irish Poetry', in *The Body and Desire in Contemporary Irish Poetry* (Dublin and Portland, OR: Irish Academic Press, 2006), pp.9, 8.

CHAPTER EIGHT

The Later Poetry
and its Critical Reception

JOHN GOODBY

'QUEER AND TERRIBLE THINGS'

The poetry of Patrick Kavanagh poses something of a problem for those wishing to understand it in terms of any normal writerly 'development'. Like other Irish poets of his generation, Kavanagh's was checked and gapped, 'his achievement all against the grain, a path scythed through the thistles of indifference, the ragwort of a new social class of post-revolutionary climbers', as John Montague has put it.[1] Moreover, one of Kavanagh's ways of responding to this indifference was to disown each preceding phase of his writing, complicating any critical response to it, or attempt to see it whole. This, in fact, was the fundamental dynamic behind his career, for he 'repudiated more of his own work than almost any other writer'.[2] 'Self-Portrait' of 1962 was only the last in a series of sweepingly self-dismissive claims made after 1959 in order to establish the primacy of the work he published in *Come Dance with Kitty Stobling* (1960) against his earlier work. '[E]xcept for a very few moments in my early years', Kavanagh proclaimed, 'I ha[ve] not been a poet. The poems in *A Soul for Sale* [1947] are not poetry and neither is *The Great Hunger* [1942]. There are some queer and terrible things in *The Great Hunger*, but it lacks the nobility and repose of poetry.'[3] That these comments appeared just after the publication of *Kitty Stobling*, whose success was still therefore relatively insecure, while *The Great Hunger* had been considered his most important achievement for twenty years, only serves to underline the vehemence of his need to define and constitute his present moment of writing through denial. In 'Self-Portrait',

Kavanagh also claimed that his later poetry did not spring from what had preceded, but was the outcome of his having been poetically 'reborn' and rebaptised while convalescing from an operation for lung cancer beside the banks of the Grand Canal in Dublin in the summer of 1955. This particular self-repudiation cast everything he had written between 1938 and 1955 as a profitless detour: 'In the beginning of my versing career', he informs us, 'I had hit on the no-caring jag [of the final poems] but there was nobody to tell me that I was on the right track'. ('No-caring' came from his claim that 'The heart of a song singing it, or of a poem writing it, is not caring'.[4])

'NEATLY SHOWCASED': KAVANAGH AMONG THE CRITICS

The negative dynamic described above, and the conflation of the different phases of his career it has allowed, has strongly influenced the way Kavanagh's œuvre has been read hitherto. It has sanctioned a levelling of distinct, salient aspects of his style, and the running together of different periods, as well as over- and under-selectivity in what is discussed. This applies to critics who both praise and dispraise the work. For Edna Longley, among the former group, Kavanagh is (with Louis MacNeice) the most important Irish poet of his generation, mediator of the poisoned chalice of modernism and inspirer of Seamus Heaney and Paul Muldoon in the north, and Paul Durcan and Brendan Kennelly in the south. (She claims the two pairs of poets respectively imploded and exploded the sonnet forms Kavanagh bequeathed.) For others, such as Declan Kiberd and Seamus Deane, Kavanagh has been worryingly over-hyped, with his influence dependent on what they regard as rural regressiveness and the baleful glamour of an Irish cult of failure.[5] Both arguments have their strong points. Longley argues that Kavanagh's 'revolutionary Irish free-verse achievement' affected his successors, and rightly stresses his border qualities: from the Free State, but also of south Ulster because of his Monaghan provenance; dislocated between country and city; speaking a language of 'internal exile'. Kiberd and Deane identify real weaknesses, too, for Kavanagh was also a destructive force, and managed to alienate himself from the successor generation of poets which included Thomas Kinsella and John Montague, before becoming an inspirational figure in the 1960s. Moreover, as Antoinette Quinn notes, his account of the genesis of his 'not-caring' late style was a mythic construct that he imposed on the chaos of his life in order to 'outwit the inconclusiveness of biography'.[6] Elements of it were in fact emerging as early as 1944, and can be observed throughout the satirical period of the late 1940s, for example. If *The Great Hunger* was something of a cul-de-sac, then the seventeen-year hiatus Kavanagh described was an invention, and this has contributed to making him a kind of poet-martyr with unimpeachable spiritual credentials down to the present.

As this suggests, disagreements about Kavanagh were magnified by the cultural effects of the Northern Irish 'Troubles' during the 1970s and 1980s, since Longley on the one hand, and Kiberd and Deane on the other, have conflicting attitudes to Kavanagh's critique of the de Valeran state. It is clear, for example, that Kiberd and Deane feel that Kavanagh should have continued the sociological vein of *The Great Hunger* into his Dublin years, and should have been an overtly nationalist writer. Similarly, Longley's essay 'Poetic Forms and Social Malformations' is conspicuous in its avoidance of poetry written after *The Great Hunger* and 'Lough Derg' (1942); of anything, that is, which cannot be used as a stick to beat the cultural impoverishment and restrictiveness of the fledgling state, and then linked to Durcan and Kennelly doing similar things in the 1980s (there are a couple of brief exceptions to this, but the post-1955 poems are not among them). Thanks largely to the work of Antoinette Quinn, however, the last decade has seen the dispelling of some of the sectarian heat surrounding this debate, in the form of a judiciously balanced critical biography (1991) and editions of the poetry and prose (in 1996, 2005 and 2003).[7]

The different narratives, and the different uses to which they have been put, raise important questions concerning the nature of Kavanagh's achievement, particularly in the poems of *Kitty Stobling*, and within them the core of eighteen 'noo pomes', as Kavanagh called them, including the famous 'Canal Bank sonnets', which were written between mid-July and October 1957. In particular, they ask us to consider questions of form and technique, particularly since the apparently relaxed style of the 'noo pomes' has had attention (sometimes negative) drawn to it by the weaker, but attitudinally similar work into which it continued in the 1960s. Indeed, even if they don't always address the 'noo pomes', the critics usually place these issues at the heart of what they have to say. For

Deane, it is such stylistic unevenness that causes his bafflement that Kavanagh 'is so obviously a lesser poet than Yeats and yet he is also so obviously more influential in Ireland that one is hard put to define his attraction or his quality'.[8] Longley's essay turns on the claim that 'Kavanagh's sonnets and problematic horizons face two ways – towards Cromwell and Quoof' – yet she fails to discuss a single Kavanagh sonnet. For the reasons given above, she prefers the long poems of the 1940s, although it may be that Kavanagh's liberties with the sonnet form clash with her rather rigid sense of the 'well-made' lyric. Deane is clearer in attacking Kavanagh's wilfully slapdash tendencies. Even so, both share what might be called a Northern Irish sense of the need to observe the proprieties of bounded, and shapely, traditional form.

Noting the distinction between those who accepted Kavanagh's formal looseness and those who did not, Michael O'Loughlin in 1985 recalled that the conflicting views were

> neatly showcased ... in a TV discussion between Anthony Cronin and Denis Donoghue, where each took opposing sides on the true value of Kavanagh. Their seemingly insoluble major/minor conflict led me to believe they were looking at Kavanagh from two radically different viewpoints; judging him in terms of two different discourses.[9]

Different 'discourses' makes a crucial point: O'Loughlin clearly feels the looseness of Kavanagh's form is not a problem, and bases his sense of his importance on a belief that he liberated Irish poetry from Yeats's example and shaping of external perceptions of Irish poetry, and into an unforced Irish vernacular. Naturally, Longley would argue that this shadow was not malign, and that it was absorbed via MacNeice; Deane that Yeats can be read as a post-colonial poet, even though he was a reactionary Anglo-Irish one. O'Loughlin is less in thrall to Yeats's canonical status than either Longley or Deane, and yet his case is weakened when he claims that Kavanagh 'showed that it was possible to break out of the terms of a given literary discourse ... by fidelity to the individual experience'.[10] Having broken with the Tweedledum-and-Tweedledee terms of the debate, the vaguely existential nature of this crucial definition is disappointing. Moreover, it replaces O'Loughlin in agreement with the other critics, since 'fidelity to individual experience' sounds very much like the empiricism of Deane and Longley and their sense of poetry as 'the act of making real'.[11]

Could it be, in fact, that the looseness that Donoghue and Deane assume as weakness, and that Longley skirts around discussing, are part of the meaning of Kavanagh, and even, up to a point, a kind of strength? If so, how might looseness, or – to put it in more literary-critical terms – the breaking of syntactic and poetic norms, the use of decentred form and conflicted, fractured identities, reflect on Cronin's and O'Loughlin's belief that Kavanagh's main virtue is his non-phoney 'fidelity', with its assumption that poetry is faithful to, and expressive of, a coherent self? Such questions point to the way that the fetishization of a limited notion of form on the one hand, and of expressivity on the other, has hamstrung criticism of Kavanagh's poetry and led to the neglect of its most characteristic aspect; namely, its radical heterogeneity, its unwillingness to settle on a pure, single 'voice' of the kind traditionally associated with the lyric.

The positions I query here have been argued most cogently in the two essays on Kavanagh (of 1975 and 1985) by Seamus Heaney, who does in fact discuss the later sonnets and 'noo pomes'. The first essay, informed by anxiety about the vulnerability of the work after 'Epic' (1951) – a relatively orthodox, 'well-made' sonnet of 1951 – deals with charges of formal weakness as they might be pressed by metropolitan criticism. Drawing the wagon-train in a tight circle, as it were, and listening to his Faber & Faber inner voice, Heaney offers *The Great Hunger* and a handful of lyrics written before 'Epic' as Kavanagh's supreme achievement. '[T]he overall impression to be got from reading the second half of the *Collected Poems*', he adds, 'is of a man who knows he can do the real thing but much of the time straining and failing.' He finds little to praise in the later Kavanagh, claiming 'when he had consumed the roughage of his Monaghan experience he ate his heart out'.[12] The second attempt, 'The Placeless Heaven: Another Look at Kavanagh', makes amends for the praising with faint damns by admitting an earlier lack of alertness to 'the liberation and subversiveness of [Kavanagh's] manner'. Heaney then likens the early Kavanagh to a Millet, painting Monaghan in 'thick and faithful pigment', the later to 'a Chagall, afloat above his native domain'.[13] Heaney now accepts that the self and the artist's inner freedom, as well as his external world, imaged in the comparison of the earthbound and the free-floating, are legitimate poetic subjects. Both essays reflect on Heaney's own poetic practice: his taste for 'the roughage of ... experience' up to *Station Island* (1984), his post-*Haw Lantern* (1987) preference for qualities he now praises in Kavanagh's 1950s poetry – its 'wise and unassertive afterlife', 'air[iness]', and 'buoyancy'. This Kavanagh, it seems, did not 'eat his heart out', but rather triumphed, 'clear[ing] a space where, in Yeats's words, "The soul recovers radical innocence ..." ... full of self-possession in the face of death'.[14]

Heaney's change of position reveals both his own growing poetic independence, and the limits of a conservative criticism bounded by realism ('roughage', or 'thick and faithful pigment') and an 'inner freedom', or transcendent mood, subsuming Catholic mysticism and Wordsworthian pietism. More alert to the technical aspects of the later poems, it nevertheless misses their excessive and unstable aspects, in which 'roughage' and 'radical innocence' are subsumed, but hardly in the stable sense Heaney proposes. This is all too clear in a concluding comparison of the Canal Bank sonnets with the *Sonnets to Apollo*, which claims that they reiterate Rilke's 'single, simple command: "You must change your life."'[15] This is not only rather pompous (Kavanagh himself had irreverently rhymed 'R.M. Rilke' with 'Clonakilty' in 'Irish Stew'), but insensitive in its attempt to impose a 'single, simple command' on what are dissonant, complex, fluid and singularly un-'single' works.[16] Although difficult to categorize, except negatively, these poems are not regressive urban pastoral or miracles of 'fidelity'; they do not 'make it real' and are not life-altering touchstones set in a sea of doggerel (although there are elements of all of these things in them). They are better described as a combination of Kavanagh's neglected heterogeneous contexts and a poetics of the casual, informed but not bound by a regard for inherited form.

'THE MEASURE OF HEAVEN ANGLE-WISE': KAVANAGH'S 'PROGRESS'

In his 1959 essay 'From Monaghan to the Grand Canal', presenting his poetry as a kind of full circle, Kavanagh gave, as two examples of his anticipation of the 'no-caring' style, 'Shancoduff' (1937), a poem which most critics would agree anticipates the post-1955 work, and 'To a Child' (1931), from *Ploughman and Other Poems*, a verse of which he cites in the essay:

Child do not go
Into the dark places of the soul,
For there the grey wolves whine,

The lean grey wolves.[17]

This is not simply the perverse attempt to redeem Ploughman that it might seem (as a collection generally regarded as weak and overdependent on Celtic Twilight clichés). For one thing, despite its title's too-obvious play for an urban Revival readership, Ploughman is not as bad as has been claimed. As Anthony Cronin points out, these are not the lyrics of a peasant-poet, but of an accomplished follower of Humbert Wolfe, AE (George Russell), Padraic Colum and Monk Gibbon.[18] The versifying ploughman-figure might have been required by Revival writers and ideologues (and Kavanagh was not the only one who obliged), and was equally welcomed as a convenient target by anti-Revivalists; but the terms of the rather polarized cultural debate in which the book tends to be read cannot hide its palpable, if modest, strengths. Shamrock Georgianism there is, but as C.H. Sisson noted, so too are many of Kavanagh's distinctive, original qualities.[19] In lines describing the Irish peasantry as 'a dark people' whose gaze is always inward, turned upon 'the liar who twists / The hill-path awry', there is already the beginning of Kavanagh's reaction against the 'Irish Thing', not to mention Heaney's 'Bogland'.[20] There is the book's variety, too, which, with the symbolist modes of the two poems above, includes the Imagism of 'Gold Watch', the Objectivist 'My Room', as well as the romantic cuteness of the title poem ('I turn the lea-green down / Gaily now, / And paint the meadow brown / With my plough').[21] It is crucial to an understanding of Kavanagh's later poems, that we grasp his unwillingness to completely abandon these styles, including the romantic, conventionally poetic one, even as he denounced them.

Indeed, in his revolt into realism, this romantic strain only appeared to vanish. Criticism has overlooked the inconsistency of Kavanagh's realism because it does not fit the narrative of a poet rejecting the Revival and embracing a valorized 'real' in the Monaghan clay and muck. Stylistic heterogeneity, however, is what we actually get. Kavanagh, as is well known, aligned himself with the sociological realism of The Bell out of distaste at being fêted as a peasant-poet, and announced his anti-pastoralism there with 'Stony Grey Soil' (1940), elaborated on in his three novella-poems Why Sorrow? (1941), The Great Hunger (1942, previously published in The Bell in 1941) and 'Lough Derg' (1942). Yet the novella-poems unashamedly mix their 'roughage' with the visionary, blatantly fustian aspects of the 1930s lyrics. Even *The Great Hunger*, where realism is most consistent, can switch, in the space of a few lines, from clayey intensity to an Arthur Rackhamish image couched in the language of the Yeats of *Crossways*:

> Primroses and the unearthly start of ferns
> Among the blackthorn shadows in the ditch,
> A dead sparrow and an old waistcoat ...
> Here with the unfortunate
> Who for half moments of paradise
> Pay out good days and wait and wait
> For sunlight-woven cloaks.[22]

The Great Hunger revolves around a contrast between true and false incarnation, the one life-denying and metaphysical only, the other life-affirming, pagan and sensual (albeit distinctly Catholic). A sense of the numinous – 'the unearthly start of ferns' – is thus to be expected. But what is really distinctive is not this aspect, or the realist touches, but the fact that the 'start of ferns' and the 'dead sparrow and an old waistcoat' coexist with the twee 'sunlight-woven cloaks'. The lack of irony in the juxtaposition will not allow it to be read as a form of modernist montage. Is it, then, simply a lapse of taste? Not really, since such slips – 'slippages' might be better – which seem troublesome failures of taste to a criticism seeking a unity of parts, occur too often to be regarded as errors. Indeed, this question might be turned around to make the argument that Kavanagh was saved from a stultifying poetics (the formulaic realism-plus-resolving-transcendent-symbol) by the stubborn survival of 'bad' habits from his very earliest poetry. Unity easily becomes unanimity, while a certain awkwardness of imagery, lexis, metre and phrasing serve to resist any homogenizing single 'voice'.

Kavanagh's difficulties with his heterogeneous influences loomed larger from the mid-1940s to the mid-1950s, a period of transition in which he came up against the aesthetic limits placed on realism in post-Independence Ireland, but was not yet able to take the plunge into a 'not-caring' outlook. Just as Sean O'Faoláin would lament the lack of a developed middle-class society capable of nurturing the novel, so Kavanagh discovered the difficulty in completing two of his three novella-poems. A turn to satire and polemic was therefore almost inevitable, although in

Kavanagh's case it took place in such a splenetic way that he managed to antagonize not only enemies like Brendan Behan, but a neutral such as Hubert Butler (who likened his critical mind to 'a monkey-house at feeding time'), and friends and natural allies, among them John Montague and Thomas Kinsella, members of the next generation of Irish poets.[23]

The cultural critique of these years was at best quixotic, at worst self-woundingly unnecessary; it ultimately failed because Kavanagh was too self-centred, too ill-equipped and too obviously steeped in the localism and narrowness he derided. Calls for sincerity and attacks on the 'phoniness' of others sat uncomfortably with his backward glances from Dublin to Monaghan, which were often wistful and confused. In the short sonnet-sequence 'Temptation in Harvest' (1945–46), for example, he betrayed a basic irresolution induced by the knowledge that 'clay could still seduce my heart / After five years of pavements raised to art', and a sense that the 'hegira' to Dublin might not have been worth the effort it had cost.[24] As Quinn notes, 'so ambivalent is the attitude to both country and city ... that returning to the farm or quitting it are both represented as temptations'.[25] Effectively, this left the poet facing both ways, a Janus-figure, self-divided and unhappy with either direction.

Kavanagh was aware that the monomania of satire stifled his lyric gift ('satire is unfruitful prayer', as 'Prelude' of February 1955 has it), but the achievement of the 'noo pomes' lay not so much in the overcoming of the irresolution and division which bred satire, as in the discovery of a way of converting these into strengths, reconfiguring their elements in a new constellation.[26] The 1945–55 period reveals Kavanagh gradually testing out various poetic strategies as he moved uncertainly away from realism (his novel By Night Unstarred, a last realist fling, was abandoned in 1950), maintaining his satirical attacks, but also writing visionary lyric poems.[27] These prolonged uncertainties, in their self-cancelling form, riddle A Soul for Sale, which collected work as various as The Great Hunger, 'Temptation in Harvest' and the title-supplying allegorical-visionary 'Pegasus' (1944). 'Pegasus' confirms Kavanagh's problem as that of uncertainty concerning the value of his poetic gift, or 'soul', which has led him in the past to treat it as 'an old horse / Offered for sale in twenty fairs', though the conclusion – that if he stopped trying to sell his gift, it would grow imaginative wings – went unheeded for another decade.[28]

By the time of 'Auditors In' (1951), however, Kavanagh had already understood the need to 'compromise / On the non-essential sides' of his work, that is, satire.[29] But there was more to the realization than this alone, for he also realized that he ought to reject the urge to be 'walking eagerly to go nowhere in particular', rushing about with a vain sense of purpose. This amounts, potentially, to a larger rejection of the work ethic, clock time, and the anxieties and neuroses which drive western civilization. Going 'nowhere' in a more general sense – 'nowhere' as authority reckons it, that is – might bring one to 'where the Self reposes, / The placeless heaven that's under all our noses'.[30] The 'self', as Heaney has noted, became a legitimate subject at this point in Kavanagh's work, and in a markedly less winsome, creakily allegorical form than the soul-horse of 'Pegasus'. The final crisis which precipitated the 'noo pomes' demanded not only Kavanagh's acknowledgement of the failure of his critical-satirical project, then, but a radical translation of its failure into a different, paradoxical kind of triumph. The triple disasters of the collapse of *Kavanagh's Weekly* in 1952, his humiliating libel case against *The Leader* in 1954, and the operation for lung cancer in March–April 1955 finally forced this on Kavanagh, making him at last see what was 'under all our noses'.

Typically, he presented this change in mythic terms, as a moment of spiritual rebirth, or return, as already noted. In reality, the 'noo pomes' were actually written after returning from a six-month sojourn in New York in the first half of 1957, or over two years after the 'rebirth', and following an encounter with Beat poetry, by which Kavanagh was much impressed. They thus had a literary as well as existential subtext, catalyzing an aesthetic and an awareness which had been latent for some time. As early as 'Bluebells for Love' (1945), for instance, the speaker tells his lover that they will look 'sideways at the bluebells in the plantation / And never frighten them with too wild an exclamation'.[31] This oblique glance is, in essence, the 'not-caring' one. This is a point Foster usefully extends to Kavanagh's metrics: 'Crookedness also works formally in [his] verse: the way, for instance, he uses three-beat lines, with their suggestion of self-mockery and facetiousness, to undercut four-beat and five-beat lines, as in "Kerr's Ass" (1950), in case his lyrical gift should tempt him into looking at the bluebells directly.'[32] Kavanagh was better at looking at things 'skew-ways' than straight ahead; and 'Bluebells for Love' mixes in the visionary with its realism ('I caught an angel smiling in a chance'), and even the humour which Kavanagh would try to claim had only arrived in 1955. Even so – like Patrick Maguire in *The Great Hunger* – in the middle years of his career this viewpoint still operated only negatively for Kavanagh, as with 'affected indifference' he '[took] the measure of heaven angle-wise'.[33]

'AWKWARDLY ALIVE': PARNASSIAN HYBRIDITY

The circularity, obliquity and textual heterogeneity I have mentioned were evident to Kavanagh himself when he regretted, in 'Self-Portrait', that 'In the beginning of my versing career I had hit on the no-caring jag but there was nobody to tell me I was on the right track', and cursed himself for having been 'too thick to take the hint', a self-misrecognition which, he argued, had betrayed him into the 'kinetic vulgarity' of *The Great Hunger*.[34] Even if the claim of circularity was mythical, it nevertheless pointed to the fundamental inadequacy of linear narratives, and to the importance of the work's mixed, hybrid nature.

'Iniskeen Road: July Evening' (1936) anticipates, like 'Shancoduff', the style of the 'noo pomes', and not only in its sonnet form and manner. Most critics have noted its vernacular assurance and evocation of the young poet's shyness, its quiet dramatization of his simultaneous belonging to, and isolation within, his community. Sitting beside the road as his neighbours go by to the evening dance in a barn, the speaker is well-attuned to their 'half-talk code of mysteries' and 'language of delight', but nevertheless isolated by his gift. His 'plight' is that of 'Alexander Selkirk', monarch of all he surveyed yet pining for human company: 'A road, a mile of kingdom, I am king / Of banks and stones and every blooming thing'.[35] There is nothing elitist in the agonizing about this condition, and it is precisely the banality of his loneliness which makes this sonnet an original work. Put a different way, its potential for post-Romantic conventionality is undermined by the peculiar hybridity of Kavanagh's sources. This quality is most apparent in 'blooming', whose punning aptness at this point in the poem has often been remarked, but without anyone noting how characteristic is Kavanagh's choice of Cowper's Alexander Selkirk (and behind him Defoe's Robinson Crusoe) as a model for poetic self-validation. Why not a Romantic, Victorian or more modern precursor? The reason, it seems to me, lies in Kavanagh's marked taste for eighteenth-century models, something evident even in his choices of titles — think, say, of 'Lines Written on a Seat on the Grand Canal, Dublin'. This is unusual — it is difficult to think of contemporaries resorting, as he so often does, to eighteenth-century exemplars. Modernism's debate was with the Romantics and the Victorians (their relationship to the eighteenth century being governed by irony and satire, as in The Waste Land), and non-modernists had no interest in classicism. But Kavanagh returns to these models continually, and to neoclassical touchstones (what else is The Great Hunger but Goldsmith's The Deserted Village reimagined for mid-twentieth-century Ireland?).

'Parnassus' is his favourite touchstone, acting as an umbrella term for many other properties — Pygmalion, Apollo, Jupiter, Styx, Charon, Pegasus, Venus, Homer, Narcissus, Jove, Mount Olympus, Prometheus, 'Agamemnon's Briseis', and so on.[36] Their function is partly indicated by the casual nature of their usage; they offer a pagan resonance rather than drawing down any mythological machinery, and contrast with the pervasive Catholicism of the poetry ('pagan' might be said to draw on a dual source; the elder faiths of Irish legend and superstition, which he occasionally mentions, and the classical). Kavanagh's fondness for them is fundamentally non-ironic, on the surface (but not thereby simply superficial), and this may be a reason why not much has been said about this area of allusion; the scattering of names seems 'unserious', a far cry from the pastiche neoclassicism of The Waste Land or the knowing Augustanisms of Auden.

Nevertheless, it is important to know what their significance might be. Michael Allen, who is specific in relating 'Parnassian' to its later, nineteenth-century French and Decadent allotropes — Théodore de Banville to Ernest Dowson, say — takes this aspect of the work as a fault: 'Another over-literary frame of reference for the poetry of this period is the ninetyish ideal of Parnassus', he opines of 'Lines Written on a Seat on the Grand Canal, Dublin', adding that 'The poem's strength resides in its "parochial" vividness', this being 'sabotaged by the clichéd attempt to fuse Kavanagh's real-life migratory experience with a symbolic Parnassian journey'.[37] But what constitutes an 'over-literary frame of reference'? Presumably Allen would not say that Ulysses suffered from having such a 'frame'; but, if so, he would surely be hard put to maintain that it was less 'literary' than Kavanagh's. In fact, the opposition between a 'ninetyish' artificiality, assumed to be a bad thing, and '"parochial" vividness', assumed to be a good thing, is critically untenable. Or, more accurately, it flows in this case from an unstated post-Movement prejudice – the influence of Donald Davie and F.R. Leavis is palpable – in favour of the 'well-made', empirical lyric.

The extent to which 'the real' is being fetishized here is apparent if the poem itself is read for evidence of the 'migratory experience' and '"parochial" vividness' allegedly being sabotaged. It opens in the rapt yet casual tone of which Kavanagh is master, with the speaker asking to be commemorated beside canal water in summer. Its locutions are clumsy and fluent, archaic and slangy, while the coinage 'Niagarously' is a flourish from the comic ballad tradition. Far from being 'sabotaged', the kind of empirical realism in which Allen is interested never gets a look in. The time and location of the sonnet is always already an unspeaking no-place suspended 'in the tremendous silence' which is not merely that of July but of meditation upon the making of the poem. 'No-one' would attempt 'to speak in prose' on these 'Parnassian islands', as Allen seems to imagine (they are more Wordsworthian 'spots of time' than geographical features in any case), and 'no-one' does. The roar of the lock is the roar of silence, of quasi-mystical transport, and right on its Mallarméan cue a swan appears 'with many apologies' – 'apologies', that is, which are Kavanagh's own for the blatant mechanics of his Parnassus. Finally, the rapt, vocative tone becomes an imperative 'And look!' as a barge, both gross and Arthurian, passes by. The whole scene is bathed in 'Fantastic light' – 'fantastic' both in its slang sense as intensifier and 'to do with fantasy' – with only the faintest attempt to realize an actual scene on the banks of the Grand Canal. Thus, the barge laden with its 'mythologies' comes from Athy / And other far-flung towns' not because it is an un-mythological place (that is, not in order to satisfy deflationary, realist requirements) but simply because it happens both to be on the canal and to provide the final rhyme for the request to be commemorated 'with no hero-courageous / Tomb – just a canal-bank seat for the passer-by'.[38]

It would be difficult to conceive of a poem which had less desire for 'parochial vividness' in the sense Allen intends. There is no 'clichéd attempt' in it to 'fuse' some 'real-life … experience' with anything 'symbolic' here; the entire poem is 'symbolic' in the sense that all of its properties, from the lock to the barge, the swan to the seat, are charged with a non-realist, blatantly symbolist significance. Athy is nowhere near

Monaghan, Inniskeen has nothing in the way of 'mythologies', and Kavanagh's passing reference to one who 'finds his way' to the canal bank in line eight can hardly be construed as a failed attempt to describe the Monaghan–Dublin *hegira*. The attempt to relate the poem to an intended realist plane of action falls flat on its face. What Allen has done, in fact, is ignore what the poem does in favour of Kavanagh's famous distinction between the provincial and the parochial imagination, which he has applied to it in Procrustean fashion, ignoring the bits that fail to fit.[39] He seeks a poem about 'real-life', one which begins in some question thrown up by empirical particulars, which it then resolves, or richly ambiguates, in symbol-epiphanic closure. But 'Lines Written on a Seat', with its brittle, hyper-elevated tonal register, its stylistic 'badness', its arch rhymes which teeter on the Byronic-comic, refuses to comply with either English 'well-made' or Leavisite critical norms, or with more sophisticated American New Critical ones; and, in refusing to accord with the 'parochial', 'vivid', expressivist model, is judged to be flawed by these qualities. Yet it seems evident that if there is a journey in the poem, it takes the form of an exploration of the nature of poetry and the poetic; what Allen dismisses in his essay as the 'vocabulary of rhetorical abstractions', forgetting that all poetry is rhetorical.

What is also overlooked, perhaps, is the extent to which Kavanagh's 'Parnassianism' reflects the prestige that classicism had in the kind of rural Irish townland in which he grew up. This prestige has a communal aspect, as is illustrated by the episode in which the narrator is given a copy of Pope's *Works* by Bob the quarry-man in *The Green Fool*. The narrator (a version of Kavanagh, since this is an autobiography of sorts) notes:

> I liked Pope. His essays on Man and Criticism were good strong truths in rhyme. At the cross-roads on Sunday morning I recited with enthusiasm to a crowd of farm-folk:

> 'Of all the causes which conspire to blind
> Man's erring judgement and misguide the mind,
> What the weak head with strongest bias rules
> Is pride, the never-failing vice of fools.'

> My hearers understood and appreciated this.[40]

It is in the light of this prestige – and poetry's ability to impart 'good

strong truths in rhyme' – that titles such as 'Intimate Parnassus', 'The
Paddiad', 'Pegasus', 'Pygmalion', 'On Looking into E.V. Rieu's Homer'
and 'Epic' can be seen to evince not affectedness or archness, but a particular rural Irish residue of respect for eighteenth-century poetry and
neoclassicism. That residue, of course, had its socio-historical basis in
the hedge-school tradition of teaching the classics (Greek as well as
Latin) in the Irish countryside during the seventeenth, eighteenth and
early nineteenth centuries, a form of schooling often (though not
always) carried out by priests. Hedge-schools are vividly described by
William Carleton, one of Kavanagh's favourite authors – he edited
Carleton's *Autobiography* – in his best-known work *Traits and Stories of the Irish
Peasantry* (1830 and 1833). The subject is also central, of course, to Brian
Friel's *Translations* (1980), which gives an idea of its cultural-political
charge. Hedge-schools had vanished by Kavanagh's day, but they were
still remembered and well-understood. They are also referenced in one
of the most famous of all Revival lyrics, Padraic Colum's 'Poor Scholar',
a poem for which Kavanagh declared a soft spot, despite the fact that he
expressed reservations about Colum on every other occasion.[41]

This specifically Irish encounter with the classics makes itself felt in
Kavanagh's poetry in several stylistic features disruptive of a homoge-
neous lyric tone and surface. Apart from the many references to classical
figures listed above, there is Kavanagh's penchant for neoclassical personification ('Schoolmistress Fancy', 'Passion's granite child', 'Truth's
manuscript' and so on), and for apostrophe ('O leafy yellowness', 'O
commemorate me', 'O wealthy me! O happy state!') – these being so
ubiquitous that one feels Kavanagh might have been speaking in his own
voice through The Poet in 'The Wake of the Books' (1947), when he
claimed to 'hear / The girl of the eighteenth century singing'.[42] To reiterate: the point about such usages is that they are neither buried and
smoothed over, nor ironically framed; they are unembarrassed, part of a
poetic texture which foregrounds them, along with other, seemingly
anomalous, non-modern stylistic markers. When Sean O'Faoláin said
that Kavanagh was guilty of 'not washing behind the ears of his poetry',
it seems to me that he was referring not simply to metrical roughness,
but to this mixed, heterogeneous quality, and to the risks taken in presenting it in this manner – its sheer difference from the standard model
of lyric, which modulates in a gradual way from empirical observation

to symbolic closure, rather than abruptly leaping between these, or mix-
ing in elements which otherwise disturb the progression of the poem.
In this sense the granular, disrupted, pasted-together quality of
Kavanagh's work goes beyond a question of mere influence.

Such neoclassicism is not the only submerged element disturbing
Kavanagh's lyric surfaces, however. I mean by this something which is
touched on in Heaney's observation that 'Much of [Kavanagh's] authority and oddity derives from the fact that he wrestled his idiom out of a
literary nowhere. At its most expressive, his voice has the air of bursting
a long battened-down silence.'[43] All of which is true enough, of course;
but Heaney simply seems to mean by this that Kavanagh validates the
'parochial vision' in using dialect words such as 'headland' (for the
County Derry 'headrig', as Heaney notes in his second Kavanagh essay),
farming terms and country turns of phrase. The effect is to valorize
Kavanagh's work in terms of dialect use and its 'spoken ... note' only;
and, although this is indeed important, as O'Loughlin observes, if
'silence' is 'an apt description of Kavanagh's effect', it is 'only apparent'.
In reality, as he points out, Kavanagh's 'ludic and confident' language use
derives from a rich, but ignored folk context:

> That voice [Kavanagh's] was still there, in the songs of the people,
> and in the Gaelic poets. Kavanagh, later in his career, stressed the
> sense of kinship he felt with the eighteenth-century Gaelic poets
> of South Ulster. But that sense of kinship was not based on any
> ostensible tradition; it was rather the quality of a response to a par-
> ticular area and a life lived there. Kavanagh did not achieve this
> tone through the study of translations, or even through great
> familiarity with the folk-songs ... To turn it around, much of
> Kavanagh's apparent oddity derived from the fact that he emerged
> from the silence all around Anglo-Irish literature – a silence made
> all the more inaudible by the voices projected into it.[44]

Revealingly, Kavanagh's tribute to the most important of the South Ulster
Gaelic poets, Art McCooey (Mac Cumhaigh), is highly oblique. Although
McCooey's name is the poem's title ('Art McCooey', 1941), the poem
itself does not mention him at all, rendering instead the contrast
between 'the time I drove / Cart-loads of dung to an outlying farm' with
one 'In Donnybrook in Dublin ten years later', a memory echoing one

in McCooey's own life (he is said to have once been so involved in the throes of composition that he kept on driving the same cartful of manure between the dunghill and his destination until he was caught in the act by his enraged employer).[45] Kavanagh later wrote about McCooey in 'A Poet's Country' in the popular publication *Ireland of the Welcomes* (in March 1953), and his poem presents local 'life lived there' in terms of name, location, idioms and proverbial wisdom, desultory chit-chat, the odd dialect word, and unspectacular events. The uneventfulness of every-day life is offered as poetry, and hence implicitly as McCooey's inspira-tion. Up to a point, it is a poem about 'real life ... experience', but Kavanagh typically mixes awkward personification ('where November dances'), the archaic 'poetic' ('Somewhere in the mists a light was laughing'), inversion ('the dreamer that the land begets'), and this het-erogeneous, unsettling quality makes us read the conclusion less as a symbolic epiphany than as a reminder that this has been a poem about the nature of poetry, emphasized by the calculatedly awkward 'but alive' polysyllabic adverbs cramped within the 'cart' of the final quatrain:

> Wash out the cart with a bucket of water and a wangel
> Of wheaten straw. Jupiter looks down.
> Unlearnedly and unreasonably poetry is shaped,
> Awkwardly but alive in the unmeasured womb.[46]

'BREAK OUT, BUT DO NOT SCATTER': BALLAD, SONG AND EPIC

O'Loughlin's concept of 'songs of the people' is somewhat essentialist, but he is correct in asserting that the 'silence' of Monaghan was mur-murous with numerous sub-literary influences. '[T]he usual barbaric life of the Irish country poor', as Kavanagh unsentimentally called it, and his reliance on local culture during his development as a poet (he was almost 35 when he went to Dublin), meant that he was steeped to an unusual degree in folksong and ballad, popular song, mumming shows, and newspaper and popular journal verse: it is no accident that he wrote an article entitled 'Schoolbook Poetry'.[47] Nor did he renounce these quite as thoroughly and as early as most poets have to in order to inte-grate into a metropolitan literary scene. Heaney, for example, discusses similar materials in the 'Reading and Rhymes' section of his essay

'Mossbawn', but these are, crucially, presented as elements which have been subsumed in childhood and thereby overcome within his later work.[48] Put in a different, more Bakhtinian way, Heaney consciously shows us how he fused and forged an individual lyric utterance, whereas Kavanagh presents, with a greater degree of casualness, a *dialogic* concatenation of materials (they are always already worked-over to some degree) aligned with, and jostling against each other, rather than fused together by what approximates to a single speaking voice.

The many barely subsumed intertexts include canonical poets, of course, several of a pre-modern vintage: among them Burns, Longfellow, Byron, Shelley (*The Cenci* makes an appearance in *The Green Fool*), Milton (*Paradise Lost* gets its separate mention), Hood, Tennyson, Swinburne and Keats. Then there are anthologies such as Palgrave's *Golden Treasury*, school poetry primers (the '*Intermediate Poetry and Prose*, by Father Corcoran, D. Litt.', mentioned in *A Green Fool*), newspapers and journals. The latter include *The Dundalk Democrat* (in which Kavanagh first published a poem), *Ireland's Own* and *World Wide Magazine*. Another source of material is religion, in the form of the Catechism and the Rosary. Aside from these materials, which have a canonical or institutional sanction, there are ballads (such as those by the local 'Bard of Callenberg', John McEnaney), and patriotic and folk song.[49]

Song and ballad were particularly important to Kavanagh, a fact which has tended to be overlooked because they have only swum into the ken of critics relatively recently, despite having featured for some time in anthologies of Irish writing as gestures to the oral tradition.[50] They were, and to some extent are still, a crucial part of the cultural background in Ireland, where there is a huge corpus of indigenous material in English, and whose importance to poetry is little-explored (after Kavanagh, the Irish poet who has used ballad and song most extensively is probably Ciaran Carson).[51] In the words of Cronin in his memoir *Dead as Doornails*:

> [Kavanagh] had an enormous love for the Irish sub-culture represented by schoolbook poems and ballads and some of the poems in schoolbooks he had airs to and would sing: 'The Burial of Sir John Moore', 'Lord Ullin's Daughter' and Richard Dalton Williams's 'From a Munster Vale They Brought Her'. He had a perfect ear and was

delighted to sing in the right company and on the right occasion. When he had the operation for cancer it damaged his vocal cords somehow ... but his ear of course remained impeccable and he simply adapted his highly individual style to the new possibilities.[52]

Kavanagh noted in 'Auditors In' that, for him, 'the dandelions at Willie Hughes's' were 'equally valid / For urban epic, peasant ballad', and 'equally' cuts both ways. Even a cursory list of songs and ballads in his work would include 'A Ballad' ('O cruel are the women of Dublin's fair city'), 'If Ever You Go To Dublin Town', 'Cyrano de Bergerac' and 'The Rowley Mile' (originally published together as 'Two Sentimental Songs'), 'Who Killed James Joyce?', 'On Raglan Road', 'Song at Fifty', 'Spring Day' ('O Come all ye tragic poets and sing a stave with me'). Two or three of these, 'If Ever You Go to Dublin Town' outstanding among them, rank with his best poems. 'Spring Day' shows that Kavanagh calculated quite precisely the subversive, plebeian effect such forms could have, explicitly directing a balladeering broadside at the 'verbal constipation' and 'inbred verses' of mid-century academic poetry:

> O Come all ye gallant poets – to know it doesn't matter
> Is Imagination's message – break out but do not scatter.
> Ordinary things wear lovely wings – the peacock's body's common.
> O Come all ye youthful poets and try to be more human.[53]

Philistine though this poem may be, it makes explicit in a thematic sense Foster's point about Kavanagh's metrical 'crookedness': the 'undercut[ting]' three-beat lines 'with their suggestion of self-mockery and facetiousness' are those of oral forms, and they are directed against the 'four-beat and five-beat lines' or standard written hexameters and iambics. This can be seen in several poems: 'Kerr's Ass', for example, opens like a ballad, with a four-stress line followed by a three-stress line. The model is then stretched a little in the more relaxed long third line, before the quatrain returns to it in the final three-stress line:

> We borrowed the loan of Kerr's big ass
> To go to Dundalk with butter,
> Brought him home the evening before the market
> An exile that night in Mucker.[54]

Kavanagh's use of popular forms, his non-ironic admixtures of eighteenth-century neoclassicism and the kind of Romanticism associated with Victorian anthology staples, points to a writing which is not simply 'oral' (another term, like 'roughage' and its synonyms, which critics of Kavanagh have tended to use uncritically), but which flaunts its dependence on a particular, rural, quasi-literary sub-culture. Something of this informs his 'parochial enthusiasm', which cuts across what Edna Longley calls 'the totalising propensities of Nationalism'.[55] From a different ideological viewpoint, David Lloyd has argued that 'the hybrid quality of popular forms constantly exceeds the monologic desire of cultural nationalism, a desire which centres on the lack of an Irish epic'. If, he continues, nationalism must (for coherent political reasons) try to supersede such hybridity, it can never entirely overcome the 'multiplicity of contending voices'.[56]

Kavanagh's rejoinder to the concept of the national epic is, of course, famously presented in 'Epic', which claims to have lived in important (parochial) places and times, bypasses 'the Munich bother', then hesitates, 'inclined / To lose my faith in Ballyrush and Gortin', until

> Homer's ghost came whispering to my mind.
> He said: I made the Iliad from such
> A local row. Gods make their own importance.[57]

The irony at the expense of monolithically conceived epic, and of a monologic nationalist project, is doubled here: Homer endorses Kavanagh's parochial poetic, but, as he would probably have known, the Homeric epics are written in a form of oral improvisatory poetry, like 'ballads and folk-songs', undoing the notion of a singular identity for the founding father of the Western canon.[58] 'Homer's ghost' is, in fact, a composite. To complicate matters further, Young Ireland, as Lloyd notes, had difficulties with existing ballads in the 1840s, because these often proved to be disfigured by their 'burlesque tone' and their heterogeneity, both internally and in collected form: 'Tonal instability ... is common, as is ... a vertiginous mixture of realism and burlesque, "high language" and slang'.

Similar 'vertiginous mixtures' can be found in the quasi-ballad 'I Had a Future' (its title is its refrain), which shifts in a near-absurd, yet strangely assured manner between 'the stretcher bed I slept on / In a room in Drumcondra Road' and 'the eerie beat / Of madness in Europe trembl[ing] the / Wings of the butterflies along the canal. / ... / O I had a future'.[59] Referring to the famous mid-nineteenth century Dublin balladeer 'Zozimus' (Michael Moran), Lloyd adds:

> To the ambiguities resulting from the refusal to differentiate the burlesque from the serious corresponds a similar indifference to cultural registers. Military language can cohabit with that of the racecourse, or classical references give way to citations of ancient and modern history, folk heroes and contemporary slang. Much of the pleasure of the street ballad, as with so many 'popular' forms, derives precisely from this indifference to cultural hierarchies.[60]

There was also, as Lloyd notes, 'an antagonism to the allegorical tendency of Gaelic poetry and the street ballads in favour of a generally symbolist aesthetic'[61] among Young Ireland critics, a shift from the metonymic to the metaphoric axis of contiguity – an antagonism which, as I have tried to show in this chapter, was replayed in the responses to Kavanagh's poetry. If Kavanagh was not quite a twentieth-century Zozimus, then, it is possible to discern clear similarities between the poetic he was searching for between 1945 and 1955 and that of the ballad-and song-makers of the past. A pragmatic, unembarrassed use of the many, often sub-literate, non-official materials to hand meant that whatever synthesis he arrived at had to allow for 'tonal instability', an anarchic-seeming, yet modulated blend of exalted and mundane cultural registers, space for allegorical and symbolic tendencies, and a tempering of the metaphoric with the metonymic. The confidence to accept instability and the heterogeneous sources of his poetry – or, better put, to actively foreground them – is what emerged from the crisis of 1955, and it is what makes the best of Kavanagh's later poetry so quicksilver and elusive of definition.

NOTES

1. John Montague, 'Patrick Kavanagh: A Speech from the Dock', in *The Figure in the Cave and Other Essays* (Dublin: Lilliput Press, 1989), p.136.
2. John Wilson Foster, 'The Poetry of Kavanagh: A Reappraisal', in *Colonial Consequences: Essays in Irish Literature and Culture* (Dublin: Lilliput Press, 1991), p.104.
3. Patrick Kavanagh, *Collected Pruse* (London: Martin Brian & O'Keefe, 1973), p.21.
4. Antoinette Quinn, *Patrick Kavanagh: Born-Again Romantic* (Dublin: Gill & Macmillan, 1991), p.398.
5. For Declan Kiberd's claim that Kavanagh's later poems were a reactionary kind of urban

pastoral, see the discussion below. Seamus Deane, who does not cover Kavanagh's work in *Celtic Revivals* (London: Faber, 1985), elsewhere describes his achievement as strictly limited by the nature of the Irish literary world of the 1940s and 1950s, where 'Talent, time and money could be wasted, drunkenness and unemployment could be given moral status and, finally, the writing itself would be imbued with something of the spirit of subversive squalor'. See Deane, *A Short History of Irish Literature* (London: Hutchinson, 1986), p.228. For Longley, see Edna Longley, 'Poetic Forms and Social Malformations', in *The Living Stream: Literature and Revision in Northern Ireland* (Newcastle upon Tyne: Bloodaxe, 1994), pp.204–26.

6. Quinn, *Patrick Kavanagh*, p.379.

7. See ibid.; Patrick Kavanagh, *Selected Poems*, ed. Antoinette Quinn (Harmondsworth: Penguin, 1996); Patrick Kavanagh, *Collected Poems*, ed. Antoinette Quinn (Harmondsworth: Penguin, 2005). Henceforward references to the poems are given for the 2005 edition of the *Collected Poems*, the most readily available, and to Patrick Kavanagh, *The Complete Poems*, ed. Peter Kavanagh (Newbridge: Goldsmith Press, 1992).

8. Deane, *Short History of Irish Literature*, p.242.

9. Michael O'Loughlin, *After Kavanagh: Patrick Kavanagh and the Discourse of Contemporary Irish Poetry* (Dublin: Raven Arts Press, 1985), p.7.

10. Ibid., p.38.

11. Richard Kirkland, *Literature and Culture in Northern Ireland Since 1965: Moments of Danger* (London: Longman, 1996), p.96. Kirkland's is easily the most incisive analysis available of the contradictions of Longley's critical position.

12. Seamus Heaney, 'From Monaghan to the Grand Canal: The Poetry of Patrick Kavanagh', *Preoccupations: Selected Prose 1968–78* (London: Faber & Faber, 1980; rpt 1984), pp.128, 130.

13. Seamus Heaney, 'The Placeless Heaven: Another Look at Kavanagh', in *The Government of the Tongue* (London: Faber & Faber, 1988), pp.9, 13.

14. Ibid., p.14.

15. Ibid.

16. Kavanagh, *Collected Poems*, p.202.

17. Ibid., p.10.

18. See Anthony Cronin, 'Patrick Kavanagh: Alive and Well in Dublin', in *Heritage Now: Irish Literature in the English Language* (Dingle: Brandon Books, 1982), p.187: 'The impression they [the lyrics in *Ploughman and Other Poems*] give is one of fully learned and absorbed accomplishment rather than otherwise. Georgian may not be the precise word, but the verse-turns and line endings suggest a man whose acquaintance with fairly recent poetic literature had been ... profitable and is being put to good literary use.' See also Foster, *Colonial Consequences*, pp.98–100.

19. See O'Loughlin, *After Kavanagh*, pp.20–1.

20. Kavanagh, *Complete Poems*, p.9.

21. Kavanagh, *Collected Poems*, pp.8, 10–11, 6.

22. Ibid., p.68.

23. See Terence Brown, *Ireland's Literature: Selected Essays* (Mullingar: Lilliput Press, 1988), pp.111–12, and Quinn, *Patrick Kavanagh*, p.275.

24. Kavanagh, *Collected Poems*, p.121.

25. Kavanagh, *Selected Poems*, p.167.

26. Kavanagh, *Collected Poems*, p.208.

27. See Quinn, *Patrick Kavanagh*, pp.322–4. On *By Night Unstarred*, see Brown, *Ireland's Literature*, p.111.
28. Kavanagh, *Collected Poems*, pp.116–18.
29. Ibid., p.181.
30. Ibid., p.182.
31. Ibid., p.120.
32. Foster, *Colonial Consequences*, pp.106–7.
33. Kavanagh, *Collected Poems*, p.80.
34. Kavanagh, *Collected Prose*, pp.20, 21, 27.
35. Kavanagh, *Collected Poems*, p.15.
36. Ibid., pp.28, 38, 43, 50, 116, 128, 184, 200, 221, 226, 230, 235. Anthony Cronin insightfully describes Kavanagh's conduct in the libel trial of 1954 as 'Parnassian'. See Anthony Cronin, *Dead as Doornails* (Dublin: Dolmen Press, 1976; rpt Poolbeg Press, 1980), p.100.
37. Michael Allen, 'Provincialism and Recent Irish Poetry: The Importance of Patrick Kavanagh', in *Two Decades of Irish Writing*, ed. Douglas Dunn (Cheadle Hulme: Carcanet Press, 1975), p.29.
38. Kavanagh, *Collected Poems*, p.227.
39. See Patrick Kavanagh, *November Haggard, Uncollected Prose and Verse of Patrick Kavanagh*, ed. Peter Kavanagh (New York: Peter Kavanagh Hand Press, 1971), p.69: 'Parochialism and provincialism are direct opposites. A provincial is always trying to live by other people's loves, but a parochial is self-sufficient. A great deal of this parochialism with all its intended intensities and courage continued in rural Ireland up till a few years ago and possibly will continue in some form forever.' Cited in Foster, *Colonial Consequences*, p.101.
40. Patrick Kavanagh, *The Green Fool* (Harmondsworth: Penguin, 1987), p.187.
41. Some of the poem's appeal for Kavanagh, one suspects, lay in its narrative: the scholar, who insists on teaching 'Greek verbs and Latin nouns', against the nationalist 'dreamer of Young Ireland' in a time and place when 'They talk Repeal the whole night long' gets the final word in the last verse, with its famous concluding line:

> And what to me is Gael or Gall?
> Less than the Latin or the Greek –
> I teach these by the dim rush-light
> In smoky cabins night and week.
> But what avail my teaching slight?
>> Years hence, in rustic speech, a phrase,
>> As in wild earth a Grecian vase!

See Padraic Colum, *The Poet's Circuits: Collected Poems of Ireland* (Dublin: Dolmen Press, 1985), p.27.
42. Kavanagh, *Collected Poems*, p.148. For examples of personification, see 'Freedom', 'Pride', 'Slavery', 'Grass of Convention', 'Frustration's holy well', 'Boredom's bed', 'Wisdom on her knees', and capitalized properties such as 'Doom' and 'the tyrants Love and Life and Time' (Kavanagh, *Collected Poems*, pp.13, 28, 31, 133, 149, 171, 196, 110, 115). For examples of apostrophe, see the poems opening 'O commemorate me', 'O the prickly sow thistle', 'O cruel are the woman of Dublin's fair city', 'O I had a future', 'O come all ye tragic poets', 'O stony grey soil of Monaghan' (Kavanagh, *Collected Poems*, pp.227, 218, 199, 190, 186, 157, 38, 222).

43. Heaney, 'From Monaghan to the Grand Canal', p.116.
44. O'Loughlin, *After Kavanagh*, p.23. O'Loughlin here follows Daniel Corkery's concept of the 'Hidden Ireland', elaborated in the 1920s and 1930s, Kavanagh's formative years. It posits that, following the dispossession of the Gaelic ruling classes during the Plantations and under Penal Law, and hence the end of their patronage, their bards and musicians merged with the Irish masses, where they enriched existing folk music and poetry.
45. Kavanagh, *Collected Poems*, p.41. See also Kavanagh, *Selected Poems*, p.151.
46. Kavanagh, *Collected Poems*, p.41.
47. Kavanagh, *Collected Pruse*, pp.14, 22.
48. Heaney, 'From Monaghan to the Grand Canal', pp.24–7.
49. See Quinn, *Patrick Kavanagh*, pp.5–7; also Cronin, *Dead as Doornails*, p.92.
50. For example, Stephen Regan (ed.), *Irish Writing: An Anthology of Irish Literature in English 1789–1939* (Oxford: Oxford University Press, 2004), which has a section on ballads, albeit these are Catholic-nationalist ones only. For a discussion of this, and the other inadequacies of this anthology, see my review in *Irish Studies Review*, 13, 1 (2005), pp.106–12.
51. Most of Carson's poetry has some kind of song presence; but see, in particular, his use of the long line and 'The Ballad of H.M.S. Belfast' in *First Language*, and the poems taking their cue from the titles of traditional Irish music tunes which make up *The Twelfth of Never*, a book which refers its readers to its 'folk-song influences' by way of Colm Ó Lochlainn's *Irish Street Ballads and More Irish Street Ballads*.
52. Cronin, *Dead as Doornails*, p.92.
53. Kavanagh, *Collected Poems*, p.157.
54. Ibid., p.173.
55. Longley, 'Poetic Forms and Social Malformations', p.208.
56. David Lloyd, *Anomalous States: Irish Writing and the Post-Colonial Moment* (Dublin: Lilliput Press, 1993), pp.89–90.
57. Kavanagh, *Collected Poems*, p.184.
58. It was the American classicist, Milman Parry (1902–35) who was the first (in 1928) to fully articulate unease concerning the existence of Homer and oral features of Homeric epic: in the words of Walter J. Ong, Parry discovered and proved that 'virtually every distinctive feature of Homeric poetry is due to the economy enforced on it by oral methods of composition'. See Walter J. Ong, *Orality and Literacy: The Technologizing of the Word* (London: Routledge, 1982; rpt 1991), p.21.
59. Kavanagh, *Collected Poems*, p.187.
60. Lloyd, *Anomalous States*, p.98. It should be noted that while both O'Loughlin and Lloyd are alert to post-colonial dimensions in Irish writing, O'Loughlin finds coherence of voice and expressivity in folk ballad and song, whereas Lloyd discovers the opposite – a disturbing incoherence which confounded attempts by Young Ireland and other Nationalist ideologues, such as Douglas Hyde, to harness such material to a unitary national voice. This mixed, 'adulterated' quality makes the form, for Lloyd, paradigmatic of Joyce's hybrid treatment of national identity in *Ulysses*. See the discussion in the next chapter.
61. Ibid., p. 98.

CHAPTER NINE

'In Blinking Blankness': The Last Poems

JOHN GOODBY

It took Patrick Kavanagh two years following his operation for lung cancer in March 1955 to produce the 'noo pomes', and another two to begin elaborating his supreme fiction of a poetic rebirth by the banks of the Grand Canal. The symbolism of the 'fiction' is bold, obvious and immediately appealing: the dirty urban waterway becomes a poetic birth canal, the water pouring from the lock gates is baptismal, sacramental, the sunshine, greenery and swans prelapsarian and Edenic. In the most general terms, it is a form of return to childhood, even the womb. It provided a perfect, if belated, rationalization for his enforced dropping of the role of journalistic gadfly and bardic prophet, and an explanation for the poems' humility and high celebratory mode. The Dublin years were now presented as a hiatus, and the poetry which recorded it was endowed with the significance of a vision vouchsafed to a saint, or the granting of a prayer to someone who has completed a pilgrimage. Yet however ineffable the sentiment, the linguistic heterogeneity of these works, as I argued in my previous chapter, undercuts any singular, transcendent message in the best poems.

Before looking at the Canal Bank sonnets in more detail, however, I want briefly to consider their contexts. One point to be made is about the form itself. Kavanagh had often used the sonnet, and taken liberties with it, yet it is more preponderant than at any other stage of his career in these poems (thirteen of the twenty-two poems in the 1956–59 section of the 2005 *Selected Poems*, for example). There is a continual play between the demands of the form and the improvisatory philosophy which attempts to destabilize and push these to breaking-point through absurd rhyme, distended line-length, hyphenated compounding, stretched syntax and so on.

A sonnet of January 1955, 'Nineteen Fifty-Four', sums up just where Kavanagh felt he stood after the awfulness of that year, and on the eve of his operation. He finds himself wanting to laugh or to cry, but unable to do either – that is, wishing to be able to surrender to some strong and simplifying emotion, or find another 'formula' capable of giving a perspective to the 'hellish scatter' of recent events. Everywhere he looks, he claims, 'a part of me is exiled from the I'. The departed year yields no frame for interpretation:

> O Nineteen Fifty-Four you leave and will not listen,
> And do not care whether I curse or weep.[1]

Within two years, however, Kavanagh would be asking himself whether it might not be better to accept precisely the 'exile' of 'a part of me ... from the I'; that is, to collapse the egocentricity and angst which a poem like 'Nineteen Fifty-Four' dramatizes and turn what seems to be a weakness into a strength. 'Wisdom', which immediately postdates his operation, begins as twelve agonized and questioning lines of the kind found in 'Nineteen Fifty-Four' ('Can you show sick heart where purpose lies?'), before breaking off and restarting as a fourteen-line block of couplets. The hiatus represents a crucial change of approach, for the seven-couplet paragraph reads as a proto-Canal Bank sonnet, one which revealingly marks the first appearance of the characteristic imagery of the 'noo pomes'. The imagery includes a walk along the banks of the canal on a summer evening, the realization that 'This was the water that mirrored our childhood eyes', and that its greenery and vegetation 'Can give the protection the soul needs'. The major insight, although it is blurred in this prototypical formulation, is that this understanding requires a humbling of intellectual pretensions; the speaker, finally, is astonished to discover that although he is one who has 'read, thought and suffered' more than most, he

> Can only offer to the hungry mass
> Unkempt water and the immortality of grass.[2]

The vision of what the soul truly needs, and therefore of what the poet can offer his fellow-citizens – 'the hungry mass', starved of spiritual sustenance

– is dishevelled, ordinary, unchanging and was under one's nose all the time. It is a vision rooted in a childlike wonder, which has explicitly Christian undertones ('unless ye be as little children').

These lines are in couplets; but two poems after 'Wisdom' in Peter Kavanagh's *Complete Poems*, comes 'The Hospital'. This has a Petrarchan rhyme scheme, and is clearly the next step along the road to the 'noo pomes'; still somewhat over-correct and formal by comparison with them, it is nevertheless clear in establishing that the importance of things lies in the way you look at them, not in the things themselves, and in its discovery of the 'heat' of love in the objects of the mundane world.

The importance of perspective, of the angle of observation, is a warning that for Kavanagh subject is becoming largely incidental – albeit, it helps if the subject is one which is commonplace, everyday, unobtrusive. 'The Hospital', which can be misread as a realist poem, is more of an indirect consideration of the workings of poetic self-consciousness than an observational piece on Kavanagh and his surroundings. It makes of those surroundings, 'the common and banal' hospital with its 'square cubicles in a row, / Plain concrete, wash basins' the medium for posing an aesthetic-spiritual question, rather than turning them into the realist details which will be symbolically transfigured.[3] That the surroundings are described as 'an art lover's woe' is a sign of this self-referential, aesthetic-spiritual focus, a complaint that is registered purely so that the speaker can demonstrate that 'nothing whatever is by love debarred'. If there are few adjectives, and description is rudimentary, this is not to satisfy a realist-symbolist impulse so much as to offer a clear model of how the imagination operates on its materials. As if to reinforce this, the sentences are clumsy, if effective, in their compression and inversion, and the octet ends with the expansive banality of 'the inexhaustible adventure of a gravelled yard' (with its echo of Keats imagining himself, in his famous 'Adam's Dream' letter to Benjamin Bailey of 1817, as a sparrow 'pick[ing] about the Gravel').[4] It is disinterested love, or *agape*, that transfigures things (such as 'The main gate that was bent by a heavy lorry') to the extent that simply 'naming' them becomes an Adamic 'love-act and its pledge'. But although told that 'we must' record 'love's mystery without claptrap', and 'Snatch out of time the passionate transitory', Kavanagh does not make the mistake of thinking that 'claptrap' includes poetic rhetoric. He spurns one kind of Parnassianism, it may be (the kind which produces 'an art lover's woe'), but does so in his own Parnassian terms.

Parnassian involves pastoral, and 'Leaves of Grass', following 'The Hospital', admits how the weeds in a Dublin street once called its speaker 'vainly from kerbstones on Bachelors Walk', singing a tale of the land he had left and calling him to return. Now, however, although he still hears their siren-like voices, he has 'hit upon the secret door that leads to the heaven / Of human satisfaction' because at last he is able to see 'the ground / Tumultuous with living, infinite variety'.[5] The terms of an urban pastoral, already hinted at in 'Wisdom', are being consolidated, willed into existence: the speaker is at last at ease in urban Dublin, no longer on a fruitless 'Bachelors Walk', having discovered a way to be wedded to the land which allows him to reconcile himself to the city. In 'October' (again a sonnet) the speaker can 'walk an arboreal street on the edge of a town' and find the rural within the urban, such that he wants to 'throw myself on the public street without caring / For anything but the prayering that the earth offers'.[6] 'Earth', like 'ground', reinscribes the land as loved rural territory within the urban scene, but Kavanagh is careful to avoid escapism by placing the speaker's new 'prayering' acceptance within the glare of mortality ('It is October over all my life ... the light is staring'), and the image of a young-old self watching the present one: 'A man is ploughing ground for winter wheat / And my nineteen years weigh heavily on my feet'. 'Winter wheat', a late fruiting, is what the 'noo pomes' are.

It is precisely the quality of this self-consciousness which, it seems to me, Declan Kiberd misses in claiming that Kavanagh ruralized Dublin in a reactionary way:

> In the familiar manner of other post-colonial capitals, Dublin was overrun by unplanned migrations of rural folk, who had no sooner settled than they were consumed by fake nostalgia for a pastoral Ireland they had 'lost'.
>
> Patrick Kavanagh was the test-case here: at first, when he was still close to his Monaghan roots, he denounced the false con- sciousness of the peasant periphery, but after a decade or more in Dublin, he fell back into line with it, going to extraordinary

lengths to recreate Baggott Street as an urban pastoral, as 'my Pembrokeshire'. And that invented Ireland proved far more attractive to poetry-readers among the new Dubliners than Kavanagh's bitter indictment of rural torpor in *The Great Hunger*. The conversion of Baggott Street into a rural idyll proved palatable to those politicians and architects intent of effecting somewhat similar transformations themselves, imposing a ruralist grid of community onto an urban setting.[7]

This is right, it seems to me, about Kavanagh's 'recreation' (which, however, applies in both senses of the word), but wrong, and in a too-literal way, in seeing it as some kind of return to Revival poetics. Above all, the poems of 1956–59 do not look to the past, or engage in the 'backward look'. Before this point, Kavanagh's celebratory lyrics – 'In Memory of My Mother', 'On Reading a Book on Common Wild Flowers', for example – had been retrospective and rural. But the new poems are all in the present tense or future-aspiring. Kiberd seems determined to ignore the fact that fantasy, humour and playfulness constitute a different yet equally valid form of radicalism to his own more political one, ignoring the fact that style itself may have its material, subversive and liberatory dimensions. He counters one form of utilitarianism (that of the 'politicians and architects'), that is, with a mirror-image of it (the preference for 'bitter indictment'), to reinforce a narrow realist paradigm. This narrowness is underlined in his assessment of *The Great Hunger*: for 'torpor' is surely inadequate to cover the anomie, spiritual death-in-life, and ground-down, distorted sexuality which Kavanagh targeted in it.

Form, at least as much as content, provides the subject of the 'noo pomes', which focus on process rather than artifactual perfection, and are open-ended, self-effacing and anti-egotistical in a self-performing manner: 'No, no, no, I know I was not important', 'Come Dance with Kitty Stobling' begins (Kitty Stobling being Kavanagh's invented name for his Muse). As Antoinette Quinn puts it, '"The self-slaved" advocates a programme of unselving', and the result is a discovery of something approximating to the state of mind of the 'green fool' of his autobiography – it is possible to agree with Kiberd on this much – whose visionary, antic disposition has been turned to self-erasing advantage.[8] The obstreperous ego has not so much vanished, of course, as metamorphosed into a new, cunningly garrulous, stylistic ebullience: the poem's final couplet claims 'I had a very pleasant journey, thank you sincerely / For giving me my madness back, or nearly'.[9] Kiberd's claim of regression has a point, then, but it lacks any kind of dialectical sense; Kavanagh returns to the visionary, but in a way which exposes and exploits aspects of the 1930s lyrics which had previously been scarcely noticed.

In elevating the mask of holy fool to that of the poet-as-seer, Kavanagh clearly drew on religious paradigms in order to fulfil the promise of 'Auditors In' and 'turn away to where the Self reposes, / The placeless Heaven that's under all our noses'. But he was also rejecting, as 'To Hell with Commonsense' has it, the 'secular / Wisdom' of churches, colleges and public life. The self has been baptismally cleansed, as 'Is' claims, and possession is now seen as unnecessary to true love:

> To look on is enough
> In the business of love ...
> Mention water again ...
> It washes out Original Sin.[10]

The poem has the future orientation Kiberd misses: Kavanagh tells himself to name the 'everydays of nature' for 'the future', abjuring the 'analytic' for an 'epic' of observation of the quotidian. The childlike wonderment conveyed by short, nursery-song-like lines and feminine rhymes ('blouses'/'houses', 'gables'/'fables') is part of the 'life of a street' Kavanagh is intent on presenting. This new self presents itself, like the Freudian Id, as pure being; existing in a single, continuous present, or no-time, future-orientated insofar as it is libidinally desiring, fluid, spending, frankly admiring the pleasures of the material world (the 'blouses' are 'red' and worn by 'girls'). This self therefore has no baggage from the past, or of anticipation in the usual sense (of work, politics, love). As 'Dear Folks' has it, it accepts the way things are, unburdening itself with a paradoxically energetic passivity, for very little 'was worth mind storage', among them memories of those women who had fallen 'for the unusual, / For the Is that Is ... The poet's'. The 'Is that Is' suggests that the speaker had a version of the new self even before this point. What is new is that memories which stem from his ability to exist solely in the present (that is, of the pleasures that accrued from that ability) are now seen to have been a contradiction in terms, and are jettisoned. He will not be mired in attachment to past romances: his 'main aim' now is to continue

> To walk Parnassus right into the sunset
> Detached in love where pygmies cannot pin you
> To the ground like Gulliver. So good luck and cheers.[11]

The main trope is one derived from religious models of dying to the world in order to find the true life of the spirit, but energized with comic gusto rather than resignation or self-pity. The poems give anarchic counsel and set verbal energies against the discourses of the powers-that-be, while counselling a merely outward, surreptitiously subversive obedience, a secular version of 'Render unto Caesar'. The examples are reminiscent of New Testament parables. But, rather than being Christ himself, the speaker is usually figured as a humble disciple relying on the charity of believers as he makes his way through the world, casually introduced, as a 'passing gift of affection / Tossed from the windows of high charity' by members of the populace not normally associated with poetry (the 'office girl' or 'civil servant'). These gifts, cheerfully bestowed, are not to be despised, and are a pretext for inner 'repose' and for offering as poetry 'praise, praise, praise' to the world – a typical triple repetition – and its simple, unremarkable being ('The way it happened and the way it is').[12]

Of course, there are objections to be made to this. What is the difference, for example, between what Kavanagh advocates and a reactionary assertion that 'Whatever is, is right'? At what point does wise passivity shade into uncomplaining acceptance of injustice and unfairness? The answer is, of course, that sometimes in Kavanagh this is what happens; but that, in the best of the poems, there is a verbal energy and ideological subversiveness which makes of passivity an active, continually challenging engagement with the world and language. There is a gender subtext, for example, which is unusual, to put it mildly, for Irish male authors in the 1950s. Thus, in 'Question to Life', as elsewhere, women are gifted with more insight into the method in the speaker's madness; rather than being written out or marginalized, they are energetic comforters, succourers, embodiments of the larger Muse, Kitty Stobling, 'Miss Universe' herself. 'Love' waits for the poet, he tells himself, with the 'violence that she chooses / From the tepidity of the common round'. She is 'beyond exhaustion or scorn' and, with calculated earthiness, is invoked for the 'sensual throb / Of the explosive body, the tumultuous thighs!', a 'Miss Universe' both of the kind displayed in a televised beauty pageant and the cosmos itself. Though vulgar, Kavanagh's point is that the 'lecher's art' has no power over the candour of such desire, even though 'she is not the virgin who was wise' according to conventional codes of sexual conduct (the final couplet echoes two of Milton's sonnets to reinforce the contrast with life-denying abstemiousness).[13]

Of course, the sexist cliché of the perfect woman – sexually experienced, yet pure – lurks here, yet its potential offensiveness is defused, it seems to me, by Kavanagh's comedy, in the bathos of 'throb', 'explosive' and 'tumultuous thighs' (the latter mocking Yeats's far more dubious 'Leda and the Swan'). 'Dear Folks' and 'Question to Life' also highlight how, while the bombast of the pre-1956 poems can grate, in the 'noo pomes' this is largely countered by the humour (often at the expense of the self) and the ragged, Skeltonic, edge-of-doggerel, style of 'the poet', who will do anything to set up his next rhyme and (like a rap performer) keep the propulsive energy flowing.

The vision Kavanagh offers is profoundly ambiguous; of a self which is a non-self, simple Being which possesses the syntactical onrush of Becoming, a commodity which rejects commodification, a wise 'Miss' who is not one of the wise virgins. There appears to be more and less at stake than previously. The poems are about 'posthumous existence', an unearned survival, and so they affect, at least, to care nothing any longer for reputation (as 'Yellow Vestment' has it, 'Do not be worried about what the neighbours will say').[14] The road to 'nothing' which leads to a 'placeless' heaven is proved to be a kind of via negativa, a route to enlightenment which runs over the ego, reflected in the poem's paradoxical treatment of its major sources of metaphor – religion, but also money, the lack of which is inverted to become a sign of election, and elevated as spiritual wealth. So, in 'Song at Fifty', the speaker 'Finds in his spendthrift purse / A bankbook writ in verse / And borrowers of purity / Offering substantial security / To him ... the ne'er- / Do-well millionaire': as 'Dear Folks' informs us, this poet is 'back in circulation'.[15]

No longer torn between town and country, the poems are aware that a correlative for the rural Monaghan vision can now be realized in Dublin in the form of a Parnassian style which mixes high and low,

learned and vernacular, classical and romantic, mythological and natu-
ralistic. This style takes the form of an urban pastoral embodied in the
two Canal Bank sonnets, as Kavanagh – in using them to open *Come Dance
with Kitty Stobling* – understood very well. As usual, the position of the
'unselving' narrator, like his disparate materials, shifts with disconcerting rapidity.

'Canal Bank Walk', the best known of the Canal Bank poems, is a case
in point. It opens with a typically brilliant Kavanaghesque stumble on
the compound 'Leafy-with-love banks', beside the canal lock and its
pouring, redemptive waters, these simultaneously symbolizing that he
is doing 'the will of God' by 'wallow[ing] in the habitual, the banal' in
being beside the canal, and encouraging him to 'Grow with nature ... as
before I grew' (that is, in childhood). The speaker notes a 'bright stick
trapped' in the water behind the lock, the slight breeze is personified as
a 'third / Party to the couple kissing on an old seat', and, in a leap of
vision, a bird is described as 'gathering materials for the nest for the Word'.
The vocative plea, which is so common in these poems, is directed at the
'unworn world' to 'enrapture me, encapture me', to feed material and
spiritual senses and 'give me ad lib / To pray unselfconsciously'. In
effect, it is a prayer for prayer, one with the same meta-narrative level of
aesthetic self-referentiality as any of the other poems in this vein for all
its language of innocence, purity and origin. It is, however, more content than most to end in paradox:

> For this soul needs to be honoured with a new dress woven
> From green and blue things and arguments that cannot be
> proven.[16]

Rather than any specific subject, it is the syntax, lexis and other formal
aspects of this sonnet which attract our attention, productive as they are
of its surging movement, expansive energies, and tonal 'wobble' (what
to make of its reference to hackneyed 'eternal voices'?). The iambic pentameter provides a ground-bass, as it were, but the sonnet opens with a
fourteen-syllable line, and there are several of fifteen and sixteen sylla-
bles each. This disconcerting metrical effect of the opening is syntactical
too: the main verb governing the first clause is a present participle
('pouring'), which has the effect of reducing the distance between the
object of the sentence (the banks and water) and what they are doing

(enacting the symbolic baptism). The first verb in the next sentence is even more unnerving; 'the bright stick trapped' may be an inversion of 'trapped' as an adjective (for 'the bright, trapped stick'), but the clause needs a verb, so we will probably at least consider 'trapped' as a verb. The question then is: 'trapped' what? Or – more likely, perhaps – we have read the intransitive 'The bright stick [that was] trapped'. However, the sense of 'trapped' as both transitive and intransitive lingers to worry the sentence, because it remains syntactically – whatever we decide – a list without a main verb or subject.

The trapped 'bright stick' had already appeared in Kavanagh's work a year earlier as a 'branch' in 'A Letter and an Environment from Dublin', in the journal *Nimbus*:

> The trouble about writing 'from Dublin' or any other place is that we may be forced by the theme to treat as exclusive to the place things that are common to all places ... I want to report about the Grand Canal bank last summer. I report on the part of the bank just to the west of Baggot Street Bridge. Most days last summer in the beautiful heat I lay there on the grass in an ante-natal roll with a hand under my head. And because that grass and sun and canal were good to me they were a particular, personal, grass, sun and canal. Nobody anywhere else in the world knew that place as I knew it. There was a branch in the water and it is still in the immortal water in my mind; and the dent in the bank can never be changed nor the wooden seat.[17]

This reinforces the point about the poem's relativism, I think. Kavanagh is claiming that his vision can be experienced anywhere, as long as the locale is internalized and loved sufficiently, and his phrasing recalls Traherne's 'orient and immortal wheat' ('immortal water') rather than any 'rural idyll', or the pieties of a specific place. The branch 'is still in the immortal water of my mind', suggesting that the hobbled syntax of the sentence in which it occurs is enacting the stasis of his mental image of the branch. The poem itself seems blithely unaware of this as a problem, in any case, and makes a principle of syntactic distortion and verbal playfulness throughout.

Take, for example, the compound adjective 'Leafy-with-love', which opens the poem so abruptly, burgeoning through connective hyphenations like the canal-side foliage it describes, or the neologism 'encapture'. 'Encapture', of course, mimics 'enrapture' two words before it, and, like it, bespeaks a relish of verbal excess for its own sake, since the prefixes could be dropped without any discernible alteration to the strict meaning of the line. But 'strict meaning' is precisely what the poem is out to sub-vert; 'encapture' may at one level be merely a gratuitous, even childish, echo, but — like the compounding and other unusual features of the poem, such as strained rhyme ('banal', 'canal') and hypermetrical lines — it contributes to its effectiveness by enacting its subject of abandon-ment, casualness, the fortuitousness of spiritual grace. It also recalls David Lloyd's point about the heterogeneity and 'adulteration' of dis-courses in Joyce, a process which ranges 'from a phenomenon of Irish colloquial speech to which Oscar Wilde gave the name "malapropism" to the ceaseless interpenetration of different discourses'. As Lloyd notes, malapropism varies from casual misspeaking, which may be intentional and critical, to a sign of lack of mastery of English (he cites Ulysses' 'syphilisation' for English civilization, or 'Don't cast your nasturtiums on my character'). The point of this is not so much a direct comparison with Joyce, as recognition that in both authors there may be 'not [so much] an opposition ... between coherent "voices", but their entire intercontamination'.[18] At this level, however, and despite the manifold differences, one may understand Kavanagh's work as partaking of 'the double voice of parody', as Bakhtin called it, a rapidity of tonal modu-lation that precludes the establishment of 'the order of probability that structures mimetic verisimilitude'. Such a process would take us back to the issue of 'roughage' and Michael Allen's critique of 'Lines Written on a Seat on the Grand Canal' discussed in the previous chapter.[19] Such 'modulation' is evident enough in the combination of a stress on the 'banal' with exalted apostrophe ('O unworn world ...'), its lumping together of cliché ('a third / Party') the archaic-spiritual ('fabulous grass and eternal voices'), and the wordplay already discussed. 'Canal Bank Walk' is simultaneously clumsily monosyllabic ('that I do / The will of God'), relishes oral tradition, and exposes the autodidact in its taste for sonorous polysyllables. The whole poem is constructed to give a sense of its 'ad lib' performativity and ultimately paradoxical, zen-like wisdom 'woven / From green and blue things and arguments that can-not be proven'. It is a riskily assembled yet shapely 'nest for the Word', and its 'overflowing speech' is contained within a sonnet, albeit in a way which almost leads to that form's dissolution.

'Lines Written on a Seat on the Grand Canal, Dublin' is both a continuation of and a reworking of 'Canal Bank Walk'. It is, in a narrative sense, what the speaker found on his 'walk' along the canal, and the poem's epigraph is evidently taken from such a seat: '"Erected to the Memory of Mrs Dermod O'Brien"'. This sonnet seems to reverse its partner's dissolutionary trend, with shorter lines (closer to the pentameter) and sentences (five as opposed to three, although they break the sonnet structure up rather more), and a centripetal rather than centrifugal movement. In citing the dedication, Kavanagh is quoting what is, in effect, a funerary inscription, and this places the poem in a *sistae viator* tradition which reaches back, through Wordsworth, Gray and the Renaissance poets, to classical antiquity (Catullus's '*Ave atque vale*'). 'Notcaring' here means a contraction of the self, a consideration of its mortality, rather than its expansion (as in 'Canal Bank Walk'), for the speaker raises the prospect of 'Athy / And other far-flung towns mythologies' only to reject them for himself: 'O commemorate me with no hero-courageous / Tomb – just a canal-bank seat for the passer-by.' But 'Lines Written on a Seat' is the first poem's companion in its subject, its verbal coinages ('Niagarously'), compounds ('hero-courageous'), weird adverbial adjectives ('stilly'/'Greeny'), flowing enjambments and apostrophes, and its sense of the poem as a cunningly ramshackle-seeming concatenation of materials held together by an 'edgy, visionary subjectivity' which confounds mundane reality.[20] The rhymes are similarly outrageous, and still more reminiscent of the approximations of ballad: 'apologies'/'bridges', 'still'/'beautiful', 'silence'/'islands'. The 'swan', 'Parnassian islands' and 'mythologies' mingle Yeats and Mallarmé, but they are thrown together with a barge and a canal-side bench, the incongruity raised to the level of paradox by the canal lock that 'roars' 'in the tremendous silence' (an echo of George Eliot's 'roar that is on the other side of silence', perhaps). 'No one will speak in prose', the speaker claims, but it is the 'will of God', we know, to 'wallow in the habitual, the banal' prose of existence, and Kavanagh manages gently to crash-land the Parnassian flight in what should sound like the dullest of throwaway lines, but which actually offers perfectly cadenced closure: 'just a canal-bank seat for the passer-by'.

Come Dance with Kitty Stobling ran to three editions within a year and made Kavanagh the single biggest influence on the emerging Irish poets of the 1960s, among them not only Heaney, Kennelly and Durcan but John Ennis, Michael Hartnett and Eavan Boland.[21] He became a cult figure in Dublin before his death in 1967, the 'King of the Kids' in Brendan Behan's phrase, a father-figure to James Liddy's Arena and Brian Lynch's The Holy Door, acknowledged even by those ostensibly at odds with his poetic, such as Michael Smith and Trevor Joyce, the editors of the tougher-minded, avant-garde-inclined The Lace Curtain (1969–76). A jointly written valedictory editorial in the second issue of this influential little magazine mentions Kavanagh's 'almost miraculous moral tenacity and integrity', and notes that '[His] survival was [his] own individual achievement; [he was] wise enough and great enough not to care for the plaudits and "respect" of uncivilized and hypocritical Dublin "educated" society. The Lace Curtain salutes the living spirit of [this] great writer.'[22] But although Kavanagh's posterity was large, by the time of Collected Poems (1964) he himself was a spent force.

It would be tempting to say that this was because the tension between form and conversational casualness had slackened to such a degree, loosened by a 'not caring' poetic, that it became mere carelessness. But this is to accept the formalist notion that there is an ideal form of the sonnet within which certain metrical, syntactic and tonal licenses are allowed to play. What I have been suggesting, however, is that Kavanagh used the sonnet form as a discursive pretext for constellating various contradictory materials which it would not otherwise have been possible to bring together, dissolving and reconstituting the form, as it were, on his own terms. 'Tension' is a New Critical category which points towards a model of autonomous resolution, ironic balance and containment which is in some crucial ways at odds with these poems. Seamus Heaney, in his two essays on Kavanagh, published in Preoccupations (1980) and The Government of the Tongue (1988), uses the image of Kavanagh as a tightrope walker to describe his daring, all-or-nothing style. However, the either – or polarity of this is still too much in thrall to the poem as artefact as opposed to process. I would suggest, instead, that the juggler, who can drop a few balls without ceasing to juggle, might be a better image for what Kavanagh does.

This is not, of course, to make a case for the 1960s poems, to argue that a poetry about inconsequentiality did not become inconsequential, that a flexibly embodied mode of poetic being did not harden into opinionatedness. In his 'Author's Note' to the Collected Poems, Kavanagh had written of having 'lost my Messianic compulsion ... in the summer of 1955', but it had not, of course, ever fully left him. Rather, as Antoinette Quinn finely observes of his prose memoir 'Self-Portrait', 'the self-cancelling syntax of [Kavanagh's claim that] "My purpose in life was to have no purpose" betrays the writer's incorrigible sense of engagement ... Here involuntariness is willed into being.'[23] It was the return of this form of a triumph of the will which eventually stifled the risky dialogism of the 'noo pomes'. Self-mockery turned outwards and became satire and protest again, rather than subversion; the complex mixture of pagan and Christian, folk and classical, vernacular and canonical was made cartoonish; the mocking dismemberment of old forms in a libidinal verbal onrush hardened into the doggerel Kavanagh had so often risked to gain his best effects.

Tragically, Kavanagh understood this only too well. 'In Blinking Blankness: Three Efforts' (1963) he admits to being nonplussed by the blank page as he sits down to write: 'But the wren, the wren got caught in the furze', he notes, '[a]nd the eagle turned turkey on my farm'. Ironically, although it alludes to a folk tradition, the poem lacks the edgy energy of the late 1950s poems (and it is one of the better efforts of this final phase).[24] The last stanza laments:

> Nature is not enough, I've used up lanes,
> Waters that run in rivers or are stagnant;
> But I have no message, and the sense
> Of no red idea can make me pregnant.[25]

'Personal Problem' (1965) shows this same lament driven to the verge of despair:

> What am I to do
> With the void growing more awful at every hour?
> I lacked a classical discipline. I grew
> Uncultivated and now the soil turns sour[26]

Again, Kavanagh seems to miss the point of his own earlier, more confident practices: he may not ever have possessed 'classical discipline' (in terms of a classical education, or a 'well-made' academic sense of the poem-as-artefact), but he had been able to deploy his residue of vernacular literary attitudes, one of which, ironically, was an ease with popular forms of eighteenth-century neoclassicism, with a controlled indiscipline that perfectly served his poetic purpose.

Such passages seem to show that Kavanagh had lost the sense, if he ever had it, of precisely what it was that had made the 'noo pomes' possible. On this point, I feel, it is not just a question of the way the discursive space, prised open by the personal crises of 1952–55, enabled such work by temporarily abolishing the desire for mastery. They also raise the question of the extent to which he knew how the poems worked. Technically, Kavanagh laboured mightily to maintain the space for writing which had opened up. In Quinn's words,

> At this stage in his career, [he] was obsessed with technique as never before, with finding modes of expression that would seem spontaneous and uncontrived. He was trying to circumvent the preacher in himself, the pundit within; to offset his tendency to the axiomatic and the abstract by stressing the importance of not being earnest, or rather of not appearing to be earnest.[27]

The qualification here is crucial, because it is often only by 'not appearing' to overcome an inner censor that it can be evaded. No successful poetry is ever completely comprehended by its author, and in order for it to be created language often has to be used to outwit the mind's internal discursive powers, the unconscious enabled to evade the conscious and controlling ego. Kavanagh's relaxation, we might say, was always under threat as an outsider, marginal writer in Dublin, his arrogance an inverted reflection of this inferior place, and such feigning of 'not caring' could not be kept up indefinitely.

In revealing and unravelling the knot of linguistic obsession which is, according to some modern accounts, the unconscious, Kavanagh did succeed for a time in allowing language to speak the poet as well as to speak his own forms of language. This enables a critic to show the inadequacy of the expressivist model of poetics so often applied to his work, and to correct the balance between the 'real' and the transcendent on the one hand, and more discursive notions of language use on the other. For Kavanagh's practices show a relinquishing of authority and a decentred, mobile sense of identity – one close to (but never quite) dissolving into the poems' structures, structures which embody the fluidity of the water they often celebrate – which irresistibly gesture towards more recent ways of reading the subject in the text than those of New Criticism, or of the Leavisism which (as Richard Kirkland has explained) have been the basis of so much recent criticism of Irish poetry.[28] Rather than removing poetry from the unconscious and from history, Kavanagh's later style suggests that it should be immersed in both more deeply.

This would involve, on the one hand, some recognition of the similarities between the style of the 'noo pomes' and Julia Kristeva's model for reading linguistic invention and disruption; that is, as a result of the pulsional pressures of the semiotic on the strictures and structures of language in the Symbolic Order. Equally, however, it requires more attention to socio-historical contexts. The period of the gestation and production of the 'noo pomes', 1955–57, marked the nadir of the fortunes of independent Ireland, immediately predating as it did the Lemass–Whitaker reforms of 1958–59. While recognizing the obvious dangers of literal and merely sociological interpretations, one needs to make the point that the coincidence of national abjection with stylistic triumph was not merely accidental. Kavanagh, for all his disdain for political-social reform (he opposed an Irish Welfare State, for example, unlike Austin Clarke), was no more immune from larger discursive pressures and public moods than most writers, and his 'not-caring' poetic at least invites a reading as a response to the times; namely, as a comic-desperate, semi-mystical dismemberment of the lyric 'I' at a time when society seemed to be imploding through economic stagnation and emigration. (We should remember that 1954, Kavanagh's personal *annus horribilis*, was the year of an essay collection entitled *The Vanishing Irish*, which calculated that the end of the nation as a viable entity would occur within two or three generations.)[29] At the same time, the chilled-out persona of the 'noo pomes' now appears almost spookily prescient of the attitudes which would arrive with international pop culture, and the prosperity and hedonism of the 1960s. Kavanagh discovered too late that he had forfeited the energies which had animated the Canal Bank poems. To state, as he did, that 'Private beauty and green happiness / Demand much courage' was a sign of the gap between a claim and its enactment through adequate linguistic and discursive daring: on the other hand –

and at the risk of making yet another contribution to the Kavanagh myth – few mid-century Irish writers had answered the call of his art with such 'courage', at once so 'casual and oracular', as he when it had been 'demanded'.[30]

NOTES

1. Patrick Kavanagh, *Collected Poems*, ed. Antoinette Quinn (Harmondsworth: Penguin, 2005), p.211.

2. Patrick Kavanagh, *The Complete Poems*, ed. Peter Kavanagh (Newbridge: Goldsmith Press, 1992), p.278.

3. Kavanagh, *Collected Poems*, p.217.

4. John Keats, *The Complete Poems*, ed. John Barnard (Harmondsworth: Penguin, 1973, rpt 1988), p.537.

5. Kavanagh, *Collected Poems*, pp.217–18.

6. Ibid., p.218.

7. Declan Kiberd, *Inventing Ireland: The Literature of the Modern Nation* (London: Jonathan Cape, 1995), p.492.

8. Antoinette Quinn, *Patrick Kavanagh: Born-Again Romantic* (Dublin: Gill & Macmillan, 1991), pp.401–2.

9. Kavanagh, *Collected Poems*, p.221.

10. Ibid., p.222.

11. Ibid., pp.224–5.

12. Ibid., p.221.

13. Ibid., p.231. See Milton's sonnets IX ('Therefore be sure ... Hast gained thy entrance, Virgin wise and pure') and XX ('He who of those delights can judge, and spare / To interpose them oft, is not unwise'). John Milton, *Milton's Sonnets*, ed. E.A.J. Honigmann (London: Macmillan, 1966), no page numbers.

14. Kavanagh, *Collected Poems.*, p.230.

15. Ibid., pp.226, 224.

16. Ibid., p.224.

17. Patrick Kavanagh, 'A Letter and an Environment from Dublin', *Nimbus*, 3, 3 (1956), p.15.

18. David Lloyd, *Anomalous States: Irish Writing and the Post-Colonial Moment* (Dublin: Lilliput Press, 1993), p.108.

19. Ibid., p.109.

20. Patrick Crotty (ed.), *Modern Irish Poetry: An Anthology* (Belfast: Blackstaff Press, 1995), p.31.

21. Eavan Boland has claimed, for example, that 'Kavanagh was a crucial poet as far as I was concerned. He still is. He was the living witness of the achieved poet for me.' See Jody Allen-Randolph, 'An Interview with Eavan Boland', in *Irish University Review:*

Special Issue on Eavan Boland, ed. Jody Allen-Randolph and Anthony Roche, 23, 1 (Spring/Summer 1993), p.118.

22. Michael Smith and Trevor Joyce, 'Editorial', *The Lace Curtain*, 2 (Spring 1970), p.2.

23. Quinn, *Patrick Kavanagh*, p.391.

24. As the note to the poem in *Collected Poems* reveals, the wren reference is to a St Stephen's Day (Boxing Day) custom, according to which groups of 'wren-boys' would call at neighbours' houses with a caged wren, reciting a verse about the 'king of the birds' and collecting money. Kavanagh uses a line from the Inniskeen wren-boys song.

25. Kavanagh, *Collected Poems*, p.250.

26. Ibid., p.259.

27. Quinn, *Patrick Kavanagh*, pp.402–3.

28. See Richard Kirkland, *Literature and Culture in Northern Ireland Since 1965: Moments of Danger* (London: Longman, 1996).

29. See John Goodby, 'Nation and Stagnation', *Irish Poetry Since 1950: From Stillness into History* (Manchester: Manchester University Press, 2000), pp.15–68.

30. John Wilson Foster, *Colonial Consequences: Essays in Irish Literature and Culture* (Dublin: Lilliput Press, 1991), p.103.

CHAPTER TEN

'The Door and What Came Through It': Aspects of Influence

BRUCE STEWART

> In any movement towards liberation it will be necessary to deny the normative authority of the dominant language or literary tradition.
>
> Seamus Heaney, 'The Redress of Poetry'

'OUR OWN DOUR WAY': KAVANAGH AND HEANEY AS ULSTER REGIONALISTS

The popularity of Patrick Kavanagh in Ireland today, north and south, is rooted in his feel for common experience, which has led Archbishop (now Cardinal) Seán Brady, for example, to identify 'In Memory of My Mother' as his favourite poem.[1] In 1985 Seamus Heaney said in a lecture at Carrickmacross, of his own first encounters with the poet, that 'Kavanagh gave you permission to dwell without cultural anxiety among the usual landmarks of your life'.[2] To that extent it could be argued that Kavanagh took the most important step of all towards the decolonization of the Irish mind. The present chapter will examine his influence upon two writers, Seamus Heaney and Brendan Kennelly, one from Northern Ireland, the other from the Republic.[3]

Heaney has much in common with Kavanagh in sociological terms: both are Ulstermen from rural, Catholic, small-farmer stock.[4] Yet Kavanagh's 'hegira' led to an impecunious existence, a cancer ward, and a briefly held extramural lectureship, while Heaney's took him from a small farm in County Londonderry to the Chair of Poetry in Oxford and beyond. Brendan Kennelly, born in County Kerry, had broad affinities with Kavanagh in social terms, but deviated from him as to career in a manner

roughly similar to that of Heaney. After a stint with London Transport fol-
lowed by a double-first at Trinity College, Dublin, and a doctorate at
Leeds, he became the first Catholic – let alone rural working-class
Catholic – to take a chair of English at Trinity in 1973.

In Heaney's case the groundwork was laid by the Butler Act of 1947,
which extended secondary education to poorer Protestants and Catholics
alike. In Kennelly's, a combination of intellectual ability and inspired
choice was matched by a growing willingness on the part of Dublin
University to be converted to Irishness. Gifts such as his would have been
wasted on University College Dublin, his natural constituency in some
ways – especially since Archbishop McQuaid still forbade Catholics to put
a toe inside the gates of Trinity College.[5] It was a perfect transaction for
all concerned. Trinity got a peasant-poet and Kennelly got the ideal platform for the literary impresario that he is. Heaney and Kennelly jointly
brought about the apotheosis of Patrick Kavanagh as the modern Irish
poet *par excellence*. There are others of no less interest as examples of
Kavanagh's literary influence: Eavan Boland, MacDara Woods, Paul
Durcan, Thomas MacCarthy, Gerald Dawe and Matthew Sweeney spring
to mind. In the same way, other critics could be cited – in the first rank
Terence Brown, whose 1975 book *Northern Voices* accorded Kavanagh his
proper place in Ulster literary tradition. But their origins on opposite
sides of the political border, with all that this implies for cross-border
cultural exchange, make these two poets uniquely representative figures
in the emergence of a new Irish sensibility, north and south, and Patrick
Kavanagh is for both men a major mediating force in that process.[6]

When Patrick Kavanagh set out from County Monaghan on his 'hegira' in the 1930s it was towards Dublin not Belfast – roughly equidistant
– that his steps tended.[7] This might seem natural given that Dublin was
the capital of the state he inhabited: Monaghan, part of Ulster, was also
part of Éire/Ireland (later the Irish Republic, from 1949). Though he
had been born some sixteen years before the island was partitioned in
1920–21, Dublin was the cultural centre to which Kavanagh always
looked, insofar as he looked anywhere beyond the 'fog of unknowing',
which he identified as the worst effect of rural poverty in *Self-Portrait*
(1964).[8] Seamus Heaney was born in County Derry and went to university in Belfast, which had by that time become host to a rather quaky
literary regionalism, a movement that exhibited many of the traits

which Kavanagh himself espoused – chiefly the privileging of the local and the vernacular, if not 'the common and banal' as in Kavanagh's more ecstatic vision.[9] If it seems natural that Kavanagh should have moved to Dublin in 1939, then Seamus Heaney's migration to the south in 1972, together with his conversion to the wider Irish tradition, was not quite as inevitable as it seems in retrospect. His endorsement of Kavanagh's influence was materially important to his stature as an Irish poet in 1975, and his renegotiation of that influence important to his status as an international writer in 1985. It could have been otherwise; but, then, everything could have been otherwise.

Heaney has sometimes written of the experience of growing up in a marginalized social group within British Ireland. In 'Frontiers of Writing', the last of his Oxford lectures in 1994, he spoke forcefully about the necessity of allowing room in Northern Ireland for anyone who viewed themselves as Irish rather than as British: 'Those who want to share that name and identity in Britain's Ireland should not be penalized ... or suspected of sinister motive because they draw cultural and psychic sustenance from an elsewhere supplementary to the one across the water'.[10] There was another side to it, of course. Nationalism in Ireland had long closed its mind to the fact of being pervasively influenced, even formed, by aspects of the dominant British culture. In the introduction to his translation of Beowulf, Heaney tells us that he was 'hampered' from adopting 'a more confident and creative way of dealing with the whole vexed question [of] nationality, language, history and literary tradition in Ireland' by the fact that the Irish and English languages were represented at his Northern Catholic school as 'adversarial' to each other.[11] While he held his chair at Oxford in the dawning days of the Northern settlement – the IRA cease-fire occurred during his stay though the Belfast Agreement would not follow until six years after – he formulated a principled conception of the cultural and political situation in the province based on his own dual heritage: 'There is nothing extraordinary about the challenge to be in two minds. If, for example, there was something exacerbating, there was still nothing deleterious to my sense of Irishness in the fact that I grew up in the minority in Northern Ireland and was educated within the dominant British culture.'[12] Educated within that culture he had indeed been, and qualified in it highly. To that extent, it was his natural constituency and the force of displacement by which he shifted from the Eng. Lit. seminar to the Irish literary salon was bound to be considerable – though in practice he moved easily enough from teaching post to teaching post in increasingly stellar regions of the academic world.

Personal and intellectual affinity with Patrick Kavanagh was virtually the fulcrum by means of which Heaney displaced himself from British into Irish Ireland. In 'The Placeless Heaven' (1985), the second of two essays that he wrote on Kavanagh, Heaney gave a chronological account of his growing acquaintance with contemporary Irish writing during his student days at the Queen's University, Belfast, and in the following year, which he spent at St. Joseph's Catholic Teacher Training College in that city. The tale that he tells reveals a gradual process of disentanglement from the hegemonic authority of English literary culture associated with the curriculum he followed as an undergraduate, then a brief flirtation with Ulster regionalism as an alternative to that somewhat alienating canon, before full immersion in the idea of Irish literature as the objective correlate of his own mind and the minds of the people to whom he gave his primary allegiance. Heaney begins his sketch by alluding to an article which has not, I think, been reprinted anywhere – perhaps uniquely among his writings. 'In 1962, while a student at St. Joseph's College of Education', he tells us, 'I had done an extended essay on the history of literary magazines in Ulster, as though I were already seeking a basis for faith in the possibility of our cultural existence as northern, Irish and essentially ourselves.'[13] He next remarks: 'It comes as something of a shock nowadays to remember that during four years as an undergraduate in the Queen's University English department I had not ever been taught by an Irish or an Ulster voice.' It is less of a shock when one reflects that the educational system in Ulster was largely adapted to the call for labour in agriculture, shipbuilding and linen manufacture up to the passing of the Butler Education Act, of which Heaney was an early beneficiary, in 1947.[14] Finally, he rattles off a list of the Irish literary contacts that he had made during this period, of which more later. In the meantime, let us consider the matter of Seamus Heaney's brief involvement in the crusade of Ulster regionalism.

In April 1964 Heaney contributed an article to *Trench*, the newly founded student magazine at St. Joseph's, where he had been lecturing for a year. (At the time of writing, his poem 'Digging' still lay four months in the future – the first poem by his own account in which he got his personal feelings 'into words'.)[15] Printed under the title 'Our Own Dour Way', the article begins: 'It is high time the North had another literary magazine.'[16] The author then goes on to note a surge of new Irish writing in the Republic, citing prognostications about the re-emergence of Dublin as the cultural centre that it had formerly been during the Irish Literary Revival. While admitting that 'Northerners have always felt this slight cultural envy', he moves on quickly to 'take a look' at several Ulster magazines which flew the flag for Ulster writing in the 1940s and 1950s, arguing that 'the work that they did in their time has not been carried on'.[17] Turning his attention to the contemporary journal Threshold (1957–), he complains that its editors have failed to take over where their predecessors had left off on Lagan (1943–46) and on Rann (1948–53). 'Why?', he asks, sardonically echoing a question posed in the first editorial of Lagan. Here is the answer that he gives: 'Because it is not essentially a northern magazine. It might as well be published in Dublin. In fact put a copy of Threshold inside a Kilkenny Magazine cover and very few people could tell the difference. Moreover, it relies on established reputations.'

At this point Heaney quotes the first editorial of Lagan, reprinted in an anthology of the journal that appeared in 1962, to the effect that 'No writer, however talented, should uproot himself in spirit from his native place … An Ulster literary tradition must spring out of the life and speech of the province … the central problem is to interpret the complex spiritual life of the province'.[18] Consulting the original, we find that John Boyd had argued the case in this fashion:

> An Ulster literary tradition that is capable of developing and enriching itself must spring out of the life and speech of the province; and an Ulster writer cannot evade his problems by adopting either a super-imposed English or a sentimental Gaelic outlook. His outlook must be that of an Ulster man. He must, therefore, train his ears to catch the unique swing of our speech; train his eyes to note the natural beauty of our towns: above all, he must study the psychology of our people.[19]

Young Heaney's response is engagingly ecumenical, if strictly regionalist for all that: 'Why could Patrick Boyle, Brian Friel, Stuart Love, Roy

McFadden and Denis Ireland not come together between limp quarterly covers and create a true artistic unity in diversity?'[20]

In this pointedly cross-community list of possible contributors the absence of Michael McLaverty is no less surprising than the presence of Stuart Love and Denis Ireland, two forgotten writers with unimpeachable liberal-Unionist credentials. This is doubly strange since Heaney would later write an obituary for the headmaster and friend who mentored him in his first teaching post at St. Thomas's on the Falls Road.[21] Much later, he would write a 13-page introduction for McLaverty's *Collected Short Stories*, edited by Sophia Hillan in 2002.[22] Such an omission from the list of Ulster regionalists was taking cultural diplomacy very far indeed, and one suspects that McLaverty himself had refused to be included. Heaney's closeness to him is recorded in 'The Placeless Heaven' where he says, 'my headmaster Michael McLaverty, himself a Monaghan man by birth but with a far gentler sensibility than Kavanagh's, lent me his copy of *A Soul for Sale* and so introduced me, at the age of twenty-three, to *The Great Hunger*',[23] while an earlier allusion to the loan of Kavanagh's 1947 collection 'late in 1962' had already appeared in the acknowledgements of *Preoccupations* (1980).[24] The growing importance of Kavanagh to Heaney at about this date is indicated by the further observation that his own copy of Kavanagh's *Come Dance with Kitty Stobling* (1960) was purchased on 3 July 1963, as his own inscription demonstrates.[25] This was the fourth impression of the book, two others having been issued in 1962, as he further tells us, indicating perhaps that he was behind the curve. The purchase was itself something of a novelty for him: 'I did not have many copies of books by living poets at that time and it is hard now to retrieve the sense of being on the outside of things ... Belfast at that time had no literary publishers, no poetry readings, no sense of a literary identity.' As Dublin presumably did.[26]

Here, then, is a transitory moment generally elided in the literary histories when liberal Catholic intellectuals in Northern Ireland were preparing to take up the regionalist cry which traditionally belonged to Protestant counterparts, decrying those who glided into the neighbouring literatures of Britain or Ireland as '*deraciné*', the pejorative dart that Boyd directs at St. John Ervine.[27] The trouble is – as Heaney was to put it in his final assessment of John Hewitt, the doyen of Ulster regionalists – that 'his regionalism suited the feeling of possession and independence of the empowered Protestants … but in his imaginings he could not include the Irish dimension in anything other than in an underprivileged way'.[28] This final judgement comes in the wake of a long series of reflections on Hewitt's poetry beginning with a warm review for Threshold in 1969 before turning circumspect in 'The Sense of Place', and finally arriving at the verdict given here. In general tendency, Heaney's unwillingness to greet Hewitt as a kindred spirit equates with Kavanagh's view of the Ulster regionalist movement as a whole. In 1948 Kavanagh had written in The Bell: 'Up in the North they are determined to produce a native culture … The worst and the best that can be said about them is that they are competent', and he called their 'perfect descriptions of nature' examples of 'excellent verse which reminds one of Robert Frost'.[29] As chief luminaries of the movement, both Hewitt and Roy McFadden are said to have all the 'material for fire' except the 'spark'.[30] In 1950 Kavanagh used his Envoy column to say: 'As for the "Ulster" writers who comprise only the Six Counties writers, they seem to be insipid, colourless and with no particular regional flavour.'[31]

When Heaney himself came to edit a special issue of Threshold in summer 1969 his contributors included Patrick Boyle, John Montague, James Simmons, Michael Longley, Mary Lavin, Thomas Kinsella and Derek Mahon, suggesting that the 'Ulster literary tradition' idea had not been entirely abandoned, if leavened with some others (Lavin and Kinsella) whose Northern connections were as negligible as anything that Heaney had critiqued in earlier issues of the journal. Kavanagh was two years dead; MacLaverty was very much alive. Hewitt had just published his Collected Poems (1968) and had seven more collections in him still, pamphlets excluded, and his absence from Heaney's Threshold, if purposed, was unkind. At the time of editing that issue, however, Heaney was rapidly moving towards the formulation of a new theory for Irish literature and, when he delivered this as 'The Sense of Place' at the Ulster Museum in 1977, Kavanagh was crucial to the argument he framed. Later, in 'Frontiers of Writing' (1994), he was to exclude Kavanagh from the list of writers who provided anchors for his fourfold schema in a vision of Irish culture as a map of 'castles', each corresponding to one of the Irish provinces which make up the 'quincunx' that forms the topographical trope of the lecture. This may not signify very much as regards his lasting estimate of Kavanagh, since the form of cul-

tural cartography involved has all to do with moderating between contending forces: Spenser, Yeats, Joyce and Louis MacNeice respectively
standing for English, Anglo-Irish, Irish Catholic and Ulster Protestant
dimensions of the Irish mind. Joyce may represent 'bourgeois Catholic'
Ireland as Heaney indicates elsewhere,[32] but no equivalent is given for
rural Ireland (Catholic or otherwise), unless the speaker feels that he
embodies that formation in himself. If so, Patrick Kavanagh's absence is
the highest form of presence considering that Heaney is speaking for
him. It is necessary to add that Heaney's quincunx was proffered as an
alternative to the 'fifth province' espoused by the *Crane Bag* writers in the
1980s and later adopted by Field Day Company as a quasi-mythological
symbol for the underlying unity of Ireland, an inveterately neo-nation-
alist idea involving a hidden centre where differences are mysteriously
resolved.[33]

MEETING THE IRISH: HEANEY AND THE DUBLIN WRITERS

It seems strange that as late as April 1964, when Seamus Heaney's essay
on the Ulster journals appeared in *Trench*, he was still intent on reinforc-
ing the literary border between Ireland, north and south. Given the date,
only months after his purchase of *Come Dance with Kitty Stobling* in
November 1963, it may be inferred that the explosive charge in that collection – like the one he had received from Michael MacLaverty a year
earlier – was on a slow fuse. Equally, the exigency of research, writing
and publication might have thrust the article into print after he himself
had parted with its ideas. It is easier, however, to suppose that he had not
properly registered the existence of an Irish literary tradition for which
Kavanagh's term 'parochialism' would give the necessary hint – a hint
which would not be available until the publication of the *Collected Prose* in
1967. Moreover, while that idea was dormant in the great sonnet 'Epic',
this was buried in *Kitty Stobling* (1960) and difficult to pick out from the
surrounding dross of Kavanagh's flailing satire. In 1975 Heaney was to
call that poem the 'magnificent coda' to such earlier pieces as
'Shancoduff', 'A Christmas Childhood', 'Spraying the Potatoes' and
'Verses from Tarry Flynn' – all of which constitute for him 'the most outstanding' poems in Kavanagh's œuvre – taking it to represent Kavanagh's
own 'comprehension of his early achievement' in those poems.[34] In 'The

Sense of Place' (1977), Heaney holds that sonnet to be Kavanagh's 'affirmation of the profound importance of the parochial',[35] something he achieves while at the same time 'abjur[ing] any national purpose, any belief in Ireland as a "spiritual entity"' – in other words, dismantling the usual Literary Revival claptrap which Kavanagh once condemned as 'a thorough-going English lie'.[36] (This, along with the notion of Dublin as 'a literary metropolis ... patented by Yeats, Lady Gregory and Synge'.)[37] Everything thereafter points to Kavanagh as the presiding spirit in Heaney's new 'region', a location that transcended conventionally regionalist or nationalist attachments by being rooted in a 'sense of place' – local and particular and often onomastically adorned with Irish place names. The great virtue of the 'sense of place' was that it enabled its devotees to eschew obvious patriotism and to worship at the fane of essential Irishness all the same. This double movement out of national-ism into a rarified conception of nationality is typical of Heaney's liter-ary discourse at the time. It was arguably characteristic of Patrick Kavanagh's also, inasmuch as he anathematized the idea of Ireland as a 'spiritual entity' but simultaneously insisted that poetry is 'mystical'.[38] Ireland, in other words, was the land of the spirit, but not the asinine 'Irish thing' that Kavanagh associated with the 'humbug', 'buckleppin', and 'bogusry' of W.R. Rodgers and – less warrantably – with Sean O'Faoláin and Frank O'Connor.

When Heaney refers to the 'shock' of realizing how hermetically sealed off from Irish writing the university was in the early 1960s, he tells it as it was. At the Queen's University, Belfast, he had heard Louis MacNeice read his poems and in 1963 had listened to Thomas Kinsella read from his second volume, *Downstream* (1962) and earlier work:

> Eventually, I got my hands on Robin Skelton's anthology, *Six Irish Poets* [1962]; on the first edition of John Montague's *Poisoned Lands* [1961], with its irrigating and confirming poem, 'The Water Carrier'; on Alvarez's anthology, *The New Poetry* [1962], where I encountered the work of Ted Hughes and R.S. Thomas.[39]

Montague's 'Water Carrier', the first poem in *Poisoned Lands* (1961) – treating of a spring or well visited with water buckets in rural childhood as 'a living source' in memory, 'the half-real / pulse in the fictive water that I feel'[40] – pioneers the theme and structure of certain poems by

Heaney and equally echoes the procedure of others by Kavanagh. For that reason alone, it is a most important poem. Its linkage between the epiphanic naturalism of Kavanagh in phrases such as 'musty smell of unpicked berries', on the one hand, and the 'supreme fiction' postulated by Wallace Stevens, on the other, reveals it as a poem that strides out of Ireland only to stride back in, informed with a capacity for heightened awareness which is modern without ceasing to be traditional, though the dominant perspective is admittedly a form of rarified nostagia. So it is with Heaney's first collection, regarding which he once reputedly said: 'I have no need to write a poem to Patrick Kavanagh; I wrote *Death of a Naturalist.*'[41]

The ardent paper-trail that Heaney manages to suggest above was probably more happenstance than the adverb 'eventually' implies. All of these sources he found 'animating', along with occasional trips to Dublin during one of which he acquired *The Dolmen Miscellany of Irish Writing* (1962), edited by John Montague and Thomas Kinsella, in which the 'strong lines' of Richard Murphy's 'Cleggan Disaster' particularly struck him.[42] *Miscellany* contained prose by Aidan Higgins, John Jordan, Brian Moore, James Plunkett, John McGahern and Montague, and poetry by Thomas Kinsella, Pearse Hutchinson, James Liddy, Richard Weber and Valentin Iremonger. Arguably, however, it was not the exposure to such a wealth of new Irish writing that made the chief difference for Heaney at this time, as much as Montague's arrival on the scene. Together, he and Heaney came to form a kind of literary think-tank in which the ideology of the newly emerging movement in Irish literature was forged, with Heaney's lecture on 'The Sense of Place' as its primary expression when it materialized in 1977. In some respects Heaney's subsequent career has been all to do with the gradual dismantling of that ideology and a corresponding distancing from former alliances with Irish poets, alive and dead, who comprised its chief exemplars. Of these, Montague and Kavanagh are the most important, as occupying almost equal space among illustrations of the main idea in that lecture. To each, however, is assigned a role: while Montague supplies the theory, Kavanagh provides the best examples; and in that sense he occupies the pride of place befitting his dignity as the subject of Heaney's slightly earlier essay, 'From Monaghan to the Grand Canal: The Poetry of Patrick Kavanagh' (1975).

This made its first appearance in Douglas Dunn's *Two Decades of Irish*

Writing (1975),[43] where it was accompanied by thirteen others sufficiently varied in provenance to justify the 'survey' sub-title, yet tending
to exhibit a fresh and distinctive critical approach to Irish literature
which might, for want of a better term, be called a new historicism —
alive to social contexts and political consequences but diametrically
opposed to the mentality that had produced the ballad poetry of Ireland.
It was not, in short, 'old whines in new bottles', to cadge a phrase from
Paul Muldoon, though it could easily become so.[44] According to Dunn,
'Seamus Deane adopts an historical perspective' while 'poets like John
Montague, Derek Mahon, and Seamus Deane himself have been unable
to ignore the subject of history, [and] a search for a comprehensive
expression of time and place is peculiarly strong in Seamus Heaney'.
Deane's contribution was a groundbreaking study of 'Irish Poetry and
Nationalism',[45] while Michael Allen's application of Kavanagh's poetic to
current Irish writing in 'Provincialism and the Importance of Patrick
Kavanagh'[46] tests some of the aesthetic premises associated with
Kavanagh which Heaney makes the main object of enquiry in his own
contribution. A striking feature of the introduction is the editor's tone of
impartial onlooker, and one suspects that the momentum for the collection rests with some of the contributors themselves. Dunn is entirely
tacit about the occasion for the collection, or his relation to the contributors other than simple 'gratitude' for the standard set by their 'practices'.[47] This doesn't prevent him noting that 'Irish writers are forced to
make decisions about their perspective on history, politics and literature', calling the thinking demanded by these things 'a catalyst to
talent'.[48]

Clearly the molecules of Irish and British culture were bonding in new
ways. This bonding proverbially originated in Philip Hobsbaum's coup in
placing three of Heaney's poems with the *New Statesman* through the influence of Edward Lucie-Smith, occasioning a letter of enquiry from Charles
Monteith at Faber which reached Heaney in January 1965. (Mary
Holland's coverage of the Belfast Festival in 1964 is also deemed to have
played a part.) Meanwhile in Dublin, John Montague had formed his
fruitful association with Liam Miller, proprietor of Dolmen Press and close
associate of Thomas Kinsella.[49] Miller had published Kavanagh's *Self-Portrait*
in 1964 and also printed *Nonplus*, a short-lived magazine edited by Patricia
Avis, one-time wife of Richard Murphy. Avis — who lived at 1 Wilton

Terrace – restored Kavanagh after he had fallen into the Grand Canal (or was pushed, by his own account) and received three of his most important essays by way of thanks.[50] Kinsella's translation of The Táin, published by Miller in 1969, with illustrations by Louis le Brocquy, supplied a Heinrich Schliemann moment for Ulster writers of that generation, though it was hardly conceived as an Ulster project.[51] His later translations in Poems of the Dispossessed (1981), also published by Miller, added a credible dimension to older Irish poetry which it had not had since Kuno Meyer. In all of this, it is difficult to avoid a sense that Miller was close to the centre of a force-field in which Montague operated as the go-between, with Kinsella and Heaney acting as the chief poles between which the cultural charge was passed.

Montague and Heaney had clearly bonded by 1967, when the former invited the latter to read a poem at Kavanagh's graveside.[52] This was an odd conjoining of very different writers, though with much in common aside from a shared experience of rural Ulster. Montague, who had attended the first performance of Allen Ginsberg's 'Howl', was certainly the Ulsterman with the best claims to literary cosmopolitanism, especially of the transatlantic kind (France was to come later), and was accordingly a strenuous opponent of the regionalist thing. In a poem entitled 'Regionalism, or A Portrait of the Artist as a Model Farmer', he laid his charge at the base of the new bawn which Heaney seemed intent on raising – though Hewitt and Kavanagh were the ostensible targets of the poem: 'Wild provincials / muttering into microphones / Declare that art / Springs only from the native part'. It ends with a parody of the peasant-poets, unnervingly like a reprise of 'Spraying the Potatoes': 'My tiny spud will comfort me / In my fierce anonymity'.[53] In 1969, however, Montague was galvanized by the Northern Irish Troubles into inventing a form of poetical bricolage with overtones of William Carlos Williams, Ezra Pound and perhaps Charles Olsen which he showcased in The Rough Field (1972). Here he set about orchestrating 'shards of a lost tradition' and 'our tribal pain'[54] in such a way as to comprise a tapestry of colonial dispossession and familial disarray that rhymes in its vision of the fragmented Irish world with Thomas Kinsella's 'The Divided Mind'.[55] This essay shared a publishing venue with Montague's own on 'The Impact of International Modern Poetry on Irish Writing'[56] in Seán Lucy's collection of critical essays, Irish Poetry in English (1973).[57] Lucy was

Professor of English at University College, Cork, where Montague held a teaching post from 1972 to 1988.

BRENDAN KENNELLY AND THE COMIC MUSE

The lecture series and collection were of immense importance in setting a new tone for Irish criticism in the 1970s. The remaining contributors – Austin Clarke, Eiléan Ní Chuilleanáin, Bryan MacMahon, Roger McHugh, Lorna Reynolds, A.N. Jeffares, Benedict Kiely, Robert Farren and Brendan Kennelly – were all either literary lights, academic stalwarts, or young Turks of the rising generation. Among them was one who had an intense imaginative affinity with Kavanagh, and was charged with writing about him the only single-author essay besides that on W.B. Yeats. Brendan Kennelly's 'Patrick Kavanagh', first published in *Ariel* in 1970, offers a strangely lucent paraphrase of Kavanagh's 'comic vision', delivered with all the heartfelt conviction of a passionate believer.[58] The central importance of Kavanagh for Kennelly can be judge from the fact that, as an undergraduate in the 1950s, he copied out *The Great Hunger* in the National Library of Ireland,[59] and his essay on Kavanagh is, in a sense, the work of a faithful copyist also.

Both internal and external evidence suggests that Heaney had read Kennelly's essay by the time he wrote his own 1975 Kavanagh essay. Internal, because he echoes the term 'comic vision' and warns against excessive faith in Kavanagh's professions about 'not-caring' which Kennelly strenuously talks up;[60] external, because the collection in which it was most widely read includes key essays by Kinsella and Montague, with whom Heaney was in contact and to whom he was closely attending. One might even speak of an element of influence. Yet, whereas Heaney focuses upon the idea of the 'parochial' as the central axiom of Kavanagh's art, Kennelly lays more stress on the exaltation of 'the Comic Muse' (or 'comic vision', in Kennelly's synoptic term,[61]) and the associated conception of 'Tragedy' as 'underdeveloped Comedy, not fully born' which Kavanagh propounds in the author's note to the *Collected Poems* (1964) – characteristically in the context of a scathing self-criticism of his own longer poem *The Great Hunger*.

In broad outline, Kennelly's evaluation of Kavanagh is a distillation of the latter's thought rather than a critique of his ideas. It is almost as though the poet's ideas were being voiced by a literary Irishman untrammelled by the 'vehemence [and] air of exhaustion' that marred so much of Kavanagh's critical prose, as Seamus Heaney has observed.[62] In one place we are told, 'The simplicity, present from the beginning in Kavanagh's work, is characteristic of his achieved comic vision' – and this is taken as the cue for a mélange of paraphrase and personal musings more redolent of the poetic disciple than the literary critic in Kennelly:

> He saw that his simplicity was a gift from the gay, imaginative God; that it was the most difficult thing in the world to achieve; and that if sophistication has any meaning at all (and no word in the English language is more abused or misunderstood) it means that the poet has the courage to be utterly himself, his best self, and that nothing else will do.[63]

Kennelly does not pause to consider that, as Antoinette Quinn has noted, Kavanagh 'was increasingly preoccupied with constructing an autobiographical myth ... representing his poetic career as a journey from simplicity to simplicity' from 1955 onwards.[64] The fact that he believed a myth was necessary to any poet does not mitigate its character as myth, and no less an 'artifice' than anything devised by Yeats. Indeed, Kavanagh's myth was constructed in some measure in emulation of Yeats's and contained some distinctly Yeatsian ingredients, including notably his adoption of the word 'gay' as in a 'gay, imaginative God',[65] and the 'gay, fantastically humorous' poets.[66] Kennelly does not invoke any such comparisons here, though he finds 'an astonishing similarity' between Kavanagh's poem 'A Personal Problem' and Yeats's 'The Circus Animals' Desertion' – both being 'triumphant expressions of the sense of failure'.[67] Later on, however, he would return to the Kavanagh–Yeats nexus in an essay on 'Irish Poetry Since Yeats' especially written for the *Selected Prose* (1994), as his editor tells us.[68] Here he notes that Kavanagh denounced Yeats in several places and suggests that 'This was Kavanagh's way of distancing himself from Yeats', adding:

> He went on to explain and express his own vision, a vision which in the end has, ironically, some remarkable similarities to Yeats's. Kavanagh called it 'comedy'; Yeats called it 'tragic joy'. Kavanagh's

castigating references to Yeats and others helped him to create for himself that space, that freedom from other poets' work (even as they are deeply aware of it) that most poets need. Poets' vicious denunciation of others can be forms of self-liberation.[69]

For Kennelly, Kavanagh is 'one of the most misunderstood and under-valued poets of our time', 'a visionary poet' to be compared with Blake and Yeats. Any supposed resemblance to Hardy, for example, is briskly overruled since '[Hardy's] poetry, at the deepest level, the level of the visionary, does not develop'. In marked contrast, 'fewer modern poets have undergone such a deep, dynamic development as Kavanagh ... His was one of the most moving, coherent, and profound visions in modern poetry.'

Kennelly's article has the drive of a good story: first there was the 'sim-plicity' of the early lyrics; then there was *The Great Hunger*. For Kennelly, this 'splendid though rather uneven work was a vital stage in his journey toward the comic vision'. Next comes the bitter chapter of his satires, cul-minating with the 'magnificent poem' 'Prelude', in which Kavanagh gives voice to the corrective notion that 'satire is unfruitful prayer'. After that, Kennelly tells us, 'Satire falls away because it is not an enduring part of the comic vision'.[70] The remainder of the essay is devoted to the stages by which Kavanagh attained the 'weightlessness' of which he once spoke, writing some of his finest poems thereafter, and some others that seem like 'a bad imitation' of himself.[71] Interwoven with this narrative there is the theme of 'poetry as a mystical thing, a dangerous thing', which Kavanagh professed in the author's note to the *Collected Poems* (1964).[72] Kennelly's response is not to interrogate the terms of that confession ('somehow or other'; 'belief'; 'mystical') but to take it as a cue for spir-ited elaboration: 'It is mystical because it is concerned with man's dia-logue with God, the foundation-stone of all Kavanagh's work, the source of his humour and sanity.'[73] This is probably an accurate paraphrase of Kavanagh's meaning, but Kennelly goes a step further in endorsing Kavanagh's intellectual outlook at every turn. It is probably this uncritical partisanship that accounts for the fact that the essay is rarely referenced in criticism today. Kennelly is not, for instance, cited in Antoinette Quinn's biography other than as an admirer of Kavanagh's work and a visitor who brought him a bottle of Scotch during his last illness (Kavanagh downed three-quarters without any noticeable effect).[74]

At one point the pitfalls of discipleship are particularly evident. In the version of the essay that appeared in *Ariel* (April 1970) and was reprinted in *Irish Poets in English* (1973), Kennelly permitted himself to take dictation from Kavanagh not only in regard to poetry and God, but also in regard to literary history as well. Kavanagh began his author's note with some remarks about the difference between himself and English writers, framing his famous sentence about poetry as 'a mystical thing' in that context:

> There is, of course, a poetic movement which sees poetry materialistically. The writers of this school see no transcendent nature in the poet; they are practical chaps, excellent technicians. But somehow or other I have a belief in poetry as a mystical thing, and a dangerous thing.

The 'school' in question is presumably The Group, associated with the name of Philip Hobsbaum, who carried its 'well-made poem' ethos to Belfast in the 1960s. Kennelly picks up Kavanagh's thread and elaborates a wider pattern:

> The English have lost a sense of the value of *naïveté* and most of their poets have substituted a passion for fatal perfection which, around the age of thirty, makes them invulnerable to criticism and usually incapable of development. This perfectionism involves a very prosaic conception of precision and concentration. It's the sort of disease against which Blake and Keats fought. (At the moment, sad traces of it can be detected in Irish writing.)[75]

Some of these observations make good sense, but others display a woeful insularity. The idea that English poetry is diseased, that it has departed from its Romantic roots, and that Irish poets should hold on to their oracular naïvety, would be less preposterous if Irish poetry were not about to take a quantum leap in 1970, expressly due to the influence of Philip Hobsbaum in his time in Belfast, while nearer home were Michael Longley and Derek Mahon, contemporaneously practising the well-made poem at Trinity College. In *Journey into Joy* (1994), Kennelly, or his editor, wisely expunged this paragraph.

PLACELESS HEAVEN: THE METAPHYSICS OF FLIGHT

In Seamus Heaney's relationship with Patrick Kavanagh there is an initial display of warm affinity, and then the check of an intellectual reserve, finally culminating in renewed friendship on terms of Heaney's own devising. In the autobiographical passages of the second Kavanagh essay, he tells us of his first response to 'Spraying the Potatoes' when he met with it in 'the old *Oxford Book of Irish Verse*':[76] 'I was excited to find details of a life which I knew intimately – but which I had always considered to be below or beyond books – being presented in a book.'[77] Generalizing from his own experience, he credibly suggests that 'Kavanagh's work probably touches the majority of Irish people ... more intimately than most things in Yeats'. This on account of 'Kavanagh's fidelity to the unpromising, unspectacular countryside of Monaghan and his rendering of the authentic speech of those parts gave the majority of Irish people, for whom the experience of life on the land was perhaps the most formative, an image of themselves that nourished their sense of themselves'.[78]

These are, of course, the true identitarian goods: sincere and forthright, and locked into reassuring measures of ordinary experience. Kavanagh's interventions were good for people, good for self-esteem: 'Kavanagh gave you permission to dwell without cultural anxiety among the usual landmarks of your life.'[79] In this sense he made room for the voice of the people in whose name the Anglo-Irish war had been fought; and, to that degree, he took what was arguably the most authentic step towards the decolonization of the Irish mind since the state was founded in 1921, offering 'a corrective to the inflations of nationalism, and the cringe of provincialism', as Heaney said on another occasion.[80] One test of this is the presence of the poet to his audience on radio – for Kavanagh broadcast from London, Belfast, Dublin and Wales on different occasions:[81]

> Over the border, into a Northern Ireland dominated by the noticeably English accents of the local BBC, he broadcast a voice that would not be cowed into accents other than its own. Without being in the slightest way political in its intentions, Kavanagh's poetry did have political effect.[82]

The implication here is that, by 'crossing the pieties of a rural Catholic sensibility with the *non serviam* of his original personality', Kavanagh raised 'the inhibited energies of a subculture to the power of a cultural resource'.[83] This is a political matter insofar as the now uninhibited energies are likely to seek democratic respite from their heretofore imposed and accepted status as second-class citizens. In this sense, the human voice with all its social and psychological inflections is the medium of social and political liberation.

That this rings true of Kavanagh as a radio personality is not surprising, and the popularity of his poetry among a wide and unpretentious readership cannot be denied; yet Heaney's attempt to demonstrate how the vernacular actually operates in a Kavanagh poem is oddly unconvincing, especially where he focuses upon the 'ambiguous word' *blooming* in the last line of the 'Inniskeen Road: July Evening': 'I am king / Of banks and stones and every blooming thing'.[84] He wants us to believe that the bicycles *going by* in twos and threes are sufficiently vernacular – 'they do not "pass by" or "go past", as they would in a more standard English voice or place'[85] – to let 'the very life blood of the place in [through] that one minute incision':[86] 'The words "go by" and "blooming", moreover, are natural and spoken; they are not used as a deliberate mark of folksiness or as separate language, in the way that Irish speech is ritualised by Synge.' Clearly not; but the trouble with 'blooming' is that it sounds less like 'Inniskeen English' than the expletive of the Cockney soldier in the closing scene of O'Casey's *The Plough and the Stars*. The real difficulty is that the 'dance in Billy Brennan's barn tonight' sits oddly with 'Alexander Selkirk knew the plight'.[87] Its effect on the uneducated reader can only be guessed, while that on the half-educated reader is likely to be a distracting element of self-congratulation. It is hard at any rate to imagine the reader who would conclude that 'the poem could carry a Wordsworthian subtitle, "Solitude"',[88] as Heaney does in his first essay on Kavanagh. Seemingly, that 'ambiguous "blooming"' adverts to the autobiographical moment framed in the last line with its 'potential flowering, its blooming, in the imagination'. Yet, in order to mean this it must mean 'blasted' or 'bloody' or – more likely – 'fecking' at the same time. At this point there is a certain throwing up of hands: 'Of course it would be wrong to insist too strongly on Kavanagh as a weaver of verbal textures. There is a feeling of prospector's luck ... about many of his best effects.' There is something of that feeling about this form of criticism, too. But Heaney has purposes here other than to debate the connotative value of a slang word. Later on he will tell us that *Tarry Flynn* 'brings to fruition the valediction to "every blooming thing" promised in "Inniskeen Road"',[89] while in another place he tells us that *The Great Hunger* is the obverse of that *Bildungsroman*, 'not about growing up and away but about growing down and in. Its symbol is the potato rather than the potato blossom.'[90] A sense emerges that allegory and symbol, rather than diction and poetics, are very much the driving force in this interpretation. If we pursue that allegory we can see that Heaney is projecting his own valedictory gesture onto the poem.

It has often been suggested that, in advancing from *Sweeney Astray* (1983) to *Seeing Things* (1991) and beyond, Heaney detached himself from the earth and took to the air. Paul Muldoon has said so: 'Doctor Heaney / the great physician of the earth / is waxing metaphysical, / has taken to "walking on air".'[91] John Wilson Foster has likewise written of a Copernican revolution in his poetry, 'a shift from the poetics of exca-vation to that of light'.[92] Yet, if Foster has some warrant for believing that 'Heaney has always intended his poetry to be ... a political poetry of considerable oblique power'[93] – and hence, that his upward flight may be a 'sublimated' form of political desire – it seems more interesting to consider that flight in its own terms. The *raison d'être* for 'Another Look at Patrick Kavanagh' was to see if the 'sense of place' ideology, with is tacit but implacable claims on Irish soil, can be dismantled – not alone for the good of the peace process but because the poetics that Heaney lives by have actually changed. There is no space in the present chapter to review his long-running debate with Derek Mahon about the meaning of the 'metaphysical' – whether it is a form of alienation or of solace – but there can be no missing the sense of his argument in *Seeing Things* when confronted by the passing of his parents and the caducity of all things.[94] It may be said in shorthand that he has passed from the real-world Irish spring where John Montague filled his enamel bucket in rural County Tyrone to the 'fictive water' which is simultaneously postulated as a 'living source' in the same poem.[95] In a poem of *Seeing Things* that remembers foot-ball games played in falling light, Heaney writes of 'Breathing [that] sounded like effort in another world'.[96] The poem caps this palpable feat of memory with a brilliant apprehension of the metaphysical edifice that the imagination tries to raise on such perceptual evidence: 'All these things entered you / As if they were both the door and what came through it. / They marked the spot, marked time and held it open'. In the light of the literally liminal and, more broadly immaterial (or idealist) tendency of the new poetry in Seeing Things, we may say that, in delivering his second lecture in 1985, at the place where Kavanagh is annually commemorated, Heaney reveals his intention of dismantling the ultimately restrictive ideology of 'place' which he arrived at through the good offices of Kavanagh's poems. At the same time – and how characteristic it is to do so – he displays his intention of bringing Kavanagh along with him in the 'weightlessness' of flight.[97]

I cannot say whether Kavanagh really shared in the non-theological (and therefore neurological) metaphysics that Heaney is implicitly offering to the Irish literary tradition as a new variant on Kavanagh's conception of poetry as a 'mystical thing'. I can only point out that in 'Another Look at Kavanagh' he re-reads poems such as 'In Memory of My Mother' to the effect that the consolation of eternal life supplied by a simpler reading gives way to the sophisticated notion that the mother is now a 'visionary presence', a 'shimmer of inner reality'[98] who, like the Duffys and MacCabes in 'Epic', are made real 'by the light of the mind that is now playing upon them'.[99] This way of thinking bears within itself a risk of solipsism, but it is unquestionably an answer to the question 'Where does the spirit live?'[100] which stands at the heart of Seeing Things.[101] Now he is looking for something that was not available to him, or even desirable, on first looking into Patrick Kavanagh. He is hoping to be 'spirited away' to a 'new place' which is 'all idea', 'not a topographical location' but 'an imagined realm, even if it can be located at an earthly spot, a placeless heaven rather than a heavenly place'.[102]

Heaney takes his altered metaphysical intuition back to the text of Kavanagh's poems and tests it there. He finds the best indication that Kavanagh will travel with him on this new road – in spite of Kavanagh's religious conventionality, his friendship with Archbishop McQuaid, and his eager reception of Extreme Unction – in that apparently subversive (even Buddhistic) line in 'Auditors In': 'The placeless Heaven that's under all our noses'.[103] I am not sure that this refers to the Heaven of religion so much as an available 'repose' for 'self' in the midst of anxiety, envy, failure and all the other 'millstones' that drag us down in temporal existence. It is probably not an eschatology at all, but it serves its purpose as an anchor in the works of the older poet, who, arguably, raised the younger 'to the power of a cultural resource'.[104] It is ironic that, having broken the provincial mould, Heaney had to break the parochial mould also: but that is the implacable logic of my epigraph, and that was just what he went to Carrickmacross to do in November of 1985.

NOTES

1. 'Eventually it came down to a choice between two Ulster poets, Seamus Heaney and Patrick Kavanagh. Finally Kavanagh won out.' See Marie Heaney (ed.), Sources: Letters from Irish People on the Sustenance of the Soul (Dublin: Town House Press,1999), p.41.

2. Seamus Heaney, 'The Placeless Heaven: Another Look at Patrick Kavanagh', in The Government of the Tongue (London: Faber & Faber, 1988), pp.3–14; p.9. The essay was originally given as an opening address at Kavanagh's Yearly, November 1985. See Heaney, Finders Keepers: Selected Prose 1971–2001 (London: Faber & Faber, 2002), p.134.

3. Heaney was born in 1939, Kennelly in 1936. Kennelly lived twelve years in the Irish Free State before the Republic was established in March 1949. Heaney was 10 when the Free State passed out of existence, though the term continued to be used in Northern Ireland for a great deal longer, usually with caustic overtones.

4. Monaghan is part of Ulster in the ancient cuigí (provinces) system of Ireland, though Ulster is politically synonymous with Northern Ireland in common parlance – that is, six of the nine counties, excluding Monaghan, Donegal and Cavan.

5. The wholesale absence of Catholics from Trinity was due, not to any university rule, but to the tender care of the diocesan Archbishop for the spiritual well-being of his flock. There was, however, a Catholic trickle – chiefly haut-bourgeois, of whom Oliver St John Gogarty is the classic example.

6. Terence Brown, Northern Voices: Poets from Ulster (Dublin: Gill & Macmillan, 1975).

7. Kavanagh's 'hegira' – as he called it in 'From Monaghan to the Grand Canal' (1959) – is usually dated from his final move to Dublin in 1939, but can reasonably be identified with his first journey to Dublin in June 1930.

8. 'Self-Portrait' [1962], in Patrick Kavanagh, A Poet's Country: Selected Prose, ed. Antoinette Quinn (Dublin: Lilliput Press, 2003), p.307.

9. 'The Hospital', in Patrick Kavanagh, Collected Poems (London: MacGibbon & Kee, 1964), p.153.

10. Seamus Heaney, 'Frontiers of Writing', in The Redress of Poetry: Oxford Lectures (London: Faber & Faber, 1995), p.210.

11. Seamus Heaney, 'Introduction', Beowulf (London: Faber & Faber, 1999), pp.xxiii–iv.

12. Heaney, Redress of Poetry, p.202.

13. Heaney, 'Placeless Heaven', p.7.

14. In Deirdre Madden's novel One by One in Darkness (London: Faber & Faber, 1996; p.60),

two characters reflect upon the change in Northern Ireland: '"What do you think is the biggest difference between now and then?", Helen asked. David replied unhesitatingly: "We are. The educated Catholic middle class. I don't think anyone fully anticipated that, or thought through what it would mean, but it should have been easy to foresee".'

15. Seamus Heaney, 'Feeling into Words', in Preoccupations: Selected Prose 1968–78 (London: Faber & Faber, 1980), pp.41–60; at p.41.
16. The title derives from an Ulster ballad of 1798: 'We men of Ulster had a word to say / And we said it then on our own dour way / And we spoke out loud and clear.' Heaney quotes the lines at the end of his article ('Our Own Dour Way', Trench, April 1964, p.4). There is a copy of the journal in the John Hewitt collection of the University of Ulster at Coleraine.
17. Ibid., pp.3–4; at p.3.
18. Lagan: A Collection of Ulster Writings (Lisburn: Lagan Press, 1962), pp.5–6.
19. Ibid., p.6.
20. Heaney, 'Our Own Dour Way', p.3.
21. Seamus Heaney, 'Michael McLaverty', Fortnight Supplement (2 May 1992), p.31.
22. Seamus Heaney, 'Introduction', in Collected Short Stories of Michael MacLaverty, ed. Sophia Hillan (Belfast: Blackstaff Press, 2002).
23. Heaney, 'Placeless Heaven', p.7.
24. Heaney, 'Foreword', Preoccupations, p.14.
25. Heaney, 'From Monaghan to the Grand Canal', Preoccupations, p.6.
26. The book was actually published by Longmans, Green in London.
27. Lagan, p.4.
28. Heaney, 'Frontiers of Writing', pp.195–6.
29. Patrick Kavanagh, 'Poetry in Ireland To-day', The Bell, 16, 1 (April 1948), p.42. I am grateful to Kelly Matthews for a copy of this article.
30. Ibid. Kavanagh revised his assessment in a footnote: 'Having read the last group of John Hewitt's poems in The Bell I have changed my mind: he has the right blaze' (p.42).
31. Patrick Kavanagh, 'Diary', Envoy, 1, 2 (January 1950), p.85.
32. Seamus Heaney, 'A Tale of Two Islands: Reflections on the Irish Literary Revival', in Irish Studies, vol 1, ed. P.J. Drudy (Cambridge: Cambridge University Press, 1980), p.18.
33. See my article, '"Quincunx": Seamus Heaney and the Ulster Regionalists', in Complicities: British Poetry 1946–2007, ed. Robin Purves and Sam Ladku (Prague: Litteraria Pragensia, 2007), pp.102–44.
34. Heaney, 'From Monaghan to the Grand Canal', p.120.
35. Heaney, 'The Sense of Place', in Preoccupations, p.137.
36. Patrick Kavanagh, 'Self-Portrait' [1962], in Quinn (ed.), Poet's Country, p.306.
37. Ibid., p.207.
38. Kavanagh, 'Author's Note', Collected Poems, p.xiv.
39. Heaney, 'Placeless Heaven', p.7.

40. John Montague, *Poisoned Lands* (London: MacGibbon & Kee, 1961; rpt Dublin: Dolmen Press, 1977), p.11.

41. Quoted by Michael Allen in 'Provincialism and Recent Irish Poetry: The Importance of Patrick Kavanagh', in *Two Decades of Irish Writing: A Critical Survey*, ed. Douglas Dunn (Cheadle Hulme: Carcanet Press, 1975), p.36.

42. Heaney, 'Placeless Heaven', p.7.

43. Dunn (ed.), *Two Decades of Irish Writing*. The contributors were Donald Davie, Stan Smith, Terence Brown, Michael Longley, Seamus Heaney, Edna Longley, Michael Smith, D.E.S. Maxwell, James Atlas, Lorna Sage, Roger Garfitt and Tom Paulin.

44. Referring to Brian Friel's play *Translations* in *Prince of the Quotidian* (1994).

45. Seamus Deane, 'Irish Poetry and Nationalism', in *Two Decades of Irish Writing*, ed. Dunn, pp.4–22.

46. Michael Allen, 'Provincialism and the Importance of Patrick Kavanagh' in Dunn (ed.), *Two Decades of Irish Writing*, pp.23–37.

47. Dunn, 'Introduction', in *Two Decades of Irish Writing*, p.3.

48. Ibid., p.2.

49. A photograph of the three men by Cartier-Bresson appears on the back of *The Dolmen Press: A Celebration*, ed. Maurice Harmon (Dublin: Lilliput Press, 2001).

50. Viz., 'Nationalism and Literature', 'Violence and Literature', and 'Suffering and Literature'. See Quinn (ed.), *Poet's Country*, p.16; also Quinn, *Patrick Kavanagh: A Biography* (Dublin: Gill & Macmillan; London: Allen Lane, 2001), pp.385–6.

51. Thomas Kinsella (trans.), *The Táin* (Dublin: Dolmen Press, 1969), reissued in a popular edition (Oxford: Oxford University Press, 1970).

52. See Seamus Heaney's feature article on Kavanagh, 'In the Light of the Imagination', *Irish Times* (21 October 2004).

53. Donald Carroll (ed.), *New Poets of Ireland* (Denver, CO: Alan Swallow, 1963), p.89.

54. John Montague, 'A Lost Tradition', in *The Rough Field* [1972], reprinted in *Collected Poems* (Dublin: Gallery Press, 1995), p.33.

55. Thomas Kinsella, 'The Divided Mind', in *Irish Poetry in English: The Thomas Davis Lectures on Anglo-Irish Literature*, ed. Seán Lucy (Cork and Dublin: Mercier Press, 1973), pp.208–18.

56. John Montague, 'The Impact of Modern Poetry on Irish Writing', in Lucy (ed.), *Irish Poetry in English*, pp.144–58.

57. Lucy (ed.), *Irish Poetry in English*.

58. Brendan Kennelly, 'Patrick Kavanagh', in Lucy (ed.), *Irish Poetry in English*, pp.159–84. It appeared first in *Ariel: Journal of International Literature in English*, 1, 3 (July 1970), pp.7–28; reprinted as 'Patrick Kavanagh's Comic Vision', in Åke Persson (ed.), *Journey into Joy: Selected Prose* (Newcastle upon Tyne: Bloodaxe, 1994).

59. See John MacDonagh, '"Tore Down à la Rimbaud": Brendan Kennelly and the French Connection', in *Reinventing Ireland through a French Prism*, ed. Eugene Maher *et al.* (Frankfurt: Peter Lang, 2007), p.181.

60. Heaney, 'From Monaghan to the Grand Canal', p.128.

61. Kennelly, 'Patrick Kavanagh's Comic Vision', pp.109–26.

62. Heaney, 'Tale of Two Islands', p.15.

63. Kennelly, 'Patrick Kavanagh', p.162.

64. Quinn (ed.), *Poet's Country*, pp.16–17.

65. Patrick Kavanagh, 'The Irish Tradition', in *Collected Pruse* (London: MacGibbon & Kee, 1967), p.233.

66. Kavanagh, 'Signposts', in *Collected Pruse*, p.25; quoted in Kennelly, 'Patrick Kavanagh', p.159. Cf. Yeats's vision of Hamlet and Lear as 'gay', their 'Gaiety transfiguring all that dread [...] Tragedy wrought to its uttermost' ('Lapis Lazuli', *Collected Poems* [London: Macmillan, 1950], p.338).

67. Kennelly, 'Patrick Kavanagh', p.184.

68. Kinsella, in Åke Persson (ed.), *Journey into Joy*, p.251.

69. Ibid., p.55. References for Kavanagh are 'Signposts', *Collected Pruse*, p.25, and Kavanagh, *Collected Poems*, p.xiv. That for Yeats is 'The Gyres', *Collected Poems* (1950), p.337.

70. Kennelly, 'Patrick Kavanagh', pp.159–60; 165; 174–5.

71. Ibid., p.176. For 'I achieved weightlessness', see 'Self-Portrait' [RTÉ 1962], in Kavanagh, *Collected Prose*, p.22; Quinn (ed.), *Poet's Country*, p.315.

72. Kavanagh, *Collected Poems*, p.xiii; Kavanagh, *Collected Pruse*, p.302.

73. Kennelly, 'Patrick Kavanagh', p.161.

74. See Quinn, *Patrick Kavanagh: A Biography*, pp.xiii, 424, 435, 446, 463.

75. Kennelly 'Patrick Kavanagh', in Lucy (ed.), *Irish Poets in English*, pp.160–1.

76. Viz., Donagh MacDonagh and Lennox Robinson (eds), *The Oxford Book of Irish Verse: XVIIth to XXth Century* (Oxford: Oxford University Press, 1958). Kinsella made a new selection for Oxford University Press in 1986.

77. Heaney, 'Placeless Heaven', p.7.

78. Heaney, 'Sense of Place', p.137.

79. Heaney, 'Placeless Heaven', p.9.

80. Seamus Heaney, in *Every Stony Acre Has a Name: A Celebration of the Townland in Ulster*, ed. Tony Canavan (Belfast: Federation for Ulster Local Studies, 1991), p.xi.

81. See Quinn, *Patrick Kavanagh: A Biography*, pp.251, 307, 424.

82. Heaney, 'Placeless Heaven', p.9.

83. Heaney, 'From Monaghan to the Grand Canal', *Preoccupations*, p.116.

84. Kavanagh, 'Inniskeen Road: July Evening', in Quinn (ed.), *Collected Poems*, p.15.

85. Heaney, ' Sense of Place', p.138.

86. Ibid. He might mean 'blood-letting' by this sentence, but I don't believe so and have emended it to make sense.

87. Kavanagh, 'Inniskeen Road: July Evening', p.15.

88. Heaney, 'From Monaghan to the Grand Canal', p.117.

89. Ibid., p.121.

90. Ibid., p.123.

91. *The Prince of the Quotidian* [1994], quoted in Nicholas Jenkins, 'Walking on Air' [review of *The Spirit Level*], in *Times Literary Supplement* (25 July 1996).

92. John Wilson Foster, 'Heaney's Redress', in *Colonial Consequences: Essays in Irish Literature and Culture* (Dublin: Lilliput Press, 1991), p.188.

93. Ibid., pp.197–8.

94. See my article '"Solving Ambiguity": The Secular Mysticism of Derek Mahon', in *Derek Mahon: A Collection of Critical Essays*, ed. Elmer Kennedy-Andrews (Gerrards Cross: Colin Smythe, 2001), pp.29–52.

95. Montague, *Poisoned Lands*, p.11.

96. Heaney, 'Markings', in *Seeing Things* (London: Faber & Faber, 1991), pp.8–9; *Opened Ground* (London: Faber & Faber, 1998), p.335.

97. Heaney, 'Placeless Heaven', p.11. See Kavanagh, 'Self-Portrait', p.22.

98. Heaney, 'Placeless Heaven', p.10.

99. Ibid., p.6.

100. Heaney, *Opened Ground*, p.372.

101. See my article '"Where Does the Spirit Live?": The Metaphysics of Unbelief in Modern Irish Poetry', in *The Irish Reader: Essays for John Devitt*, ed. Michael Hinds *et al.* (Dublin: Otior Press, 2007), pp.133–46.

102. Heaney, 'Placeless Heaven', p.4.

103. Kavanagh, 'Auditors In', *Collected Poems*, p.126; Quinn (ed.), *Collected Poems*, p.182.

104. Heaney, 'Sense of Place', p.116.

Select Bibliography

WORKS BY PATRICK KAVANAGH

Kavanagh, Patrick, *Ploughman and Other Poems* (London: Macmillan Contemporary Poets Series, 1936).

Kavanagh, Patrick, *The Green Fool* (London: Michael Joseph, 1938; Harmondsworth: Penguin Books, 1975; rpt 1987).

Kavanagh, Patrick, *The Great Hunger* (Dublin: Cuala Press, 1942, limited edition).

Kavanagh, Patrick, *A Soul for Sale* (London: Macmillan, 1947).

Kavanagh, Patrick, *Tarry Flynn* (London: Pilot Press, 1948; rpt London: Martin Brian & O'Keeffe, 1972; Harmondsworth: Penguin, 1978).

Kavanagh, Patrick, *Recent Poems* (New York: Peter Kavanagh Hand Press, 1958).

Kavanagh, Patrick, *Come Dance with Kitty Stobling and Other Poems* (London: Longmans, Green, 1960; Chester Springs, PA: Dufour, 1964).

Kavanagh, Patrick, *Self-Portrait* (Dublin: Dolmen Press, 1964; Dufour, 1964); text of a RTÉ TV documentary (1962).

Kavanagh, Patrick, *Collected Poems* (London: MacGibbon & Kee, 1964; rpt London: Martin Brian & O'Keeffe, 1972; New York: Devin-Adair, 1964).

Kavanagh, Patrick, introduction to W. Steuart Trench, *Realities of Irish Life* (London: McGibbon & Kee, 1966).

Kavanagh, Patrick, *Collected Pruse* (London: MacGibbon & Kee, 1967; Martin Brian & O'Keefe, 1973).

Kavanagh, Patrick, Preface to *The Autobiography of William Carleton* (London: MacGibbon & Kee, 1968).

Kavanagh, Patrick, *Lapped Furrows: Correspondence 1933–1967 Between Patrick Kavanagh and Peter Kavanagh with Other Documents*, ed. Peter Kavanagh (New York: Peter Kavanagh Hand Press, 1969).

Kavanagh, Patrick, *November Haggard, Uncollected Prose and Verse of Patrick Kavanagh*, ed. Peter Kavanagh (New York: Peter Kavanagh Hand Press, 1971).

Kavanagh, Patrick, *The Complete Poems of Patrick Kavanagh*, ed. Peter Kavanagh (New York: Peter Kavanagh Hand Press, 1972).

Kavanagh, Patrick, *The Complete Poems*, ed. Peter Kavanagh (Newbridge: Goldsmith Press, 1972; rpt 1992).

Kavanagh, Patrick, *By Night Unstarred*, ed. Peter Kavanagh (Newbridge: Goldsmith Press, 1978) (conflation of two unpublished novels).

Kavanagh, Patrick, *Lough Derg*, with a foreword by Paul Durcan (London: Martin Brian & O'Keeffe, 1978; The Curragh: Goldsmith Press, 1978).

Kavanagh, Patrick and Peter Kavanagh, *Kavanagh's Weekly* (Dublin: Goldsmith Press, 1981) (facsimile of the paper published in thirteen issues, 12 April–5 July 1952).

Kavanagh, Patrick, *Selected Poems*, ed. Antoinette Quinn (Harmondsworth: Penguin, 1996).

Kavanagh, Patrick, *A Poet's Country: Selected Prose*, ed. Antoinette Quinn (Dublin: Lilliput Press, 2003).

Kavanagh, Patrick, *Collected Poems*, ed. Antoinette Quinn [2004] (Harmondsworth: Penguin, 2005).

Shorter Prose Pieces Published Separately
'Three Glimpses of Life', *The Bell*, VIII (July 1944).
'The Cobbler and the Football Team', *The Irish Press* (6 March 1946).
'Stars in Muddy Puddles', *The Irish Press* (14 April 1946).
'One Summer Evening in the Month of June', *The Irish Press* (15 June 1946).
'Four Picturizations', *The Bell*, XIV (May, June, July, September 1947).
'Feasts and Feasts', *The Standard* (4 April 1947).
'The Good Child', *The Standard* (24 December 1947).
'The Gallivanting Poet', *Irish Writing*, III (November 1947).
'Three Pieces from a Novel', *The Bell*, XVII (August 1951).
'Pages from a Literary Novel', *The Bell*, XIX (February 1954).

Columns in Journals
'City Commentary', *The Irish Press*, twice weekly, 14 September 1942–18 February 1944.
'The Literary Scene', *The Standard*, weekly, 26 February–11 June 1943.

Film reviewing, *The Standard*, weekly, 22 February 1946–8 July 1949.
'Diary', *Envoy*, monthly, December 1949–July 1951.
Kavanagh's Weekly, with Peter Kavanagh, 12 April–5 July 1952.
Creation, monthly, June–December 1957.
Irish Farmers' Journal, weekly, 14 June 1958–9 March 1963.
National Observer, monthly, July 1959–January 1960.
RTV Guide, weekly, 17 January 1964–30 October 1967.

BOOKS AND ARTICLES ABOUT OR WITH RELEVANCE TO KAVANAGH

Agnew, Sr, Una, *The Mystical Imagination of Patrick Kavanagh: A Buttonhole in Heaven?* (Dublin: Columbia Press, 1998).
Allen, Michael, 'Provincialism and Recent Irish Poetry: The Importance of Patrick Kavanagh', in *Two Decades of Irish Writing*, ed. Douglas Dunn (Cheadle Hulme: Carcanet Press, 1975), pp.23–36.
Allison, Jonathan, *Patrick Kavanagh: A Reference Guide* (New York: G. K. Hall, 1995).
——— 'Patrick Kavanagh and Antipastoral', in *The Cambridge Companion to Contemporary Irish Poetry*, ed. Matthew Campbell (Cambridge: Cambridge University Press, 2003), pp.42–58.
Brown, Terence, 'Conclusion: With Kavanagh in Mind', in *Northern Voices: Poets from Ulster* (Dublin: Gill & Macmillan, 1975; Cheadle Hulme: Carcanet Press, 1975), pp.214–21.
——— Ireland: *A Social and Cultural History 1922–1979* (London: Fontana, 1981); revised as Ireland: *A Social and Cultural History 1922–1985* (London: Fontana, 1985), and as Ireland: *A Social and Cultural History 1922–2002* (London: HarperPerennial, 2004).
——— 'After the Revival', in *Ireland's Literature: Selected Essays* (Mullingar: Lilliput Press, 1988).
Butler, Hubert, 'Envoy and Mr Kavanagh' [1954], reprinted in *Escape from the Anthill* (Mullingar: Lilliput Press, 1985).
——— 'Envoy and Mr Kavanagh' [1954], reprinted in *The Sub-Prefect Should Have Held His Tongue*, ed. Roy Foster (Dublin: Lilliput Press 1990), pp.83–91.
Cantalupo, Catherine, 'Patrick Kavanagh', in *Dictionary of Literary Biography* (Ann Arbor, MI: Edwards Brothers, Inc., 1983), vol.22, pp.192–200.

Casey, Daniel J., 'Kavanagh's Calculations and Miscalculations', Colby Library Quarterly, 12, 2 (1976), pp.65–82.

Corcoran, Neil (ed.), The Chosen Ground: Essays on the Contemporary Poetry of Northern Ireland (Bridgend: Seren Books, 1992).

———— After Yeats and Joyce: Reading Modern Irish Literature (Oxford: Oxford University Press, 1997).

Cronin, Anthony 'The Great Humour', feature article in Magill (October 1997), p.51.

———— 'Patrick Kavanagh', in Dead as Doornails: A Chronicle of Life (Dublin: Dolmen Press, 1976; rpt. Dublin: Poolbeg Press, 1980).

———— 'Patrick Kavanagh: Alive and Well in Dublin', in Heritage Now: Irish Literature in the English Language (Dingle: Brandon Books, 1982), pp.185–96.

Crotty, Patrick (ed.), Modern Irish Poetry: An Anthology (Belfast: Blackstaff Press, 1995).

Davis, Victoria Ann, 'Restating a Parochial Vision: A Reconsideration of Patrick Kavanagh, Flann O'Brien, and Brendan Behan' (unpublished Ph.D. thesis, University of Texas at Austin, 2005), at www.lib.utexas. edu/etd/d/2005/davisv09008/davisv09008.pdf.

Dawe, Gerald, 'Brief Confrontations: The Irish Writer's History', in Against Piety: Essays in Irish Poetry (Belfast: Lagan Press, 1995), pp.19–29.

———— 'How's the Poetry Going?' in How's the Poetry Going? Literary Politics and Ireland Today (Belfast: Lagan Press, 1993), pp.25–37.

Deane, Seamus, Celtic Revivals: Essays in Modern Irish Literature (London: Faber, 1985).

———— A Short History of Irish Literature (London: Hutchinson, 1986).

————'Boredom and Apocalypse: A National Paradigm', in Strange Country: Modernity and Nationhood in Irish Writing Since 1790 (Oxford: Clarendon Press, 1997).

Duffy, Patrick J., 'Patrick Kavanagh's Landscape', Éire-Ireland, 21, 3 (1986), pp.105–18.

———— 'Patrick Kavanagh's Rural Landscape', Baile (1968), pp.3–5.

Dunn, Douglas (ed.), Two Decades of Irish Writing: A Critical Survey (Cheadle Hulme: Carcanet Press, 1975).

Durcan, Paul, A Snail in My Prime (London: Harvill, 1993).

———— 'The Drumshanbo Hustler: A celebration of Van Morrison', Magill (May 1988), p.56.

———— 'Foreword' to Patrick Kavanagh, Lough Derg (London: Martin Brian & O'Keeffe, 1978), pp.vii–ix.

Fallis, Richard, The Irish Renaissance: An Introduction to Anglo-Irish Literature (Dublin: Gill & Macmillan, 1978).

Fallon, Peter and Derek Mahon (eds), 'Introduction' to Penguin Book of Contemporary Irish Poetry (Harmondsworth: Penguin, 1990).

Fleischmann, Ruth, 'Old Irish and Classical Pastoral Elements in Patrick Kavanagh's Tarry Flynn', in Literary Interrelations: Ireland, England and the World, vol. 2, Comparison and Impact, ed. Wolfgang Zach and Heinz Kosok (Tübingen: Guntar Narr Verlag, 1987), pp.311–22.

Foster, John Wilson, 'The Geography of Irish Fiction', in The Irish Novel in Our Time, ed. Patrick Rafroidi and Maurice Harmon (Lille: Presse de Université de Lille, 1975–76), pp.90–103.

———— 'The Poetry of Kavanagh: A Reappraisal', in Colonial Consequences: Essays in Irish Literature and Culture (Dublin: Lilliput Press, 1991), pp.97–113.

Foster, R.F., Modern Ireland 1600–1972 (Harmondsworth: Penguin, 1989).

Frawley, Oona, Irish Pastoral: Nostalgia and Twentieth-Century Irish Literature (Dublin: Irish Academic Press, 2005).

Freyer, Grattan, 'Patrick Kavanagh', Éire-Ireland, 3, 4 (Winter 1968), pp.17–23.

Garratt, Robert F., 'Tradition and Continuity II: Patrick Kavanagh', in Modern Irish Poetry: Tradition and Continuity from Yeats to Heaney (Berkeley and Los Angeles: University of California Press, 1986), pp.137–66.

Goodby, John, Irish poetry since 1950: from stillness into history (Manchester: Manchester University Press, 2000).

Greacen, Robert, Rooted in Ulster: Nine Northern Writers (Belfast: Lagan Press, 2001).

———— 'Sixty Years On', Books Ireland (February 2002), p.17.

Gunston, Sharon R. and Jean C. Stine, 'Patrick (Joseph Gregory) Kavanagh', in Contemporary Literary Criticism, ed. Sharon R. Gunston and Jean C. Stine (Detroit, MI: Gale Research Company, 1982), vol.22, pp.234–44.

Harmon, Maurice, 'Patrick Kavanagh: Touched by God', in Selected Essays, ed. Barbara Brown (Dublin: Irish Academic Press, 2006), pp.121–32.

Heaney, Seamus, The Redress of Poetry: Oxford Lectures (London: Faber and Faber, 1995).

———— 'From Monaghan to the Grand Canal: The Poetry of Patrick Kavanagh', in *Preoccupations: Selected Prose 1968–78* (London: Faber and Faber, 1980; rpt 1984), pp.115–30; first published in Douglas Dunn (ed.), *Two Decades of Irish Writing* (Cheadle Hulme: Carcanet Press, 1975), pp.105–17.

———— 'In the Light of the Imagination', *Irish Times* (21 October 2004).

———— 'Our Own Dour Way', *Trench* (April 1964).

———— 'The Placeless Heaven: Another Look at Kavanagh', in *The Government of the Tongue* (London: Faber and Faber, 1988), pp.3–14.

———— 'The Sense of Place', in *Preoccupations: Selected Prose 1968–78* (London: Faber & Faber, 1980; rpt 1984), pp.131–49.

———— 'Strangeness and Beauty', *The Guardian* (1 January 2005).

Hewitt, John, 'The Cobbler's Song: Poetry of Patrick Kavanagh', *Threshold*, 5, 1 (Spring/Summer 1961), pp.45–51.

Jeffares, A. Norman, *Anglo-Irish Literature* (Dublin: Gill & Macmillan, 1982).

Johnston, Dillon, 'Kavanagh and Heaney', in *Irish Poetry after Joyce* (Dublin: Dolmen Press, 1985; Notre Dame, IN: Notre Dame University Press, 1985), pp.121–66.

Kavanagh, Peter, *The Garden of Golden Apples: A Bibliography of Patrick Kavanagh* (New York: Peter Kavanagh Hand Press, 1972).

———— *Sacred Keeper: A Biography of Patrick Kavanagh* (Newbridge: Goldsmith Press 1979; Maine: National Poetry Foundation, 1988).

———— (ed.), *Patrick Kavanagh: Man and Poet* (Maine: National Poetry Foundation, 1986; Newbridge: Goldsmith Press, 1987).

Kearney, Richard, *Transitions: Narratives in Modern Irish Culture* (Manchester: Manchester University Press, 1988).

———— 'Post-Revival Demythologizers', in *Postnationalist Ireland: Politics, Culture, Philosophy* (London: Routledge, 1997), pp. 124–26.

Kennelly, Brendan, 'Patrick Kavanagh', *Ariel*, 1, 3 (July 1970), pp.7–28.

———— 'Patrick Kavanagh', in *Irish Poetry in English: The Thomas Davis Lectures on Anglo-Irish Poetry*, ed. Seán Lucy (Cork and Dublin: Mercier Press, 1973), pp.159–84.

Kenner, Hugh, 'Two Eccentrics', in *A Colder Eye: The Modern Irish Writers* (Harmondsworth: Penguin, 1984), pp.293–317.

Kiberd, Declan, *Inventing Ireland: The Literature of the Modern Nation* (London: Jonathan Cape, 1995).

————The Irish Writer and the World (Cambridge: Cambridge University Press, 2005).

———— 'Underdeveloped Comedy: Patrick Kavanagh', Irish Classics (London: Granta, 2000), pp.590–601.

Laird, Nick, 'Not a Damn Thing', London Review of Books (18 August 2005).

Liddy, James, 'Open Letter to the Young about Patrick Kavanagh', The Lace Curtain: a magazine of poetry and criticism, 1 (Winter 1969), pp.55–7.

Lloyd, David, Anomalous States: Irish Writing and the Post-Colonial Moment (Dublin: Lilliput Press, 1993).

Longley, Edna, 'Poetic Forms and Social Malformations', The Living Stream: Literature and Revision in Ireland (Newcastle upon Tyne: Bloodaxe, 1994), pp.204–26.

Lucy, Seán (ed.), Irish Poetry in English: The Thomas Davis Lectures on Anglo-Irish Poetry (Cork and Dublin: Mercier Press, 1973).

MacManus, Francis (ed.), The Years of the Great Test 1929–39 (Cork: Mercier Press, 1967).

Mahon, Derek, 'Patrick Kavanagh', The Dublin Magazine, 7, 1 (Spring 1968), pp.6–8.

May, Hal and Susan M. Trosky, 'Patrick Kavanagh', in Contemporary Authors, ed. Hal May and Susan M. Trosky, vol. 123 (Detroit, MI: Gale Research Company, 1988), pp.199–202.

[Mercier, Vivian], 'Kavanagh's Explosive Legacy', Profile (1973), pp.41–3 (unsigned review article of the Letters).

Montague, John, 'Monaghan Man', review of Antoinette Quinn, Patrick Kavanagh: A Biography, Irish Times, weekend supplement (17 November 2001).

———— 'Patrick Kavanagh: A Speech from the Dock', in The Figure in the Cave and Other Essays (Dublin: Lilliput Press, 1989), pp.136–46.

Muri, Allison, 'Paganism and Christianity in Kavanagh's The Great Hunger', Canadian Journal of Irish Studies, 16, 2 (December 1990), pp.66–78.

Nemo, John, Patrick Kavanagh (London: George Prior; New York: Twayne, 1979).

———— 'The Green Knight, Patrick Kavanagh's Venture into Criticism', Studies 63 (Autumn 1974), pp.282–94.

———— 'A Joust with the Philistines: Patrick Kavanagh's Cultural Criticism', Journal of Irish Literature, 4 (1975).

———— 'Patrick Kavanagh: A Bibliography of Materials by and about

Patrick Kavanagh', Irish University Review, 3, 1 (Spring 1973), pp.81–106.

O'Brien, Darcy, Patrick Kavanagh (Lewisburg, PA: Bucknell University Press, 1975).

O'Connor, Frank, 'The Future of Irish Literature', Horizon, 5, 25 (1942), pp.55–63.

Ó Drisceoil, Prionsias (ed.), Culture in Ireland: Regions, Identity and Power (Belfast: Queens University Belfast, Institute of Irish Studies, 1993).

O'Grady, Desmond, 'Paddy Kavanagh in Rome, 1967', Poetry Ireland Review (Spring 1992), pp.14–24.

O'Grady, Thomas B., '"The Parish and the Universe": A Comparative Study of Patrick Kavanagh and William Carleton', Studies (Spring 1996), pp.17–25.

O'Loughlin, Michael, After Kavanagh: Patrick Kavanagh and the Discourse of Contemporary Irish Poetry (Dublin: Raven Arts Press, 1985).

Peacock, Alan, 'Received Religion and Secular Vision: MacNeice and Kavanagh', in Irish Writers and Religion, ed. Robert Welch (Gerrards Cross: Colin Smythe, 1992), pp.148–68.

Quinn, Antoinette,Patrick Kavanagh: A Biography (Dublin: Gill & Macmillan, 2001; 2nd edn 2003).

——— Patrick Kavanagh: Born-Again Romantic (Dublin: Gill & Macmillan, 1991).

Redshaw, Thomas Dillon, '"We Done Our Best When We Were Let": James Liddy's Arena, 1963–1965', The South Carolina Review, 38, 1 (Fall 2005), pp.97–117.

Ryan, John, Remembering How We Stood: Bohemian Dublin at the Mid-Century (Dublin: Gill &Macmillan, 1975).

Sealy, Douglas, 'The Writings of Patrick Kavanagh', The Dublin Magazine, 3 (Winter 1965), pp.5–23.

Smith, Michael and Trevor Joyce, 'Editorial', The Lace Curtain, 2 (Spring 1970), p.2.

Smyth, Gerry, 'The Moment of Kavanagh's Weekly', in Decolonisation and Criticism: The Construction of Irish Literature (London: Pluto Press, 1998), pp.103–12.

Stack, Tom, No Earthly Estate: The Religious Poetry of Patrick Kavanagh (Dublin: Columba Press, 2002; Chester Springs, PA: Dufour Editions, 2002) (an anthology of Kavanagh's religious poems with biographical and critical commentary).

Stewart, Bruce, '"Quincunx": Seamus Heaney and the Ulster Regionalists', in *Complicities: British Poetry 1946–2007*, ed. Robin Purves and Sam Ladku (Prague: Litteraria Pragensia, 2007), pp.102–44.

Thornton, Weldon, 'Virgin or Hungry Fiend? The Failures of the Imagination in Patrick Kavanagh's *The Great Hunger*', *Mosaic*, 2, 3 (Spring 1979), pp.152–62.

Warner, Alan, *Clay is the Word: Patrick Kavanagh 1904–1967* (Dublin: Dolmen, 1973).

———— 'Patrick Kavanagh', in *A Guide to Anglo-Irish Literature* (Dublin: Gill & Macmillan, 1981), pp.72–108.

Welch, Robert, 'Language as Pilgrimage: Lough Derg Poems of Patrick Kavanagh and Denis Devlin', *Irish University Review Special Issue: The Long Poem*, 13, 1 (Spring 1983), pp.54–66.

Whelan, Kevin, 'The Bases of Regionalism', in *Culture in Ireland – Regions: Identity and Power*, ed. Prionsias Ó Drisceoil (Belfast: Queens University Belfast, Institute of Irish Studies, 1993).

UNCOLLECTED POEMS

Some poems not included in Kavanagh's *Collected Poems* are made available on the website of The Patrick Kavanagh Centre to readers and students for study and scholarly use: http://www.patrickkavanaghcountry.com/index.html

From MS Collections

Buffalo (1938–39) (State University of New York at Buffalo).

Verses (Harry Ransom Center for Humanities Research, Texas, 1938).

The Lady of the Poets (Harry Ransom Center for Humanities Research, Texas, 1938).

The Seed and the Soil (National Library of Ireland).

To Anna Quinn (National Library of Ireland).

To Anna Quinn (2) (National Library of Ireland).

Poems (c.1929–1940) (National Library of Ireland).

From Published Books

Ploughman and Other Poems

A Soul for Sale

Uncollected MS Poems
Betjeman Poems (1942) (University of Victoria smalltext, BC, Canada).
Hilda Poems (1945–47).
UCD B3 (University College Dublin).
UCD B4 (University College Dublin).
UCD B6 (University College Dublin).

Uncollected Published Poems
City Commentary Poems (1942–44).
Irish Times Poems.

The Patrick Kavanagh Centre

The Patrick Kavanagh Centre
Inniskeen, Co. Monaghan, Ireland
Tel: +353 42 93 78560
Email: infoatpkc@eircom.net

Hours: from 15 January to 31 May: Tuesday to Friday, 11a.m. to 4.30p.m. Closed Saturday, Sunday and Monday. From 1 June to 30 September: Tuesday to Friday 11a.m. to 4.30p.m. Closed on Monday. Run by the Inniskeen Enterprise Group, the centre houses exhibitions on local history and on Kavanagh, a sixty-seat audio-visual theatre, and a research library. On view are twelve specially commissioned paintings illustrating Kavanagh's poem 'The Great Hunger', a miniature model depicting 'A Christmas Childhood', the poet's death mask, and other memorabilia associated with him. The performance tour of Kavanagh Country takes in many local sites immortalized by the poet, with anecdotes, historical facts, wild rumours and even the odd poem along the way. The tour rounds off back at the centre with a half-hour one-man show by Inniskeen actor, Gene Carroll. Membership of the 'Friends of Patrick Kavanagh' organization includes free admission to the centre.

Index

A

aisling poems, 100
alcohol, 30, 33, 177–8
Allen, Michael, 8, 132–4, 155
  'Provincialism and the Importance of
  Patrick Kavanagh', 173
Allison, Jonathan, 9
Alvarez, Al, 171
Anglo-Irish Treaty (1922), 7, 93
Arensberg, Conrad, 16
Ariel , 175, 178
Arnold, Matthew, 27
Auden, W.H., 96, 118, 132
Avis, Patricia, 173–4

B

Bakhtin, Mikhail, 138, 155
Barry, Kevin, 34
Beat poetry, 130
Beckett, Samuel, 43–4, 113
  Murphy, 44, 116
Behan, Brendan, 5, 128, 157
Belfast, 164–5, 166–7, 171, 173
The Bell , 28, 31, 40, 55, 57, 127, 169
Beltaine, 55
Bhabha, Homi, 45
Big House, the, 27
Blake, William, 95–7, 177, 178
Boland, Eavan, 4, 157, 164
borderlands, Irish, 7–9, 122, 164
Boyd, John, 167, 168
Boyle, Patrick, 167, 169
Brady, Archbishop Sean (now
  Cardinal), 163
Brown, Terence, 15, 49, 94
  Northern Voices, 164
Budgen, Frank, 17
Butler, Hubert, 129
Butler Education Act (1947), 164, 166

C

Carleton, William, 135
Carson, Ciaran, 138
Catholicism, 24, 30, 132, 147, 151,
  164, 168, 170
  1937 Constitution and, 15, 110–11,
  117
  Christmas poems and, 114–15,
  117–18
  The Great Hunger and, 93, 94–5,
  99–100, 101, 110, 111, 112, 115,
  128
  Literary Revival and, 27, 45
  in 'Lough Derg', 104–5
  PK and, 24, 45, 102, 105, 163, 182
  A Soul for Sale and, 112–13, 115
  Tarry Flynn and, 99–100
censorship, 13, 15, 28, 29, 31, 109
Censorship of Publications Act (1929),
  15, 28, 109
An Claidheamh Soluis, 55
Clare, John, 9
Clarke, Austin, 32, 39, 43–4, 50, 58,
  61, 62, 67, 160, 175
  Pilgrimage and Other Poems , 45
classicism, 134–5
Coffey, Brian, 4
Coleridge, Samuel Taylor, 41
colonial themes, 10, 11, 27, 77, 78
  decolonisation, 64, 66, 69, 179
  post-colonial writing, 6, 11, 27,
  45–6, 56, 59, 61–2, 64, 66, 77–8,
  124
Colum, Paidraic, 127, 135
comedy/comic spirit, 14, 23, 25, 28,
  40, 46, 49, 117, 152, 175, 176–7
Conditions of Employment Bill
  (1935), 15
Connolly, Cyril, 28
contraception, 15

Corcoran, Neil, 8
Corkery, Daniel, 67, 80
Costello, John A., 33, 57
Crabbe, George
  The Village, 9
The Crane Bag , 8, 170
Crawford, Robert, 46
Criminal Law Amendment Act (1935),
  15
'critical mind, the', 62, 129
Cronin, Anthony, 124, 125, 127
  Dead as Doornails , 13, 138–9
Cross, Dorothy, 118
Cuala Press, 7, 28, 109
Curry, Patrick, 30

D

Dante, 117
Davie, Donald, 133
Dawe, Gerald, 8, 164
  'How's the Poetry Going?', 5–6
de Valera, Eamon, 1, 15, 16–17, 45,
  57, 62, 117, 123
  1943 St. Patrick's Day broadcast,
    27–8, 114
  PK on, 102–3, 109
  rural Ireland and, 27–8, 49, 94,
    109, 110–11, 117
Deane, Seamus, 12–13, 42, 56, 64,
  116, 122, 123, 125, 173
  'internal schism' and, 12, 116
  'Irish Poetry and Nationalism', 173
  on PK and Yeats, 124
decolonisation, 64, 66, 69, 179
Devlin, Denis, 4
divorce, 15
Dolmen Press, 172, 173
Donoghue, Denis, 124, 125
Dublin, 4, 14, 44, 60, 63, 94
  Canal Bank sonnets, 12, 90, 123,
    145, 153–6, 160
  Heaney and, 170–5
  Joyce and, 1, 17, 44, 63, 68
  PK and, 1, 5, 13, 148–9
  PK's move to (1939), 9, 22, 26,
    29–30, 85–6, 107–8, 129, 164, 165
  literary elite, 15, 25, 30, 32
  migration to, 13, 85, 148–9
  theatre, 59–60
  universities, 34, 59, 164, 178
  The Dublin Magazine, 25

Duck, Stephen
  The Thresher's Labour, 9
The Dundalk Democrat, 98, 101, 138
Dunn, Douglas
  Two Decades of Irish Writing, 173
Durcan, Paul, 3–4, 7, 8, 122, 123,
  157, 164
  'November 1967', 3

E

Eliot, T.S., 44, 49, 50, 95, 97, 111, 132
  The Waste Land , 49, 50, 95, 97, 111,
    132
Emergency Powers Act (1939), 109
emigration, 16, 28, 57, 93, 113
Empson, William, 76
enclosure of land, 10
Ennis, John, 157
Envoy, 31, 40, 42, 57, 58, 59, 169
Eriu, 57
Ervine, St. John, 168

F

Fallon, Peter
  Penguin Book of Contemporary Irish Poetry ,
    2
'familism', 16
famine, Irish, 15–16, 93
Farran, Robert, 32, 175
Field Day Company, 170
film criticism, 30, 40
folk songs and ballads, 3–4, 11, 136,
  137, 138–9, 140–1
Folklore Commission report (1935),
  111
Foster, John Wilson, 46, 116, 117,
  130, 139, 181
Foster, Roy, 16–17, 110–11
Freud, Sigmund, 98, 118, 119, 150
Friel, Brian, 135, 167
Frye, Northrop, 48

G

Garratt, Robert F., 44, 81
Geary, Frank, 30
Gibbon, Monk, 127
Ginsberg, Allen, 174
Gogarty, Oliver St. John, 25, 39
Goldsmith, Oliver

The Deserted Village, 9, 132
Goodby, John, 85
Gregory, Lady Augusta, 22, 27, 107, 171

H

Hardy, Thomas, 177
Harmon, Maurice, 66
Hartnett, Michael, 157
Heaney, Seamus
  background of, 7, 163, 164, 165
  Dublin writers and, 170–5
  The Great Hunger and, 125, 168, 181
  Kennelly and, 175, 176
  move to the Republic (1972), 165,
    166
  on PK, 2, 8, 95–6, 117, 125–6, 130,
    157, 170–1, 182
  PK's influence on, 2, 8, 9, 122, 157,
    163–6, 168–70, 171, 172, 182–3
  on PK's language, 136, 179, 180–1
  rural life and, 2, 10, 90, 179
  Ulster and, 7–8, 9, 164–5, 166–70
  Yeats and, 1–2, 179
  WORKS OF, 137–8, 165, 173, 174,
    179–83
    Death of a Naturalist, 8, 172
    'Digging', 166–7
    'From Monaghan to the Grand
      Canal', 8, 125, 172
    'Frontiers of Writing', 165,
      169–70
    The Government of the Tongue, 8, 157
    Haw Lantern , 125
    'The Placeless Heaven: Another
      Look at Kavanagh', 8, 125, 166,
      168, 181,182
    Preoccupations, 8, 157, 168
    'The Redress of Poetry', 163
    Seeing Things, 181–2
    'The Sense of Place', 2, 8, 169,
      171, 172
    Station Island, 125
    Sweeney Astray, 181
Hedge School tradition, 135
Hewitt, John, 168–9
Higgins, Aidan, 172
Higgins, F.R., 31, 42, 43, 67
Hillan, Sophia, 168
Hirsch, Edward, 10–11
Hobsbaum, Philip, 173, 178
Holland, Mary, 173

Homer, 17, 140
Horace, 41
Horizon , 28, 32, 50, 109
Howes, Marjorie, 15, 16
Hughes, Ted, 171
Hutchinson, Pearse, 172
Hyde, Douglas, 10

I

Inniskeen (Co. Monaghan), 7, 24–5,
  28, 32, 34, 90, 107
Ireland
  1916 Easter Rising, 12, 116, 117
  1919-23 period, 7, 12, 48, 86, 93,
    116, 117, 164, 179
  1930s/40s, 13, 15, 48, 50, 86
  1937 Constitution, 12, 15, 27,
    110–12, 117, 118–19, 120
  1950s, 56, 57–67, 160
  aisling poems, 100
  borderlands, 7–9, 122, 164
  'familism', 16
  literature and, 5–7, 27, 59, 60–1,
    68–9, 80, 86, 91, 171
    see also Literary Revival; parochial,
    the; pastoral tradition
  'national myth', 42–3, 45, 62, 66–7
  sexual conservatism, 15, 16, 49, 50,
    93, 102, 104, 110
  urbanisation, 85, 86–7, 88, 90, 91,
    113
  woman and the mother theme,
    28–9, 98–103, 104–6, 111–12,
    118–19
Ireland, Denis, 168
Ireland of the Welcomes, 40, 137
Ireland's Own, 138
Iremonger, Valentin, 172
Irish -American audience, 43
Irish Farmers' Journal, 31
Irish Independent, 30
Irish language, 27, 79, 165
Irish Press, 30, 32, 39
Irish Statesman, 25, 41, 55
Irish Times, 21, 30, 33, 47–8, 50, 108
Irish Weekly Independent, 25
Irish Writing, 31, 40

J

Jackson, Tessa, 118

jazz, 3
Jeffares, A. Norman, 11, 175
Johnston, Dillon, 49, 80
Jordan, John, 172
journalism, 22, 30–2, 39–40, 47–8,
   59–67, 75, 83, 90, 169
journals, 55–8
   see also *Kavanagh's Weekly*
Joyce, James, 10, 27, 64, 75, 76, 132,
   155, 170
   Dublin and, 1, 17, 44, 63, 68
   The Great Hunger and, 97, 106, 112
   PK and, 32, 41, 42, 44, 63, 65, 68,
      73, 115–16
   WORKS OF
      'The Dead', 106
      Finnegans Wake, 41, 76, 112
      A Portrait of the Artist as a Young Man,
         41, 115–16
      Ulysses, 17, 41, 42, 44, 68, 75,
         132, 155
Joyce, Trevor, 5, 157

K

Kavanagh, Patrick
   1930 pilgrimage to Dublin, 25,
      48–9, 51, 81, 82
   1960s poems, 157–9, 160–1
   autobiographical elements in work,
      21, 24–5, 28–9, 39, 47–9, 180
   autobiographical myth (from 1955),
      145, 176
   biographical information, 7, 14–15,
      23, 24, 25, 26, 29–30, 33, 34, 37,
      58
   criticism of fellow artists, 31, 32,
      40, 43, 62, 67–8
   critics and, 122–6
   death of (1967), 3, 34
   family of, 6, 24, 29, 31, 33, 34, 40,
      58
   Grand Canal 'illumination' (1955),
      14, 23, 33, 46, 117, 122, 130,
      145
   health of, 14, 23, 33, 34, 46, 122,
      130, 145, 146, 163
   influence of, 2, 3, 4, 7–8, 122, 157
   influence on Heaney, 2, 8, 9, 122,
      157, 163–6, 168–70, 171, 172,
      182–3
   influence on Kennelly, 9, 122, 157,
      164, 175–8
   marriage (1967), 34
   move to Dublin (1939), 22, 26,
      29–30, 85–6, 107–8, 129, 164,
      165
   poetics *see* parochial, the; pastoral
      tradition; poetic style of PK; realism
   political views, 160
   radio broadcasts, 179–80
   religion and, 177, 178, 182
      see also Catholicism
   repudiation of own work, 14, 15,
      23, 25, 40, 87, 112, 117, 121–2,
      131, 175
   sources of material, 131, 137–40,
      156
   Ulster regionalism and, 169
   WORKS OF
      'Advent', 114–15, 119
      'Ante-Natal Dream', 32
      'Art McCooey', 41, 114, 117–18,
         136–7
      'Auditors In', 4, 32–3, 129, 139,
         150, 182
      'A Ballad', 139
      'Bluebells for Love', 113, 114,
         130
      Canal Bank sonnets, 12, 90, 123,
         145, 153–6, 160
      Christmas poems, 12, 114–15,
         117–18
      'A Christmas Childhood', 115,
         117–18, 119, 170
      'Christmas Eve Remembered', 86,
         114
      'Christmas in the Country', 109
      Collected Poems, 15, 28, 34, 109, 117,
         125, 157, 158, 175, 177
      Collected Prose, 39, 40, 97, 170
      'Coloured Balloons', 31
      *Come Dance with Kitty Stobling and Other
      Poems*, 12, 34, 58, 64, 91, 121, 123,
         149–50, 151, 157
         Canal Bank sonnets, 12, 90, 123,
            145, 153–6, 160
         Heaney and, 168, 170
         'noo pomes', 12, 123, 125, 129,
            130, 131, 145–52, 158–60
      Complete Poems, 28, 147
      'Cyrano de Bergerac', 139
      'Dark Ireland', 14
      'Dear Folks', 150–1, 152

'The Defeated', 32
'Epic', 2, 5, 17–18, 32, 45, 125, 135, 140, 170–1, 182
'Father Mat', 112–13, 115, 119
'From Monaghan to the Grand Canal', 46–7, 51, 126–7
'The Gallivanting Poet', 31, 42, 43
'Gold Watch', 127
The Great Hunger, 7, 13, 27–8, 58, 80, 106, 123, 129, 130
  1937 Constitution and, 27–8, 110–12
  Blake and, 96–7
  Catholicism and, 93, 94–5, 99–100,101, 110, 111, 112, 115, 128
  censorship laws and, 15, 28, 109
  cycle of nature and, 103–5
  expurgated version, 28, 58, 109–10
  great famine and, 15–16, 93
  Heaney and, 125, 168, 181
  Joyce and, 97, 106
  Kennelly and, 175, 177
  'Lough Derg' and, 32, 104–5
  pastoral tradition and, 11, 87–90, 91, 103–4
  PK's rejection of, 14, 15, 23, 40, 87, 112, 117, 121, 131, 175
  realism and, 11–12, 17, 44, 49, 50, 87, 91, 127–8, 149
  sexual themes, 16, 28, 100, 101, 102, 114, 149
  spiritual hunger and, 15–16, 93–5
  Tarry Flynn and, 98–100
  The Waste Land and, 95, 97, 111
  woman and the mother theme, 99, 101, 102, 104
The Green Fool, 12, 24–5, 28, 29, 39, 47–9, 51, 134
'The Hospital', 51, 147–8
'I Had a Future', 140
'If Ever You Go To Dublin Town', 139
'In Blinking Blankness: Three Efforts', 158
'In Memory of My Mother', 149, 163, 182
'Inniskeen Road: July Evening', 25, 41, 131, 180, 181
'Intimate Parnassus', 134
'Irish Stew', 126

'The Irish Tradition', 98
'Is', 150
'Kerr's Ass', 130, 139
'Leaves of Grass', 51, 148
'Lines Written on a Seat on the Grand Canal, Dublin', 131, 132–4, 155–6
'The Long Garden', 114, 115
'Lough Derg', 12, 32, 104–5, 123, 127
'Miss Universe', 151–2
'My People', 108–9, 111
'My Room', 127
'Nationalism and Literature', 42–3, 51, 72, 84, 100
By Night Unstarred, 129
'Nineteen Fifty-Four', 146
'noo pomes', 12, 123, 125, 129, 130, 131, 145–52, 158–60
Canal Bank sonnets, 12, 90, 123, 145, 153–6, 160
'October', 148
'On Looking into E.V. Rieu's Homer', 134
'On Raglan Road', 3, 100, 102, 139
'On Reading a Book on Common Wild Flowers', 149
'The Paddiad: Or the Devil as a Patron of Irish Letters', 32, 43, 134
'The Parish and the Universe', 73, 97–8, 101
'Peasant Poet', 25, 84
'Pegasus', 30, 32, 36, 129, 130, 134
'A Personal Problem', 158, 176
'The Ploughman', 5, 127
Ploughman and Other Poems, 11, 24, 25–6, 27, 41, 95–6, 126–7
'Poet', 84
A Poet's Country: Selected Prose, 40, 108, 109, 137
'Prelude', 129, 177
'Pygmalion', 134
'Question to Life', 151, 152
Recent Poems, 34, 58
'The Rowley Mile', 139
'The Rustic', 84–5
'Sanctity', 115
Selected Poems, 145
Selected Prose, 176
Self-Portrait, 5–6, 26, 33, 34, 39, 121–2, 164, 173
  The Green Fool and, 12, 25, 29, 47

inconsistencies in, 34–5
Literary Revival and, 13–14, 27
poetry of 'not caring', 46, 131
Quinn on, 35, 158
Tarry Flynn and, 12, 29, 47, 82
'Shancoduff', 126, 131, 170
'Song at Fifty', 139, 152
A Soul for Sale, 5, 12, 28, 32, 58, 59,
    107, 109, 114–17, 121, 129
1937 Constitution and, 112, 117
Catholicism and, 112–13, 115
Heaney and, 168
'Spraying the Potatoes', 100–1, 170,
    174, 179
'Spring Day', 139
'Stony Grey Soil', 32, 35–6, 37, 127
Tarry Flynn, 24, 39, 51, 58, 59, 89,
    97, 170, 181
    censorship laws and, 15, 29
    The Great Hunger and, 98–100
    PK on, 12, 29, 46–7, 61, 82
    rural life in, 28–9, 49, 50,
        98–100
    Self-Portrait and, 12, 29, 47, 82
    woman and the mother theme,
        28–9, 98–100, 101–2
'Temptation in Harvest', 116, 129
'Threshing Morning', 97
'To a Child', 84, 126
'To Knowledge', 84
'Two Ways', 21
'The Wake of the Books', 31, 135
'Who Killed James Joyce?', 139
'Why Sorrow?', 127
'Wisdom', 146, 147, 148
'Yellow Vestment', 152
Kavanagh, Peter, 6, 31, 34, 40, 58, 147
Kavanagh Centre (Inniskeen), 7, 199
Kavanagh's Weekly, 6–7, 14, 27, 31, 33,
    40, 44, 57–8, 59–69, 101, 130
Kearney, Richard, 13–14, 56
Postnationalist Ireland , 13
Keats, John, 41, 97–8, 147, 178
Kennelly, Brendan, 9, 122, 123, 157,
    163–4, 178
PK and, 9, 122, 157, 163–4, 175–8
WORKS OF
    'Irish Poetry Since Yeats', 176–7
    Journey into Joy , 178
    'Patrick Kavanagh', 175–8
Kenny, Mary, 1
Kiberd, Declan, 13, 74, 75, 112,

113–14, 122, 123, 148–50
Kiely, Benedict, 175
Kimball, Solon, 16
Kinsella, Thomas, 8, 122, 129, 169,
    171, 172, 173, 175
    'The Divided Mind', 174–5
    Dolmen Miscellany of Irish Writing, 172
    Poems of the Dispossessed, 174
    The Tain translation, 174
Kirkland, Richard, 160
Kristeva, Julia, 160

L

The Lace Curtain, 4–5, 157
Lagan, 167
Lavin, Mary, 67, 169
The Leader, 33, 39, 98, 130
Leavis, F.R., 133, 134, 160
Lee, Joseph, 57
libel actions, 23, 25, 33, 39, 98, 101,
    130
Liddy, James, 157, 172
    'Open Letter to the Young about
    Patrick Kavanagh', 4–5
literary criticism, 56, 62, 65–6, 67,
    68, 69, 75
Literary Revival, 26, 44, 113, 135,
    149, 167
    Catholicism and, 27, 45
    The Great Hunger and, 11, 12, 87, 89
    PK and, 5, 45, 46, 48, 49, 61, 72–4,
        80–1, 107–8
    PK influenced by, 27, 83–4, 127
    PK's hostility to, 13–14, 22, 27, 30,
        31, 32, 40, 42, 72, 75, 78, 116,
        171
    mythologising spirit of, 12, 13–14,
        22, 27
    pastoral tradition and, 72, 73–4, 75,
        77–81, 83–4, 86, 87, 89
    peasantry and, 10–11, 13, 22, 25,
        26, 42, 49, 61, 78, 80–1, 127
    Protestantism of, 27, 45
    romanticism of, 22, 25, 27, 29, 49,
        77, 78
Lloyd, David, 140, 141, 155
localism and regionalism, 40, 43, 44,
    165, 174
    see also parochial, the
London, 24, 26, 85
Longley, Edna, 7–8, 9, 75, 122, 123,

124, 125, 140
Longley, Michael, 10, 169, 178
Love, Stuart, 167, 168
Lucie-Smith, Edward, 173
Lucy, Sean, 174–5
Irish Poets in English , 175, 178
Lynch, Brian, 157

M

MacBride, Sean, 57
MacCarthy, Thomas, 164
MacDiarmid, Hugh, 46
MacDonagh, Donagh
  Poems from Ireland , 7
MacGreevy, Thomas, 4
MacLaverty, Michael, 168, 169, 170
Macken, Walter, 67
MacNeice, Louis, 2, 122, 124, 170,
  171
Mahon, Derek, 169, 173, 178, 181
  Penguin Book of Contemporary Irish Poetry, 2
malapropism, 155
Mallarmé, Stephan, 156
Mangan, James Clarence, 100
marriage, 16, 49, 111–12, 113–14
Martin, Augustine, 50
McEnaney, John, 138
McFadden, Roy, 167–8, 169
McGahern, John, 10, 172
That They May Face the Rising Sun , 49
McHugh, Roger, 175
McMahon, Bryan, 175
McManus, M.J., 32
McQuaid, Archbishop, 164, 182
Meyer, Kuno, 57, 174
Miller, Liam, 173–4
modernism, 4, 21, 49, 50, 122, 132
Moloney, Katherine Barry, 34
Monaghan, Co., 13, 24, 29, 41, 46, 58,
  72, 90, 125, 127, 137, 152
  as borderland, 7–8, 122, 164
  countryside of, 2, 85, 179
  nostalgia for, 85, 86
  speech of, 2, 179
  in 'Stony Grey Soil', 32, 35–6, 37, 127
Montague, John, 122, 129, 169, 172,
  173, 174, 175, 181
  on PK, 13, 22, 121
  PK's influence on, 2, 8, 171–2
  WORKS OF
    Dolmen Miscellany of Irish Writing, 172

'The Impact of International
  Modern Poetry on Irish Writing',
  174–5
Poisoned Lands, 171–2
'Regionalism, or A Portrait of the
  Artist as a Model Farmer', 174
The Rough Field , 174
'Water Carrier', 171–2
Monteith, Charles, 173
Moore, Brian, 172
Moore, George, 63, 65, 73, 102
  Hail and Farewell , 44
Moran, Michael, 141
Morrison, Van, 3, 7
Morton, H.V.
  In Search of Ireland, 47
mother and woman theme, 28–9,
  98–103, 104–6, 111–12, 118–19
Muir, Edwin, 46
Muldoon, Paul, 122, 173, 181
  Faber Book of Contemporary Irish Poetry, 8
Munich crisis (1938), 17, 45, 140
Murphy, Richard, 172, 174
music, 3–4, 11, 136, 137, 138–9,
  140–1
mythology
  classical, 14, 17, 36, 44
  Revivalist, 12, 13–14, 22, 27

N

The Nation, 55, 56
National Observer, 31
nationalism, 43, 46, 63–4, 68–9, 72,
  140, 165, 170
  cultural, 40, 42–3
Nemo, John, 23
neoclassicism, eighteenth-century, 132,
  135, 139, 159
New Criticism, 134, 157, 160
The New Poetry, 171
New Statesman, 173
ni Chuilleanain, Eilean, 175
Nimbus , 40, 154
'no caring', style of, 23, 46, 50, 122,
  123–6, 128, 147, 152–7, 159,
  160
  early examples, 123, 130, 131,
  145–6
Nonplus, 173–4
Norden, Irene Gilsenan, 119
Northern Ireland, 123, 165, 166, 174

see also Ulster
Northwestern University, Chicago, 34

O

O'Brien, D., 81
O'Brien, Flann, 1, 5, 10, 13
O'Brien, John Anthony
  The Vanishing Irish , 160
O'Casey, Sean, 32, 180
O'Connor, Frank, 31, 50, 59, 61, 171
O'Donnell, Peadar, 31
O'Faolain, Sean, 10, 28, 31, 50, 55,
  59, 61, 66, 128, 135, 171
O'Flaherty, Liam, 94
O'Grady, Standish James, 78
O'Loughlin, Michael, 124, 125, 136,
  137
Olsen, Charles, 174
O'Sullivan, Maurice
  Twenty Years A-Growing, 47
O'Sullivan, Seamus, 25
Oxford Book of Irish Verse, 179

P

Palgrave's Golden Treasury, 47, 138
Parnassus theme, 132–5, 148, 151,
  153, 156
parochial, the, 14, 22, 43, 47, 49,
  63–7, 68, 72–4, 97–8, 132–3
  'Epic' and, 2, 140, 170
  Heaney and, 2, 136, 170–1, 175,
    183
  and provincial distinction, 1, 2, 14,
    27, 44–6, 63, 73, 97, 134, 183
  woman and the mother theme,
    100–1
pastoral tradition, 9–10, 11–12, 32–3,
  72–4, 79–80, 83–9
  anti-pastoral modes, 9, 11, 72–4,
    84, 89, 90, 91, 127
  classical, 76, 84, 87, 88
  English, 11, 74, 76, 77, 78, 79, 84,
    88
  The Great Hunger and, 11, 87–90, 91,
    103–4
  history of, 76–7
  Irish, 11, 72, 74, 75–8, 79–80, 83,
    87–91
  Literary Revival and, 72, 73–4, 75,
    77–81, 83–4, 86, 87, 89

post-colonial writing and, 77–8
  urban and rural modes, 9–10, 13,
    90, 91, 148–9, 152–3
Patrick Kavanagh Centre (Inniskeen), 7,
  199
peasant, the, 10, 22, 25–6, 49, 67, 87,
  89, 95, 127
  Literary Revival and, 10–11, 13, 22,
    25, 26, 42, 49, 61, 78, 80–1, 127
  PK's role-playing, 80–4
PEN, Irish
  Concord of Harps, 67
periodicals, 55–8
  see also *Kavanagh's Weekly*
Plunkett, James, 172
poetic style of PK, 1, 3–4, 5, 131–7,
  139–41, 146–61, 180–1
  comedy/comic spirit, 14, 23, 28,
    40, 46, 49, 117, 152, 175, 176–7
  formal looseness, 123–6, 130–1,
    139, 145–6, 147, 152, 153–4,
    155–6
  formulae and, 41, 42
  inspiration and, 40–2
  'outrageous rhymes', 4, 117–18,
    156
personal poetry, 25–6, 32–4
  sincerity and, 21–4, 31, 32, 33,
    34–7
  style of 'no caring', 23, 46, 50, 122,
    123–6, 128, 147, 152–7, 159, 160
  style of 'no caring', early examples
    of, 123, 130, 131, 145–6
post-colonial writing, 6, 11, 27, 45–6,
  59, 61–2, 64, 66, 124
pastoral tradition and, 77–8
periodicals and, 56
postmodernism, 22
Pound, Ezra, 44, 174
prose writing, 29, 39–41, 42–3,
  44–51, 72–3, 75, 154
  journalism, 22, 30–2, 39–40, 47–8,
    59–67, 75, 83, 90, 169
  literary criticism, 56, 62, 65–6, 67,
    68, 69, 75
  see also Kavanagh, Patrick: WORKS OF:
  Self-Portrait; *Tarry Flynn*; *The Green Fool*
Protestantism, 27, 31, 45, 170
provincialism, 1, 2, 14, 27, 44–6, 63,
  73, 97, 134, 183

Q

Queen's University, Belfast, 164, 166, 171
Quinn, Antoinette, 41, 45, 63, 107, 122–3, 129, 149, 159, 177–8
  The Great Hunger and, 15, 50, 93, 110
  on The Green Fool, 25, 47
  on PK's autobiographical myth, 176
  on PK's role-playing, 80–1, 83–4
  on Self-Portrait, 35, 158
  Patrick Kavanagh: A Biography, 14, 177–8
  Patrick Kavanagh: Born-Again Romantic, 14, 123
  A Poet's Country: Selected Prose (ed.), 40, 108, 109, 137

R

radio broadcasts, 179–80
Rann, 167
realism, 1, 27, 31, 42, 46, 47, 49, 50, 51, 127–8
  fantasy and, 12, 116, 119
  The Great Hunger and, 11–12, 17, 44, 49, 50, 87, 91, 127–8, 149
  move away from, 129, 147
  parochialism and, 40, 43, 44, 73
Reynolds, Lorna, 175
Rieu, E.V., 98
Rilke, R.M., 126
Robinson, Mary, 7
Rodgers, W.R., 67, 171
romanticism, 21, 36, 40, 41, 85, 86, 97–8, 127, 139–40
Revival, 22, 25, 27, 29, 49, 77, 78
RTV Guide, 31, 40
rural life, 41, 93–5, 108–10, 112, 117, 136–7, 164
  classicism and, 134–5
  de Valera and, 27–8, 49, 94, 109, 110–11, 117
  departure theme, 26, 28, 29, 33, 116
  in The Green Fool, 24–5, 47–8
  Heaney and, 2, 10, 90, 179
  late marriage and, 16, 113–14
  migration from, 85, 86–7, 88, 90, 91, 113, 144–5
  in Tarry Flynn, 28–9, 49, 50, 98–100
  see also Kavanagh, Patrick: WORKS OF: The Great Hunger; pastoral tradition; peasant, the
Russell, George (Æ), 25, 41, 48–9, 51, 55, 58, 60, 61, 81, 127

Ryan, John, 57

S

Said, Edward, 77
Samhain , 55
satire and polemic, 22, 32, 85, 128–30, 158, 170, 177
Scotland, 46
Second World War, 26, 57, 58, 86, 107, 108, 109
self-consciousness, 23, 33, 36, 37
Selkirk, Alexander, 41, 131, 180
sexual themes, 11, 99–101, 102, 104–5, 113, 114, 117–20, 152
  The Great Hunger and, 16, 28, 100, 101, 102, 114, 149
Sheridan, Niall, 39
Simmons, James, 169
sincerity, 21–4, 31, 32, 33, 34–7
Sisson, C.H., 127
Skelton, Robin
Six Irish Poets, 171
slang, 4, 118, 180, 181
Smith, Michael, 5, 157
Smyllie, Bertie, 30, 32
sonnet form, 145–8, 153–4, 156, 157
speech, rendering of, 2, 179, 180
Synge and, 67, 68, 180
St. Joseph's Catholic Teacher Training College (Belfast), 166–7
  The Standard, 30, 39–40
stereotypes (stage Irishry), 10, 42, 47, 75, 78, 80–1, 82
Stevens, Wallace, 172
Studies, 40, 57
Sweeney, Matthew, 164
Synge, John, 27, 40, 42, 74, 75, 78–9, 80, 108, 171
  The Aran Islands, 78–9
  peasantry and, 10, 22, 67
  rendering of speech and, 67, 68, 180

T

The Tain , 174
Theocritus, 76
Thomas, R.S., 171
Threshold, 167, 169
tourism, 27, 47–8, 89
Traherne, Thomas, 154
Trilling, Lionel, 22, 36

Trinity College, Dublin, 164, 178

U

Ulster, 7–9, 122, 136, 163, 164–5
   literary magazines in, 166, 167–8
   literary tradition, 164, 167–8, 169
   regionalism, 164–5, 166–70
   The United Irishman, 55
University College Dublin, 34, 59, 164
urbanisation, 85, 86–7, 88, 90, 91,
   113

V

Virgil, 76, 87

W

Walsh, Maurice, 32
Weber, Richard, 172
Whitman, Walt, 51
Wilde, Oscar, 155
Williams, Richard Dalton, 138
Williams, William Carlos, 174
Wolfe, Humbert, 127
women, 15, 117, 151–2
woman and the mother theme, 28–9,
   98–103, 104–6, 111–12, 118–19
Woodham-Smith, Cecil, 93
Woods, MacDara, 164
The Workers' Republic, 55
World Wide Magazine, 138

Y

Yeats, George, 28
Yeats, William Butler, 22, 32, 44, 55,
   61, 112, 124, 128, 156, 170
   critique of own nostalgia, 78, 79, 86
   Heaney and, 1–2, 179
   PK, comparisons with, 1, 2, 4, 5,
      124, 179
   PK, influence on, 27, 42, 80, 176–7
   PK on, 34, 42, 63, 68
   PK's hostility to, 40, 42, 75, 116
   Literary Revival and, 13, 22, 27, 40,
      42, 75, 78, 107, 171
   multiple masks and, 21, 83
   pastoral tradition and, 74, 75, 76,
      78, 79, 80, 87, 90, 91
   peasantry and, 10, 22
   poetic style, 1, 4, 12
   WORKS OF
      'The Circus Animals' Desertion',
         176
      'Easter 1916', 7
      'The Lake Island of Innisfree', 79
      'Leda and the Swan', 152
      'Towards Break of Day', 79
Young Ireland movement, 140, 141

Z

Zozimus, 141